Harvard Semitic Monographs

Volume 6

Studies in the Text of Jeremiah

J. Gerald Janzen

Harvard University Press

Cambridge, Massachusetts

1973

## PREFACE

This study of the text of Jeremiah was first undertaken in 1963, and was presented to Harvard University as a doctoral dissertation. The original study was done under the direction of Professor Frank Moore Cross, to whom I am indebted for my understanding of matters pertaining to the study of the text of the Old Testament. I wish to express my appreciation also to Monsignor Patrick Skehan who read the manuscript, and who spotted several errors and made a number of suggestions for improvement; to Miss Joan Ryan, editor at the Harvard University Press, whose close reading of the text led to many points of stylistic improvement; and to Miss Carol Cross who with dauntless skill and good humour prepared the typescript as it appears in this book.

J. Gerald Janzen
Indianapolis, Indiana
March 21, 1973

CONTENTS

# ABBREVIATIONS AND SIGLA

ALQ[2]

Frank Moore Cross, *The Ancient Library of Qumrân*, rev. ed. Garden City, New York: Doubleday and Co., Inc., 1961.

BA

*The Biblical Archaeologist.*

BANE

G. E. Wright, ed., *The Bible and the Ancient Near East.* Garden City, New York: Doubleday and Co., Inc., 1961.

BASOR

*Bulletin of the American Schools of Oriental Research.*

Bright

John Bright, *Jeremiah*. The Anchor Bible, XXI. Garden City, New York: Doubleday and Co., Inc., 1965.

CBQ

*Catholic Biblical Quarterly.*

Cornill

C. H. Cornill, *Das Buch Jeremia*. Leipzig: C. H. Tauchnitz, 1905.

Duhm

B. Duhm, *Das Buch Jeremia*, Kurzer Hand-Kommentar zum Alten Testament, XI. Tübingen: J. C. B. Mohr, 1901.

Ehrlich

A. B. Ehrlich, *Randglossen zur Hebraischen Bibel*, vol. IV. Leipzig: J. C. Hinrichs, 1912.

Giesebrecht

F. Giesebrecht, *Das Buch Jeremia*, second edition, Handkommentar zum Alten Testament, III.2. Göttingen: Vandenhoeck and Ruprecht, 1907.

Graf

K. H. Graf, *Der Prophet Jeremia*. Leipzig: T. O. Weigel, 1862.

Hitzig

F. Hitzig, *Der Prophet Jeremia*, second edition, Kurzgefasstes exegetisches Handbuch zum Alten Testament, III. Leipzig: S. Hirzel, 1866.

HTR

*Harvard Theological Review.*

Hyatt

J. P. Hyatt, *Jeremiah: Introduction and Exegesis*, The Interpreter's Bible, vol. V. New York: Abingdon Press, 1956.

IDB

*Interpreter's Dictionary of the Bible.* New York: Abingdon Press, 1962.

IEJ

*Israel Exploration Journal.*

JAOS

*Journal of the American Oriental Society.*

JBL

*Journal of Biblical Literature.*

JCS

*Journal of Cuneiform Studies.*

JTS

*Journal of Theological Studies.*

Nötscher

F. Nötscher, *Das Buch Jeremias*, Die Heilige Schrift des Alten Testaments, VII.2. Bonn: Hanstein, 1934.

Rudolph

W. Rudolph, *Jeremia*, second edition, Handbuch zum Alten Testament, XII. Tübingen: J. C. B. Mohr (Paul Siebeck), 1958.

| | |
|---|---|
| Scholz | A. Scholz, *Der masorethische Text und die LXX-Uebersetzung des Buches Jeremias*. Regensburg: G. J. Manz, 1875. |
| Scholz, *Comm.* | A. Scholz, *Commentar zum Buche des Propheten Jeremias*. Würzburg: L. Woerl, 1880. |
| Skinner | J. Skinner, *Prophecy and Religion*. Cambridge: at the University Press, 1961. |
| Streane | A. W. Streane, *The Double Text of Jeremiah*. Cambridge: D. Bell and Co., 1896. |
| Volz | P. Volz, *Studien zum Text des Jeremia*. Leipzig: J. C. Hinrichs, 1920. |
| Volz, *Comm.* | P. Volz, *Der Prophet Jeremia*, Kommentar zum Alten Testament, X. Leipzig: A. Deichert, 1922. |
| VT | *Vetus Testamentum.* |
| Wambacq | B. N. Wambacq, *Jeremias, Klaagliederen. Baruch, Brief van Jeremias*, De Boeken van het Oude Testament, X. Roermond en Maaseik: J. J. Romen & Zonen, 1957. |
| Weiser | A. Weiser, *Das Buch des Propheten Jeremia*, fourth edition, Das Alte Testament Deutsche, XX-XXI. Göttingen: Vandenhoeck and Ruprecht, 1960. |
| ZAW | *Zeitschrift für die Alttestamentliche Wissenschaft.* |
| Ziegler, *Beiträge* | J. Ziegler, *Beiträge zur Ieremias-Septuaginta*. Göttingen: Vandenhoeck and Ruprecht, 1958. |
| Ziegler, *Ieremias* | *Septuaginta: Vetus Testamentum Graecum*. Göttingen: Vandenhoeck and Ruprecht, 1958. |

When any of these works is cited without page reference, the citation refers to the primary discussion of the passage in question.

In general, the sigla in this book are those used in the Göttingen Septuagint, and in the Cambridge Larger Septuagint. The following are also used.

| | |
|---|---|
| $\mathfrak{G}$ | The Old Greek text, as critically reconstructed. |
| $\mathfrak{G}^{zi}$ | Ziegler's critical text of the Septuagint of Jeremiah (used to indicate Ziegler's text when my reconstruction of the Old Greek text differs from his). |
| καιγε | A recension of the Greek Old Testament, identified by D. Barthélemy in *Les Devanciers d'Aquila* (Leiden: E. J. Brill, 1963). |
| $\mathfrak{M}$ | Masoretic text, according to *Biblica Hebraica*, third edition (= BH³), ed. R. Kittel (Stuttgart: Privilegierte Württembergische Bibelanstalt, 1937). |
| Syr | Syriac text, according to Codex Ambrosianus (A. M. Ceriani, *Translatio Syra Pescitto Veteris Testamenti, ex codice Ambrosiano, etc.*, 2 vols. (Milan, 1876-1883) and the Urmia text, published by the Trinitarian Tract Society (London). |

Targ     Targum, according to A. Sperber, *The Bible in Aramaic* (Leiden: A. J. Brill, 1959-1962).

Vulg     Vulgate, according to *Biblia Sacra, Juxta Vulgatam Clementinam* (Rome, 1956).

Jer α and  Chapters 1-29 and 30-52, respectively, of the Septuagint
 Jer β   text of Jeremiah, according to the analysis of H. St.-John Thackeray, *The Septuagint and Jewish Worship* (London: The British Academy, 1921).


*Note:* The most recent addition to the collection of manuscript witnesses to the text of Jeremiah, *Papyrus Bodmer XXII*, is not mentioned in this monograph. The reasons are these: the Coptic text of Jeremiah 40.3-52. 34, contained in this papyrus, is basically a witness to the Greek text. From the remarks of the editor (*Papyrus Bodmer XXII et Mississippi Coptic Codex II*, ed. Rodolphe Kasser [Cologny-Genève: Bibliothèque Bodmer, 1964], pp. 25-26), it appears that the deviations from the Greek text used in this study (that is, Ziegler's Göttingen text) amount to just over a dozen, and these of an inconsequential sort. Because I do not control Coptic, the work of weighing the handful of Coptic variants for their bearing on the further establishment of the Greek text must be left to someone else.

Studies in the Text of Jeremiah

# I Introduction

The discovery of a rich corpus of biblical manuscripts among the
documents from the caves of Qumrân, and subsequently from other sites in
the wilderness surrounding the Dead Sea, has given a fresh impetus to the
textual criticism of the Old Testament, and especially to the study of
the Septuagint as a tool of criticism. To date this corpus is only partly
published, with much of the most significant material awaiting its *editio
princeps*. But already it is clear that old problems and issues are open
to investigation from new perspectives and with a degree of precision and
evidential control hitherto not possible.[1]

One such problem, indeed one of the most dramatic in the field of
textual criticism, concerns the radical divergence in length between the
Masoretic and Greek texts of the book of Jeremiah. This divergence
attracted scholarly attention from the beginning through the end of the
nineteenth century. But the past fifty years or so have seen only sporadic and anticlimactic treatment of the problem, with a general tendency
to mediate between earlier positions. While Orlinsky's verdict that the
problem of the short and long texts in Jeremiah has not yet received com-
petent study[2] is too harsh, he is correct in his contention that the
problem has not yet been finally solved. Now, new evidence from Qumrân
has re-opened the debate and points to a final solution of at least some
of the issues.

The divergence in length, consisting of some 2700 words[3] which are
present in 𝔐 but absent in 𝔊, may be described briefly as follows. The
Greek omissions, or zero variants,[4] comprise single words, phrases, sentences, and some entire passages, the longest amounting to about 180
words. There are also, of course, the usual number of what we would call
content variants, and the whole transposition and differing order of the
Oracles against Foreign Nations. But these textual problems are not
directly relevant to this study, and except for incidental comment will
be left to one side.

The modern discussion of the relationship between 𝕸 and 𝕲 in Jeremiah begins with Eichhorn,[5] who proposed that the two text traditions
originated in successive editions of the book by Jeremiah himself.
According to his hypothesis, a first edition was composed in the fourth
year of Jehoiakim, augmented in Egypt with subsequent oracles, and in
this form was sent to Babylon for the use of the exiles there. An identical copy was kept in Egypt, not in one continuous document, but in a
series of smaller booklets. From this copy Jeremiah prepared a second
edition, whose various additions were typical of the elaborations, retouching, and up-dating which go into any revision. This revised edition
was sent to Palestine, where it entered the Hebrew canon and became the
prototype of the received text. Meanwhile, the copy of the first edition,
which remained in Egypt, was transmitted in its unrevised form (though in
somewhat different order because of reshuffling of the small booklets in
which it was contained) and eventually was translated into Greek. Eichhorn thus explained the divergence not as a textual, but as an editorial,
phenomenon.

Spohn was the first to devote a full-length monograph to the problem.[6] He agreed with Eichhorn that the problem could not have been one
merely of inner-Greek corruption, but that "Graecus...interpres ea, quae
omisit, *aut ante oculos non habuit, aut lecta bis vertere noluit.*"[7] In
contrast to Eichhorn, however, he laid the origin of the differences at
the feet of the translator. This judgment he based on the observation
that, of the several doublets in Jeremiah (25 by his count), the second
occurrence of 6 (or 7) of them was absent from 𝕲. In his view, the translator simply declined to translate those materials which he had already
treated earlier. He proposed to meet the objection from the many doublets
which *were* doubly rendered, by pointing out that the latter occurred at
widely spaced intervals, and therefore the translator could have forgotten
that he had rendered them earlier; that in some instances omission of the
second occurrence would have disturbed the context; and that, in at least
one instance (49.19-20//50.44-45), the difference in the two translations
suggests the work of different translators. But why would the translator
omit such large passages? He was a private individual, who translated
the Hebrew text not by public authority but for his own use, and who
therefore was free to omit what he wished.[8] Spohn supposed that, where
the translator omitted passages, he placed a suitable sign in the margin

to tell him which earlier passage belonged there.  A later copyist, not
understanding the signs, omitted them.  In addition to omitting second
occurrences of doublets, Spohn maintained, the translator also omitted
material which was not exactly paralleled elsewhere.

With the study of Movers in 1837,[9] the debate over the worth of the
Septuagint text was joined.  Movers took a position diametrically opposite
to that of Spohn, holding that 𝕲 represents an older text than 𝔐 and is
to be preferred.  This is seen first of all, he argued, from an examination of Jeremiah 52 together with the parallel text in 2 Kings 25.  In
almost a score of instances, Jeremiah 𝕲 and 2 Kings 25 agree against Jeremiah 𝔐.  The additional materials in the latter are secondary glosses,
drawn from similar usage.  Similarly, elsewhere in Jeremiah 𝔐 has a great
number of plusses which are to be taken as expansions from usage elsewhere.  Such additions occur also in 𝕲, but to a lesser extent.  As for
the absence of second occurrences of doublets, examination reveals that
they are secondary on internal grounds; in fact, Movers suggested, the
doublets common to 𝔐 and 𝕲 probably are also due to secondary development,
which in this case occurred before the rise of the Alexandrian recension.
Another series of expansions in 𝔐 arose, not from parallel places or
familiar usage, but from scribal tendency to embellish, clarify, and
otherwise elaborate the text.  Furthermore, 𝔐 is characterized by the
addition of synonyms.  Admittedly, in some instances 𝕲 omissions are the
result of chance scribal lapse.  For example, there are a number of instances of homoioteleuton in 𝕲.  But the great number of demonstrably
secondary 𝔐 plusses disposed Movers generally to prefer the simple reading to the complex.

The impact of Movers' study is indicated by the fact that for the
next generation discussion of the problem developed in terms of agreement
or disagreement with his conclusions.  We may pass over the details of
the debate[10] and describe the two main positions as they were presented
by Graf (1862) and Scholz (1875).

Leaving open, to begin with, the question whether or not the translator rendered his Hebrew *Vorlage* literally, Graf[11] asked the question:
does 𝔐 look like a text which grew out of the Alexandrian text through
additions, expansions, and glosses?  Or does 𝕲 look like a text which is
shortened from 𝔐 by omissions and abridgements?  Graf observed that many
frequently occurring expressions (אלהי ישראל, צבאות, כה אמר יהוה, נאם יהוה)

and many common surnames and titles are missing from ¢; it is as likely,
he maintained, for a later person to omit these recurrent, and indiffer-
ent, formulas and names, as it is unthinkable that a later person added
them when they were not originally there.

This Graf took as evidence of "eines Strebens nach Weglassung des
als überflüssig Erscheinenden."[12] This tendency he identified elsewhere,
in cases where many synonyms and pleonastic expressions and sentences are
missing from ¢. The reason for omitting these superfluous items is
easily recognized, while "es gar nicht zu erklären wäre, wie 'ein Ueber-
arbeiter es über sich gewinnen konnte, den ohnehin breiten Stil durch
entbehrliche Zusätze noch breiter und Schleppender zu machen.'"[13] Other
larger sections are omitted (e.g., in 42.20-21, 34.11-12, 5.15-16), where
the deletion disturbs the context. Again, ¢ omits specific details which
would have seemed irrelevant and therefore superfluous to a later person,
but which could not possibly have arisen as later glosses (e.g., in 28.3-
4, 36.9, 44.24). Also, difficult (e.g., 4.30 שדוד, 25.25 זמרי) or offensive (e.g., איש סריס) expressions are deleted. Finally, larger passages
which are paralleled elsewhere in Jeremiah are omitted, so as not to have
to repeat them. Where, on the other hand, parallel passages are translated in both places, this is due only to the inconsistency and wilfulness
of the translator's method, because he forgot that the passage had already
been translated elsewhere.

The above considerations led Graf to conclude that the Greek text
is a mutilated and corrupted form of the Hebrew text which is extant
today. These mutilations and corruptions are not to be laid to copyists
of the Hebrew tradition behind ¢, for what scribe would dare so to tamper
with the publicly disseminated Hebrew text? Rather, they are the work of
the translator. Indeed, of the wilfulness of the translator almost every
page gives testimony.[14] Graf closed his analysis with this statement:

> Bei den unzähligen Beweisen der Eigenmächtigkeit und Willkürlichkeit
> des alexandrinischen Uebersetzers ist es ganz unmöglich seiner Bear-
> beitung--denn Uebersetzung kann man es kaum nennen--irgend eine
> kritische Auctorität zuzuerkennen und daraus auf eine von der uns
> überlieferten verschiedene Gestalt seines hebräischen Textes zu
> schliessen.[15]

Graf's presentation of this point of view is extreme; yet his arguments basically are representative of those who have upheld the superiority of M, and his extremeness consists mainly in the severe terms in which

he couches his strictures against the translator. Somewhat removed from
this extreme view, shared by Kueper, Haevernick, Wichelhaus, Hengstenberg,
and Keil, were those who, influenced by Movers' study, acknowledged that
in at least a number of instances the shorter text of ₵ is original, and
that at these points 𝔐 is expansionist. At the same time, they doubted
that the Greek translator could be completely exonerated from wilful
mutilation of the text. This middle, or compromise, position is reflected
in the Introductions of Ewald and de Wette, and in the Commentary of
Hitzig.

Scholz,[16] however, stood squarely against the Grafian view. Acknowledging the truth of Keil's assertion that none of the advocates of a special text recension underlying ₵ had taken the trouble to discover the
precise nature of the translation, Scholz began his study with an inquiry
into the character of the translation of Jeremiah. His results were as
follows:[17]

As Movers had pointed out, the translation was careful and literal.
Unknown words were guessed from context. The meaning of difficult words
was sometimes sought in cognate languages. At times the same Hebrew word
was variously rendered in different places. Often the translation conveyed the sense, without troubling with the otherwise known etymology.
Some Hebrew words were translated with similar-sounding Greek words, yet
so as to convey the correct meaning. Some words or expressions were
taken for proper nouns and transcribed. The translation followed Hebrew
construction, against Greek idiom. Even sentences which gave no support-
able sense (as rendered) were translated. Recurring passages were rendered in similar phrases. Some passages which occur twice were rendered
only the second time.[18] ₵ is minus some passages which occur only once
in the book, and which make good sense (17.1-4, 25.14, 27.7, etc.).

From these observations, Scholz argued as follows: since the translation is very literal, even to following Hebrew word order against Greek
usage, it is in the strictest sense a translation. But if this is so,
places which seem to depart from this literal standard may well represent
a different *Vorlage*. In other instances, a Greek rendering which seems
to miss the meaning of a Hebrew word or phrase suggests that the latter
language was known, not from living use, nor from scholarly work, but by
traditional understanding of the passage. In these instances the translation reflects this traditional understanding, and not the individual

caprice of the translator.

Further, the instances where ₵ transliterated an unknown word, or
wrestled to translate a difficult sentence, producing nonsense, shows the
baselessness of the view that such words and passages were omitted.
Finally, if it were a principle to omit the second occurrence of doublets,
how could the translator so ignore this principle as to use it only in a
few places, and faithfully to translate second occurrences elsewhere?  In
short, ₵ is a translation in the strictest sense of the term, and the
movement from ₵ to its *Vorlage* is legitimate.

Scholz pointed out that the plusses in both texts are to be seen
against the background of textual translation in antiquity.  All much-
read books of antiquity suffered through glosses, the proliferation of
which necessitated the recensional labors, for example, of Aristarchus on
the text of Homer.  Similarly in Jeremiah, only a few ₵ plusses are original, and an examination of M plusses leads to the same judgment.  In
neither text was anything intentionally deleted.  Therefore, the presumption stands against each addition, and only specific grounds in each individual case can show the genuineness of a plus.

The study of Workman[19] may be passed over without extended comment.
His method of retroversion from Greek to Hebrew and his predisposition to
exalt the Greek text at every point nullify those individual points which
are valid, and the work has had no influence on the subsequent discussion.[20]

In the introduction to his commentary, Giesebrecht set out, in the
manner of Graf, to ascertain the character of the translation and from
this a clue to the omissions in ₵.  His argument is summarized in chapter
V and so will not be sketched here.  He carried forward the mediating
position of Hitzig, acknowledging the presence of much secondary material
in M but maintaining also that ₵ manifests a definite tendency to abridge
verbose passages, to omit frequently occurring phrases and passages, and
in general to translate with culpable freedom.

The last systematic discussion of the problem of the two text types
is that of Streane.[21]  Streane's position concerning the character of the
two texts is basically that of Movers and Scholz, that ₵ generally is the
preferred text and that M is a later, heavily expanded text.  While
Scholz's discussion of passages was organized topically, Streane followed
a short introductory essay with an examination of variants in the order
of their occurrence in the book of Jeremiah.

Of commentators since Giesebrecht, Duhm, Cornill, and Hans Schmidt
generally prefer the text of $\mathcal{G}$.  On the other hand, Volz, Condamin, Rudolph,
Weiser, Wambacq, and Bright, while varying in the degree to which they use
$\mathcal{G}$ to retore the text of Jeremiah, agree in principle with the position of
Giesebrecht.  This middle position is reflected also in Eissfeldt's Introduction,[22] and in the dictionary articles of Wildberger[23] and Muilenburg,[24]
and appears to be in process of becoming the consensus view.  The following statement by Rudolph is a good summary of this position.

> Die Frage, ob $\mathcal{G}$ gekürzt oder ob der hebräische Text nach der Fertig-
> stellung von $\mathcal{G}$ Erweiterungen erfahren hat, lässt sich nicht einheit-
> lich beantworten. *Dass $\mathcal{G}$ nach Kürzung strebt, ist unverkennbar* und
> bei der Breite der Quellen B und C wohl begrieflich, aber auch unab-
> sichtliche Auslassungen, vor allem durch Homoioteleuton, sind bei $\mathcal{G}$
> nicht selten (das umfänglichste Beispiel ist 39.4-13); auf der
> anderen Seite jedoch fehlen in $\mathcal{G}$ Stücke oder Verse oder Versteile,
> die aus inneren Gründen als Zusätze in $\mathcal{M}$ betrachtet werden müssen
> (Hauptbeispiel 33.14-26).  Besonders lehrreich dafür, dass man hier
> nicht schematisieren darf, ist Kap. 27.... Auch über das Plus von $\mathcal{G}$
> kann nur von Fall zu Fall geurteilt werden.[25]

Since the studies of Giesebrecht, Streane, and Volz, there have been
new developments in the general field of textual criticism, and with respect to the textual witness to Jeremiah.

We now possess improved tools for recovering the old Greek text of
Jeremiah, in the form of the critical edition of the Septuagint in the
Göttingen series, edited by Joseph Ziegler.  This superb edition, with its
definitive commentary on the text families and recensions, makes possible
a new level of precision in analysis.

New manuscript evidence for the Hebrew text of Jeremiah has come
from Qumrân.  While three of the four manuscripts have yet to be published,
this much can be said from preliminary notices:  4QJer[a], dated about 200-
175 B.C., reflects the early development of the proto-Masoretic text type.[26]
4QJer[b], with its $\mathcal{G}$ readings, confirms the methodological validity of
attempts to move from $\mathcal{G}$ by retroversion to its supposed Hebrew *Vorlage*.[27]

Current studies based on the biblical manuscripts from Qumrân are
presenting a new picture of the history of the biblical text in its broad
outlines and are vindicating the method which seeks to use the Septuagint
as a witness to a text tradition at times substantially divergent from $\mathcal{M}$.
As a result, the whole approach which minimizes the divergence between $\mathcal{G}$-
*Vorlage* and $\mathcal{M}$, and seeks to explain divergent Greek readings as resulting

from transmission technique or *Tendenz*, is seriously called into question.
For example, the time is past when one could approach the Greek text pri-
marily as a source for learning the exegetical method of the translator.[28]
The bearing of this general development upon our problem is obvious.

The unsatisfactory character of the present-day approach to the
text of Jeremiah demands that the problem be examined again.  In his
*Studien zum Text des Jeremia*, Volz offered no systematic discussion of
the origin of ₵ omissions (i.e., zero variants), but the study reflects a
point of view in basic agreement with Giesebrecht.  Since Volz, scholars
usually have been content with a summary statement of earlier studies and
tend to adopt the middle position between ₥ and ₵ and to minimize the difference between the two.  For example, Hyatt says that "generalizations
regarding the superiority of the Septuagint over the Hebrew text, or of
the latter over the Septuagint, are dangerous.  Every instance of variation between the two must be carefully considered on its own merits."[29]
To the extent that this statement is not a truism, it is misleading.  For
some strange reason, almost everyone who has had occasion recently to comment on the text of Jeremiah makes the same comment about explaining each
reading for itself, as though this were a *result* of the study of the text.
But it is *axiomatic* in textual criticism that every instance of textual
variation must be treated *de novo*, that one must not, in the first instance, move from generalizations about the character of the texts involved to the interpretation of specific readings.  In Housman's apt
figure, textual problems must be given the individual attention that a
dog gives to hunting fleas.[30]  But, if we may extend the figure, it is
not out of place to observe that some dogs have more fleas than others
and to hope to find out why.  We cannot suppose that the radical variation
in length between ₥ and ₵ is the end result of an overwhelmingly high
number of individual and unrelated textual corruptions.  When we compare
this divergence with the much smaller number of zero variants in most
other books of the Septuagint, we are driven to look for causes which can,
legitimately, be expressed in generalizations.[31]

In the course of our research, attention has been directed primarily
to what we have called the zero variants.  We must ask two questions concerning these variants.  Does the shorter reading of ₵ arise from the
tendency of the translator to abridge his text, or does it reflect a

Hebrew *Vorlage* with the shorter reading?  If 𝔊 reflects a *Vorlage* with the
shorter reading, is this reading superior or inferior to the longer reading
of 𝔐?

The first question can be answered satisfactorily only by detailed
examination of all the zero variants.  It is fair to say at the outset,
however, that in view of the general absence of a tendency to condense in
the Greek Old Testament,[32] and especially now in view of Hebrew support
for the short text of 𝔊,[33] the burden of proof lies with those who would
continue to hold a theory of condensation.  As I will argue (see especially chapter V), the ad hoc arguments for such a view are singularly
unconvincing.

We cannot answer the second question simply by appeal to the axiom
*brevior lectio potior.*[34]  For one thing, like many other principles of
textual criticism (e.g., *lectio difficilior* versus *lectio facilior*) it
has its converse.  For though, as this axiom indicates, it is a common
tendency for texts to grow in transmission,[35] haplography is perhaps the
most common scribal error.  Thus, in the books of Samuel, "the [Rabbinic]
text...is remarkably defective, and its shortness is the result of a long
history of losses by haplography, the commonest error by far in a text
which has not undergone systematic recensional activity, or which has not
become mixed by infection from a different textual tradition."[36]  Both
types of textual change find ample illustration in the book of Jeremiah.
As I will show, 𝔊 not infrequently is short by haplography, which usually
has occurred already in its *Vorlage*.  But this in itself gives valuable
evidence of the history and character of the Egyptian text.  On the other
hand, instances of conflation and expansion in 𝔐 are far more frequent
and rule out the ascription of all 𝔊 zero variants to scribal error or
carelessness.

## II   Double Readings

By double readings, or conflations, I mean those readings which com-
bine variants from two or more manuscripts.  Such readings may arise from
more or less systematic collation of divergent text traditions,[1] or (perhaps more often) from ad hoc comparison of manuscripts, or memory of
another reading.  The scribal motive behind the development of such readings often is the concern to ensure that the correct reading of the passage is not lost to the text tradition.

The development of variant members of a double reading may come
about variously.  Some variants are purely stylistic or synonymous alternatives.  Others involve a difference of content when, from one cause or
another, one of the readings is a corruption or secondary development of
the other.[2]

In this chapter I will discuss first the double readings in 𝔐, then
the double readings in 𝔊, and then I will assess the significance of
these readings for understanding the history of the respective text types.

### *Double Readings in 𝔐*

1.   1.15  לכל משפחות ממלכות צפונה [ πασας τας βασιλειας απο βορρα
της γης.  𝔐 may simply be expanded from 25.9 כל משפחות צפון (so Rudolph
in Biblia Hebraica[3]).  But in view of the synonymous and interchangeable
character of the two words (cf. Jer. 10.25//Ps. 97.6),[3] it is more likely
that 𝔐 is the result of conflation of two variant readings of 1.15.

2.   2.17-18  בעת מוליכך בדרך B ועתה מה לך לדרך מצרים A] και νυν
τι σοι και τη οδω Αιγυπτου.  It is clear from the context that (B) is
original and (A) intrusive.  Bright (cf. Cornill) comments, "may be a
corrupt dittography."  More likely, 𝔐 conflates (B) with a variant tradition (A), which developed from a misreading of ועתה מה לך לדרך under the
influence of preceding המוליך אתנו במדבר (verse 6).[4]

3.  2.34 דם נפשות אביונים נקיים] αιματα ψυχων αθωων. ℳ may be expanding with אביונים from similar contexts with נפש אביון (Jer. 20.13, Ps. 72.13, Jb. 31.35); or ℳ conflates synonymous variants אביונים/נקיים.[5]

4.  7.24 וילכו במעצות בשררות לבם הרע] αλλ επορευθησαν τοις ενθυμημασι της καρδιας αυτων της κακης. It is not clear which word 𝔊 translates, as in this phrase elsewhere the rendering of שררות varies: 3.17 ενθυμηματων; 9.13, 16.12, 18.12 αρεστων; 23.17 θελημασιν.[6] But since the word occurs only in the phrase שררות לב, its precise meaning may not have been clear, so that in the various contexts the translator may have offered alternative renderings. In any case, in 7.24 one of the words is superfluous, and the question is, which one is original to the passage? In view of the set character of the phrase with שררות elsewhere in Jer. (3.17, 9.13, 11.8, 13.10, 16.12, 18.12, also Dt. 29.18, Ps. 81.13; on 23.17, see note 6), במעצות seems intrusive.[7] However, it is not simply an addition from Ps. 81.13 (Cornill, Rudolph in BH[3]), as in this case we should expect וילכו במעצותיחם (ו)בשררות לב. The impossible syntax of ℳ is best explained as being due to conflation of variants וילכו [במעצות/ בשררות] לבם. It may be significant that there is no Hexaplaric or other correction of 𝔊 toward the conflate text of ℳ.

5.  8.10b-12] om. 𝔊. This passage is a doublet of 6.13-15. Variant positions of the passage have been conflated in ℳ. For details see pp. 95-96.

6.  8.19 הנה קול שועת לת עמי] ιδου φωνη θυγατρος λαου μου. ℳ conflates synonymous variants קול/שועה (cf. Ps. 18.7, and the use of the two terms in similar contexts in the Psalter). The presence of both words overloads the meter.

7.  9.14 הנני מאכילם את העם הזה לענה] ιδου εγω ψωμιζω αυτους αναγκας; cf. 23.15 הנני מאכיל אותם לענה. ℳ conflates variants מאכיל את העם הזה/מאכילם. Similarly, numbers 23, 31, 43, 53 below; also, on 52.50, see pp. 109-112.

8.  10.25 כי אכלו את יעקב ואכלהו ויכלהו ואת נוהו השמו] οτι κατεφαγον τον ιακωβ και εξανηλωσαν αυτον και την νομην αυτου ηρημωσαν/ Ps. 79.7 omits ואכלהו ויכלהו. ℳ conflates variants ואכלהו/ויכלהו (cf. Ziegler, Beiträge, p. 87). ואכלהו would have arisen as a variant to ויכלהו,[8] under the influence of the previously written אכלו. In view of Ps. 79.7, it is likely that neither verb after יעקב is original, and that ויכלהו in turn may have arisen as a corruption of כי אכלו.

9. 11.13 מזבחות לקטר לבעל B מזבחות למשת A שמתם] εταξατε βωμους
θυμιαν τη Βααλ. βωμος translates במה in its five other occurrences in
Jeremiah, so that 𝔊-*Vorlage* may have read במות לקטר לבעל. On the other
hand, βωμος does mean altar, and renders מזבח in Ex. 34.13, Num. 23.1,
Dt. 7.5, etc. Most likely, 𝔐 conflates the variants (A) and (B), which
were created by the otherwise well-known replacement of בעל by משת. The
original text may have read simply מזבחות לבעל, with לקטר entering the
variant common to 𝔐 and 𝔊 from passages like 11.17.

10. 14.3b,4b בשו אכרים חפר ראשם B ... בשו והכלמו וחפו ראשם A] 𝔊
omits (A). (A) and (B) contain old variants והכלמו/אכרים which arose
through confusion of ל and ר.

11. 23.8 אשר העלה ואשר הביא] ος συνηγαγεν; cf. 16.15 אשר העלה.
It is difficult to be sure which word 𝔊 is translating, as the other 3
occurrences of העלה (v. 7, and 16.14,15) are rendered αναγω. It would
seem simplest to take συναγω as = הביא, with 𝔐 אשר העלה an inner manuscript conflation from 16.15. But συναγω never = הביא elsewhere in Jer.,
and only rarely in the O.T., and several times elsewhere in Jer. (e.g.,
2.7, 3.4) הביא = εισαγω, which we would expect here. It is possible that
𝔊 originally read ος ανηγαγεν, which by dittography or auditory error
became ος συνηγαγεν.[9] In any case, 𝔐 is conflate.

12. 23.8 את זרע בית ישראל] το σπερμα Ισραηλ; Syr ישראל לבני; cf.
16.15 את בני ישראל. 𝔐 appears to be conflation of synonymous variants
ישראל [זרע/בית.[10]

13. 23.10 כי מנאפים מלאה הארץ B כי מפני אלה אבלה הארץ A] 𝔊 omits
(A). 𝔐 conflates two variants, of which (B) seems the preferable reading.

14. 23.18 𝔐 and 𝔊 differ at three points: וַיֵּרָא]וְיֵרֶא 𝔊 Syr Vulg;
וישמע 1°] om. 𝔊; דברו] om. 𝔊. Following a suggestion by Cross, I would
propose that 𝔐 conflates variants. The resultant text yields much better
poetry (3+3):

מי עמד בסוד יהוה וַיֵּרָא

דברו מי הקשיב וישמע = 𝔊
מי הקשיב דברו וישמע = 𝔐*

15. 23.29 הלוא כה דברי כאש נאם יהוה] ουτως οι λογοι μου λεγει
κυριος ουχι οι λογοι μου ωσπερ πυρ. On these variants, see Ziegler, *Beiträge*, p. 100. The old variants are הלוא and כה, conflated differently in
in 𝔐 (cf. nos. 1, 4, 16, 52) and 𝔊 (cf. nos. 10, 18, 19, 38).

16. 24.9 ונתתים לזועה לרעה לכל ממלכות הארץ] 𝔊 omits לרעה, which

clearly is intrusive here (cf. 15.4, 29.18, 34.17; Dt. 28.25). The addition is best explained as conflation (cf. Ziegler, *Beiträge*, p. 87), from
a manuscript in which לזועה was transcribed as לרעה.

17.   25.6-7 /ולא הכעיסו אותי במעשה ידיכם ולא ארע לכם A (v. 6)
οπως [(v. 7) ולא שמעתם אלי נאם יהוה B/ למען הכעיסוני במעשה ידיכם לרע לכם
μη παροργιζητε με εν τοις εργοις των χειρων υμων του κακωσαι υμας και ουκ
ηκουσατε μου. That (A) and (B) form a doublet is commonly recognized.
However, the reading common to M and ₲ is *not* (A) (so BH[3] *et al.*) but (B),
as the following observations show: οπως μη παροργιζητε με does not translate ולא הכעיסו אותי.   A survey of occurrences of οπως μη in the Septuagint reveals that it rarely if ever translates the simple negative לא, but
predominantly the purposive negatives פן, לבלתי, למען אשר לא, למען לא.
Accordingly, ₲-*Vorlage* must have read למען לא הכעיסוני.[11] Whatever του
κακωσαι υμας translates,[12] it clearly does *not* translate ולא ארע לכם, but
some version of the parallel phrase in (B). Thus, as in the doublet in
41.10 (see p. 17, no. 32), ₲ reads one half of the doublet, but in the
position occupied by the other half in M. This is clear indication that
M represents conflation of two old variants, and ולא שמעתם אלי in verse 7
is to be taken as the last clause before the new paragraph in verse 8.

18.   25.24 ואת כל מלכי ערב A] και ואת כל מלכי הערב/השכנים במדבר B
παντας τους συμμεικτους τους καταλυοντας εν τη ερημω/ Syr ולכלהון מלכא
דמתחמין חד עם חד ולכלהון דערביא דשכין במדבר.   To begin with, M has conflated variants (A) and (B), which originally were (A) את מלכי ערב and (B)
את מלכי הערב (= ₲).[13]   Now, when it is noted that the phrase ואת כל הערב
has occurred already in verse 20, the suspicion is aroused that only one
of the three occurrences is original. Comparison of v. 23b with 9.25
ואת כל (כל קצוצי פאה הישבים במדבר) suggests that 25.23b-24 ought to read
קצוצי פאה השכנים במדבר, and that both (A) and (B) are intrusive in v. 24.
We propose tentatively that the text developed as follows: the phrase is
original in v. 20; it was dropped by haplography; the marginal correction
found its way, in various forms, into verse 24 (attracted perhaps to the
phrase השכנים במדבר--cf. 3.2 כערבי במדבר); ₲ and M represent conflation
of the original reading in v. 20 with a secondary reading in v. 24; in
addition, M represents a further stage of development, in which variant
forms of the incorrect restoration in v. 24 were conflated there.

19.   25.25 ואת כל מלכי זמרי ואת כל מלכי עילם] και παντας βασιλεις
Αιλαμ. In a list such as this, it is of course possible that ₲ (or

₡-*Vorlage*) is defective by haplography. But explanations of זמרי as a
place name are doubtful, and the word probably is a corruption of זמכי,[14]
an *atbash* cipher for עֵילָם[15] in which case Ⲙ has conflated the two forms.[16]

20.  25.34  והתפרצותיכם ונפלתם ככלי חמדה] και πεσεισθε ωσπερ οι κριοι
οι εκλεκτοι.  Ⲙ is metrically too long, and one of the verbs would appear
to be secondary.  But a second variant, ככלי/ου κριοι, may be connected
with the two verbs, arising from the following variants:[17] והתפרצותיכם A
ככלי B ונפלתם כאילי /חמדה.  Ⲙ has conflated the two verbs, apparently in
an (A)-type base text.

21.  25.38  ומפני חרון אפו] ₡ omits.  The phrase also occurs in v.
37 (מפני חרון אף יהוה/απο προσωπου οργης θυμου μου).  It would appear
that the line fits best at the end of v. 38,[18] reading מפני[19]חרב היונה
ומפני חרון אפו//.  The position in ₡ would then be due to faulty restoration of an omission, and misreading אפו as אפי.  Ⲙ has conflated the two
readings, expanding one to אף יהוה in accordance with the form of the
phrase in 12.13, 30.24, 51.45.

22.  26.22  וישלח המלך יהויקים A/ אנשים מצרים B את אלנתן בן עכבור
ואנשים אתו אל מצרים] και εξαπεστειλεν ο βασιλευς ανδρας εις Αιγυπτον.  Ⲙ
preserves shorter and longer variants.  (For discussion, see S. Talmon,
*Textus* 1 [1960], 180, and below, p. 100.)

23.  27.8  לא יעבדו [אתו/את נבוכדנאצר]מלך בבל.  ₡ is defective by
haplography (לא 1° to 2°).  But it is likely that, as in 41.3 (see p. 17,
no. 31), Ⲙ represents conflation of את/אתו[20](נבוכדנאצר) מלך בבל.

24.  28.1  ויהי בשנה ההיא בראשית ממלכת צדקיה מלך יהודה בשנת הרבעית
בחדש החמישי B-S Bo Aeth Arab και εγενετο εν τω τεταρτω ετει Σεδ. βασιλεως
Ιουδα εν μηνι τω πεμπτω A-106′ 130-239-538 Sa Q-V-(omn.) C′ και εγενετο
εν τω τεταρτω ετει βασιλευοντος Σ.β.Ι. εν μηνι τω πεμπτω O-233 L′ Arm και
εγενετο εν τω ετει εκεινω εν αρχη βασιλευοντος Σ.β.Ι εν... (= Ⲙ).  This
complex reading cannot be separated from the reading in 27.1 and the question of the date of the events of 27.3:  In 27.1, בראשית ממלכת יהויקם בן
ויאשיהו מלך יהודה...לאמר] om. ₡.  The name יהויקם is impossible here (cf.
verses 3, 12 צדקיהו).  On the other hand, צדקיהו in ⲘKenn 3 mss Syr[21] probably is later correction.  The date בראשית ממלכת is unlikely, the events
of chapter 27 occurring most probably in the fourth year of Zedekiah's
reign.[22]  27.1 probably is secondary from 26.1.  Whether the chapter ever
had a date formula after incorporation of chapters 27-29 into the book,
we cannot tell.  Certainly, Ⲙ is no help in reconstructing one.

Returning to 28.1, 𝔐 clearly is a conflation of two variant traditions which may be represented thus: ויהי [A‏ בשנה הרביעית‏]‏ל‏ /B‏ במשנה ההיא
בראשית ממלכת[ צדקיהו מלך יהודה.‏  The superiority of (A) (= 𝔊) is two-
fold: it fits better into the general historical picture (cf. Bright, in
note 22 above); if (B) were original, it would be difficult to explain
the development of (A),[24] whereas the secondary development of (B) is
easily explained.  The latter arose after the secondary addition of 27.1,
in order to preserve the temporal connection between the two chapters
(perhaps for the sake of the common "yoke" theme).  When the two texts
were conflated in proto-𝔐, the (B) variant constituted the base text, and
the (A) variant, at first probably a marginal variant, subsequently was
taken in before the month date.

     25.  31.15  [רחל מבכה/A‏ על בניה/מאנה להנחם/B‏ על בניה/כי איננו  𝔊$^B$
omits (A) / 𝔊$^{A\ Q-V\ L}$ Syr Matthew 2.18 omit (B).  The variant position of
the prepositional phrase is conflated in 𝔐.

     26.  32.14  לקוח את הספרים האלה את ספר המקנה הזה ואת החתום ואת ספר
הגלוי הזה ונתתם[  λαβε το βιβλιον της κτησεως τουτο και το βιβλιον το
ανεωγμενον[25] και θησεις.  It is clear from verses 10, 11, 12, 16, that
only *one* "book" or document was involved in the transaction of 32.6-25.
Contracts and deeds from Elephantine and Palestine illuminate the significance of verse 11 את ספר המקנה את החתום···ואת הגלוי:  the document con-
sisted of two parts, one rolled up, bound and sealed, the other rolled
loosely and left open for reference.[26]

     In verse 14, therefore, את הספרים האלה and (נתת)ם reflect scribal
misunderstanding of, or inattention to, the nature of the document being
drawn up.  Now, it is to be noted that the Hexaplaric correction is not
in complete agreement with 𝔐.  For את הספרים האלה, compare Syh Arm το
βιβλιον τουτο; 88 ✳ συν× τω βιβλιω τουτω (only α'-Syh reads τα βιβλια
ταυτα).  Note also for (ונתת)ם: 𝔊 θησεις/ + αυτο B L Co Aeth Arab/ + αυτα
1 Syh-mg.  Further, ספר 2° is ungrammatical before הגלוי.  From verse 11
we would expect to read here simply ואת הגלוי, i.e., the open part of the
one document.  Therefore, ספר is best taken as an early expansion (it is
in 𝔊) from את ספר המקנה הזה, as is הזה 2° (om. 𝔊).  If את הגלוי belongs
in verse 14, ואת החתום (om. 𝔊) is required also, though the conjunction
should be deleted with the Hexaplaric and Lucianic correction (again only
α'-Syh agrees precisely with 𝔐).  𝔊-*Vorlage* probably suffered haplography,
את 3° to 4°.  We propose that at one time there were variant traditions:

A] את הספר הזה B/‏ את ספר המקנה הזה [את החתום והגלוי ונתתו בכלי חרש לקוח.
M has conflated (A) and (B). With addition of ספר 2° and הזה 2° (see
above), את הספר הזה developed to את הספרים האלה.

Another development of this type may be seen in verse 12: ואתן את
המקנה הספר/‏ ואתן אתו = και εδωκα αυτο. M expanded from verses 11, 12aβ.
But its present text is awkward, and may well reflect conflation of two
stages of expansion: A] ואתן את הספר B/‏ את ספר המקנה [אל ברוך. Here,
המקנה of (B) has been added to a proto-M text base with (A).

While on this passage, we may consider also the reading in verse
11: המצוה והחקים [om. ₵. The M phrase is elliptical and, if genuine, is
in apposition to the preceding, referring to the content of the document.
But its position (between את החתום and ואת הגלוי) is awkward, unless the
sealed portion is the only full statement of purchase and the open portion is only an abstract.[27] The close graphic resemblance between (A)
המקנה את החתום and (B) המצוה והחקים may have produced haplography in ₵-
Vorlage.[28] Or, it is possible that (B) represents a corruption of (A)[29]
later conflated with it.

27.  32.30  /‏ A‏ כי היו בני ישראל ובני יהודה אך עשׁיט הרע בעיני מנערתיהם
B] ‏ כי בני ישראל אך מכעסים אתי במעשׁה ידיהם נאם יהוה οτι ησαν υιοι Ισραηλ
και υιοι Ιουδα μονοι ποιουντες το πονηρον κατ οφθαλμους μου εκ νεοτητος
αυτων. ₵ may be defective by haplography. However, not only do the three
כי clauses of verses 30-31 seem unduly repetitious, but (A) and (B) are
virtually identical. הכעיסרני במעשׂה ידי/‏- and עשׂה הרע בעיני are frequent
in Deuteronomic literature, and the latter especially in Jeremiah (compare their usage together, in Dt. 31.29 and 1 Kgs. 16.7). We suspect,
therefore, that M has conflated alternative synonymous expressions.

28.  34.1  וכל ממלכות ארץ ממשׁלת ידו] και πασα η γη αρχης αυτου. M
conflates synonymous expressions A. ‏ כל ארץ ממשׁלתו/‏B‏ כל ממלכות הארץ‏[30] Eb
22 and Kennicott 4, 96, 145 still have the definite article (הארץ), which
may reflect the conflation before subsequent smoothing.[31] In such a
case, (B) would represent the proto-M base text and (A) (= ₵) the variant.

29.  40.5  ארחה ומשׁאת] δωρα  B-S-130-239 A-106' Bo Aeth Arab; εστιατοριαν V-26-46-86'-534-538-544 Olymp; εστιατοριαν και δωρα Q-613 O-233 L'
C' Arm; εστιατοριαν και λημμα α'-86. M may conflate variants ארחה (=
εστιατοριαν; cf. Jer. 52.34, 2 Kgs. 25.30, etc.) and משׂאת (= δωρα). V-
etc. would reflect a Greek tradition revised to a proto-M text which contained only ארחה,[32] while Q-613, O-233 Arm, L', C' are revision to M.

30.  40.8  ויוחנן ויונתן בני קרח [om. ויונתן  ¢; also 2 Kgs. 25.23.
𝔐 conflates variants caused by corruption of יוחנן to יונתן in one manu-
script tradition (cf. J. Ziegler, *Beiträge zur Ieremias-Septuaginta*
[Göttingen: Vandenhoeck and Ruprecht, 1958], p. 87).

31.  41.3  אתו [A/ את גדליהו/במצפה B]  ¢ and 2 Kgs. 25.25 omit (B).
𝔐 has a pronounced tendency to fill out personal names (see chapter IV).
Here, 𝔐 conflates the earlier pronominal and the later nominal variants.
Similar conflations occur in 9.14, 27.8, 42.2, 51.56, in 𝔐.

32.  41.10  וישב ישמעאל A/ את כל שארית העם אשר במצפה/את בנות המלך/
B] ואת כל העם הנשארים במצפה/אשר הפקיד נבוזראדן רב טבחים את גדליהו בן אחיקם
και απεστρεφεν Ισμαηλ παντα τον λαον τον καταλειφθεντα εις Μασσηφα και
τας θυγατερας του βασιλεως ας παρεκατεθετο ο αρχιμαγειρος τω Γοδολια υιω
Αχικαμ.  It is to be noted that ¢ translates the *second* of the two variants, but in the place occupied by the *first*, agreeing with the first
variant on the proper place of the clause.[33]  When conflation occurred,
(A) was in the base text (and in proper position before ראת בנות), while
(B) (= ¢) was marginally noted.  Later, the marginal variant was taken in
after ראת בנות, and the conjunction was moved from ראת בנות to ראת כל העם.
Variant (A) probably is original, while (B) was produced by attraction to
the phrase in verse 16.  It is possible that 𝔐 conflation has obscured an
original reference of אשר הפקיד specifically to the king's daughters (cf.
¢ τας θυγ....ας παρεκ.), whom the רב טבחים then may have appointed to be
with Gedaliah in order to strengthen his position as governor in the
absence of the king.

33.  42.2  ¢ [והתפלל /A בעדנו אל יהוה אלהיך /B בעד כל השארית הזאת
omits (A)/ Syriac omits (B).  𝔐 is conflate.

34.  43.1  אשר שלחו יהוה אלהיהם אליהם [om. אלהיהם  ¢.  It is most
probable[34] that 𝔐 conflates two traditions, אלהיהם/אליהם.  Verse 2 provides another example of these variants, unconflated: 𝔐 אלהינו ¢ אלינו.[35]

35.  44.3  לקטר לעבד] om. לעבד  ¢.  𝔐 conflates synonymous variants
קטר (cf. verses 5, 8, 15, and 1.16, 19.4) and עבד (cf. 11.10, 13.10, 16.11,
13, 22.9, 25.6, 35.15).[36]

36.  44.3  𝔐 Vulg Targ ידעום המה אתם ואבתיכם [Eb 22 ידעום המה
ידעו אנון הנון ואבהיהון Syr /(ידעתם =) ¢ εγνωτε אבתיכם/ .  The above readings probably originated in the old variants (A) ידעום (B) ידעתם.[37]  From
here, expansion moved in various directions: in an (A)-type text, addition of המה ואבותיהם (= Syr) from 19.4; in a (B)-type text, addition of

אתם ואבותיכם from 16.13.  Eb 22 may represent the A-type partly influenced by the B-type, or smoothing of 𝔐; 𝔐 conflates the A-type and the
B-type.

37.  44.9  𝔐 (= Targ Vulg)  את רעות אבותיכם ואת רעות מלכי יהודה ואת
בישא דאבהיכון ובישא דמלכא דיהודא Syr [רעות נשיו ואת רעתכם ואת רעת נשיכם
ובישא דנשיהון.  The Greek evidence is diverse, and will be cited in full.
For convenience of arrangement, an asterisk will represent (και) των κακων
(των):[38]

G$^{zi}$     *πατ. υμων *βασ. Ιουδα *αρχ. υμων *γυν. υμων

C'-613    *πατ. υμων *βασ. υμων *αρχ. υμων *γυν. υμων

L'$^{-36}$    *πατ. υμων *υμων *βασ. Ιουδ. *γυν. αυτων *γυν. υμων

  36     *πατ. υμων *υμων *βασ. Ιουδα *αρχ. αυτων *γυν. υμων

Aeth    *πατ. υμων *βασ. Ιουδα *αρχ. αυτων *γυν. υμων

Syh Arm *πατ. υμων *βασ. Ιουδα *γυν. αυτων *υμων *γυν. αυτων

88      *πατ. υμων *β. υμων *β. Ιουδα *αρχ. υμων *γυν. αυτων *γυν. υμων

Verses 17 and 21 are also pertinent to this problem:[39]

17          אנחנו ואבחינו מלכינו ושרינו

21  אתם ואבותיכם מלכיכם ושריכם ועם הארץ

Methodologically, two factors would seem most likely to be involved in
the above textual variants: the occurrence of serial clauses would tend
to give rise to haplography; the threefold occurrence of a séries (verses
9, 17, 21) would give rise to harmonizing tendencies.  It would be simplest, therefore, to view 𝔊 om. ואת רעתכם and Syr om. ואת רעתכם ואת רעת
נשיכם as owing to haplography, and 𝔊 αρχοντων υμων as owing to harmonization.  But a closer look at the data suggests a more complex textual
development.

        (a)  ואת רעתכם is grammatically out of place in this series which
lists, not the evil deeds of Jeremiah's hearers, but those of a number of
*third* parties (אשר עשר; cf. also verse 10 דכאו, הלכו, יראו).  Moreover,
the orthography of the phrase is peculiar.  It is pointed to harmonize
with the rest of the series; but after the threefold *plene* רעות, it is
difficult to see this as a doubly defective plural noun with plural suffix.  Rather, it is to be pointed רָעָתְכֶם (cf. 1 Sam. 12.17, Hos. 10.15) and
taken as conflation from a manuscript tradition in which the three earlier
רעות were also read as רעת.  In the latter tradition, ואת רעתכם arose by
expansion, from the sense of verses 17, 21.  Insofar as 𝔊 does not have
this phrase, then, its text is superior.

(b) ‏ואת רעת נשיכם‏. If ‏ואת רעתכם‏ is secondary in ‏M‏, the presence
in the series of the following phrase becomes odd. In view of the probable significance of the orthography of ‏ואת רעתכם‏, the defective orthography renders this phrase suspect also.[40] While Syr probably has suffered haplography (‏דנשיהון‏‏/‏‏דנשיכון‏‏>‏, or the like), it may reflect a
shorter, more nearly original tradition.

(c) ‏נשיו‏ does not fit the grammatical context. It probably arose
in a text which read ‏מלך יהודה‏ by haplography. It is interesting that
most recensional Greek texts read ‏נשיהם‏ (L[‏'‏-36] O Arm (!); cf. Syr ‏נשיהון‏).
G[zi] αρχοντων υμων reflects ‏שׂריכם‏. Methodologically, it is plausible to
prefer ‏נשי‏‏>‏‏הם‏‏<‏ and to explain ‏¢‏ *Vorlage* as owing to harmonization with
verses 17, 21. But it is equally likely that the original ‏שׂריכם‏ ‏>‏ ‏נשיכם‏
by anticipation of the context of verses 15-26. We consider it doubtful
that in the original form of the passage this stock sentence would contain such a variant between verse 9 and verses 17, 21.

We therefore propose the following development of verse 9:

(α) Original text: ‏ואת‏ [41]‏מלכי יהודה'‏ ‏ואת רעות‏ ‏ואת רעות אבותיכם‏
‏רעות שׂריכם‏.

(β) Rise of variant ‏נשיכם‏, from graphic similarity to ‏שׂריכם‏, and
anticipation of the content of verses 15-26.

(γ) Transmission of the passage in various forms: ‏שׂריהם‏‏/‏‏שׂריכם‏
‏נשיהם‏‏/‏‏נשיכם‏.

(δ) ‏¢‏ preserves conflation of α and β, while Syr preserves one of
the variants (‏נשיהון‏). Alternately (so, e.g., Giesebrecht), ‏¢‏ *γυναικων
υμων could be taken as secondary correction to a Hebrew text which had
added ‏נשיכם‏.

(ε) ‏M‏ preserves another conflation in which ‏נשיו‏ (cf. c above)
may have formed the base text of proto-‏M‏, while the phrases ‏ואת רעתכם‏
‏רעת נשיכם‏ were conflated from a divergent manuscript.

38. 44.12 ‏בחרב וברעב ימתו‏ B/ ‏···‏‏בחרב ברעב יתמו'‏ A] ‏¢‏ omits (B).
‏M‏ conflates variants ‏יתמו‏‏/‏‏ימתו‏.[42] We can hardly have both here, especially with the repetition of the cliché again in verse 13.

39. 48.7 ‏במעשיך ובאוצרותיך‏] ‏¢‏ εν οχυρωμασι σου/ Syr ‏על חסניכי‏
‏ועל גזיכי‏ /Targ ‏באוצרך ובבית גנזך‏/ Vulg *in munitionibus tuis et in the-*
*sauris tuis.* ‏M‏ ‏מעשׂיך‏ is odd here, unless it is a very general term for
what one makes to defend oneself ("works"). It is difficult to know
whether Targ Syr Vulg read something like ‏מעזיך‏, with ‏M‏ suffering ‏ז‏ ‏>‏ ‏שׂ‏

(auditory error?),[43] or whether they "exegete" the bland word by its
synonym (the latter is suggested at least by Targ, whose words are synonymous; but cf. Syr).

Just what 𝕲 renders is not certain. במבצרותיך commends itself,
since οχυρωμα translates it in verse 18, Lam. 2.2, 5, cf. 49(29).22;
also, οχυρος translates מבצר 5 times in Jer. (once in 5.17, in similar
context) and בצר once. במצדותיך is another good possibility,[44] as οχυρωμα translates this word in verse 41. מעזיך is also possible[45] (though
rendered by οχυρωμα only twice, outside of Jeremiah); it is attractive,
as providing a textual bridge between οχυρωμα and מעשה. In any case,
48.7a 𝔐 is metrically overloaded, and we take ובאוצרותיך (?מעזיך) במעשה
as conflation of old variants.

40.  49.4 מה תתהללי בעמקים זב עמקך הבת השובבה]τι αγαλλιασῃ εν
τοις πεδιοις, θυγατερ ατιμιας. The study of this verse has been put on
a new footing by M. J. Dahood's observation that עמק here means "strength,"
as in Ugaritic, and not "valley."[46] However, 𝔐 is metrically too long,
and we would agree with most earlier commentators (against Dahood and
Bright) that one phrase or the other is secondary. 𝔐 probably conflates
variant readings:

מה תתהללי A] בעמק-ם[47] [48]B/ זב עמק] הבת השובבה

(A) Why boast in (your) strength, O faithless daughter?
(B) Why boast? your strength has ebbed, O faithless daughter.

41.  50.2 הביש בל חת מרדך B/ הבישר עצביה חתו גלוליה A] κατῃσχυνθη
[βηλ] η απτοητος η τρυφερα [παρελυθη Μαρωδαχ]. On 𝕲 as an inner-Greek
doublet of (A) (later correction to 𝔐 in square brackets), see Ziegler,
*Beiträge*, p. 96. 𝕲 translates only (A); (B) represents conflation of a
text tradition in which the divine names were displaced, in part pejora-
tively, by עצביה and גלוליה.[49]

42.  50.9 כי הנה אנכי מעיר ומעלה על בבל] οτι ιδου εγω εγειρω επι
Βαβυλωνα. 𝔐 conflates synonymous variants מעיר (cf. 51.1, and Isa. 13.17,
Ezek. 23.22, Joel 4.7) and מעלה (cf. 33.6, and Isa. 8.7).

43.  51.56 כי בא עליה על בבל שודד] om. עליה 𝕲 Syr. 𝔐 conflates
variants consisting of a pronoun and its (probably expanded) noun form.

44.  52.15 ומדלות העם/ואת יתר העם הנשארים בעיר ואת הנפלים אשר A
נפלו אל מלך בבל ואת יתר האמון הגלה נבוזראדן רב טבחים/B ומדלות הארץ] και
τους καταλοιπους του λαου/ 2 Kings 25.11 omits (A); cf. Jer. 39.9. Phrase
(A) clearly is secondary; its textual support is weak, and it is

intrusive—Nebuzaradan would hardly have taken some of the poor to Baby-

lon! The phrase arose as a variant to ומדלות הארץ in verse 16,[50] and

(A) and (B) in 𝔐 represent conflation of the two text traditions. If

now we suppose that 𝔊-*Vorlage* read ומדלות העם in verse 16, we may account

for the 𝔊 omission in 52.15-16 (הנשארים'''ומדלות הארץ) as owing to hap-

lography: (15) ואת יתר העם הנשארים'''(16)(ומדלות) העם השאיר.

45.   52.34   עד יום מותו B כל ימי חייו A] 𝔊 omits (B) / 2 Kings

25.30 omits (A). An excellent example of the conflating tendency of Jer.

𝔐.[51]

The above passages are taken as providing clear cases of double

readings in 𝔐. The following cases are taken as less clear but probable.

46.   4.12   מאלה 𝔊. om. [רוח מלא מאלה יבוא לי. מאלה may be corruption

of a variant construed with רוח as feminine: מלאה (cf. Ziegler, *Beiträge*,

p. 87).

47.   15.12-14 and 17.1-4. On the omission of the latter passage

in 𝔊, see p. 117. For our proposal that 15.12-14 is a conflation of a

variant of 17.1-4, see p. 133.

48.   23.27   להשכיח את עמי שמי] του επιλαθεσθαι του ονοματος μου =

לשכח את שמי. The doublet probably arose through graphic confusion, ש/ע

(cf. Ziegler, *Beiträge*, p. 45).[52]

49.   26.20   על העיר הזאת ועל הארץ הזאת] περι της γης ταυτης. 𝔊

(or its *Vorlage*) may have suffered haplography. But in view of other

עיר/ארץ variants in the book,[53] and the reference in 26.11, 12, to Jere-

miah's prophecy אל העיר הזאת, 26.20 𝔐 may represent conflation of vari-

ants על [העיר/הארץ]הזאת.

50.   26.21   המלך יהויקים וכל גבוריו וכל השרים] ο βασιλευς Ιωακιμ

και παντες οι αρχοντες. Again, 𝔊 may be due to haplography (וכל 1°2°).

But 𝔐 is suspect in the position of גבוריו before השרים (we would expect

השרים'''גבוריו; cf. 2 Kgs. 24.14, Ezr. 7.28, 1 Chr. 29.24, 2 Chr. 32.3);

and in the shift from determination by suffix to determination by defi-

nite article which, if not grammatically wrong, seems odd. We would sug-

gest conflation of variants: וכל השרים/וכל גבוריו.

51.   26.21   וישמע אוריהו וירא ויברח ויבא מצרים] και ηκουσεν ουριας

και εισηλθεν εις Αιγυπτον. Once again, haplography is possible in 𝔊-

*Vorlage* (וירא'ויבא), or we may have conflation of variants (cf. 1 Kgs.

11.40 ויקם ירבעם ויברח מצרים):

וישמע/וירא] אוריהו [ויברח/ויבא] מצרים

Thus, in 26.20-22 we have *four* variants (see p. 14, no. 22), all
of which could be due to haplography. But in verse 22 the conflate character of 𝔐 is clear and in verse 21a it is probable. In verses 20 and
21b the correct interpretation is not clear; but since the passage contains other conflations, perhaps we should interpret these readings similarly.

52.   29.23   ועד הוידע [ואנכי   και εγω μαρτυς. The history of the
reading הוידע is not entirely clear. It would be easy for an original
אנכי (ה)ידע to become אנכי (ה)עד, or vice versa, and 𝔐 probably conflates variants thus developed.

53.   37.7   מצרים לארצו [שב   εις γην Αιγυπτου; O-233 (om. την) Arm
εις την Αιγυπτον; L' εις την γην εαυτων εις γην Αιγυπτον (cf. Targ
למצרים (לארעהון); α'-Syh^mg εις γην αυτου. O probably is inner-Greek.
The conflation in L, combined with the reading of 𝕲 and Targ, suggests
that 𝔐 may be conflate: לארץ מצרים/לארצו] שב. But we cannot be sure.

54.   37.15   לבית עשו אתו כי הספר יהונתן בית האסור אתו ונתנו
[הכלא   και απεστειλαν αυτον εις την οικιαν Ιωναθαν του γραμματεως, οτι
ταυτην εποιησαν εις οικιαν της φυλακης. 𝕲 may have suffered haplography
(בית/οικιαν 1°⌢2°). But האסור בית and הכלא בית are synonymous, and 𝔐
may conflate variants.

55.   40.3-4   שמעתם ולא ליהוה חטאתם כי דבר כאשר יהוה ויעש ויבא
הנה ועתה הזה דָּבָר_לכם והיה [בקולו   και εποιησε κυριος οτι ημαρτετε αυτω
και ουκ ηκουσατε της φωνης αυτου. ιδου. The combination ויבא ויעש is
odd;[54] but something is required after יהוה 1°. We propose, tentatively,
that 𝔐 has conflated the following variants: [ויעש B/A ויבא A] [יהוה A] לכם
הנה ועתה בקולו שמעתם ולא לו חטאתם כי [דבר כאשר B/הזה דבר<ה>. 𝕲 may be
defective by haplography, הנה''' (4) ''והיה, or (less likely) לי דבר כאשר.
On ליהוה/לו, see p. 74, reading (q).

56.   41.13-16 This passage contains a number of other variants
in addition to conflate readings. For convenience it is reproduced in
full, with 𝕲 omissions bracketed:

(13)   שרי (כל) ואת (בן קיח) יוחנן את ישמעאל את אשר העם כל כראות ויהי
(המצפה מן ישמעאל שבה אשר העם כל (ויסבו (14); (וישמחו) אתו אשר החילים
במשנה נמלט (בן נתניה) וישמעאל (15) : קרח) (בן יוחנן אל (וילכו) וישבו
שרי וכל קרח) (בן יוחנן ויקה (16) עמון) בני אל וילך (יוחנן (מפני אנשים
המצפה מן נתניה (בן ישמעאל מאת השיב אשר העם שארית כל את אתו אשר החילים
השיב אשר וסרסים וטף ונשים המלחמה אנשי גברים (אחיקם בן גדליה את הכה אחר
מגבעון:

The other versions (Syr Targ Vulg) agree with M, except that in verse 14
Syr reads והפכו כלה עמא דשבא אישמעיל מן מצפיא ואתו לות יוחנן בר קורח.

The majority of these variants are characteristic expansions in M:
בן קרח in verses 13, 14, 16: בן נתניה in verses 15, 16; כל in verse 13;
וישמחו in verse 13 (elaborating gloss); מפני יוחנן in verse 15.[55] Three
readings are of primary concern to us here:

(a) verse 14 וישבו וילכו(`···`)[ויסבו(`···`)] και ανεστρεφαν/ Syr והפכו
(`···`)ואתו. 𝕲 translates וישבו,[56] but it is difficult to be sure what
Syr translates, as הפך may render either שוב or סבב. The use of אהפך
for השיב in verse 16 (twice) may suggest the same here. In any case,
Syr has only one of the first two verbs. We suspect M to be a conflation of old variants וישבו/ויסבו, virtually synonymous in this context,
and easily confused both graphically and phonetically. וילכו may be general expansion.

(b) and (c), in verses 14-16:

A  v.14   `····`כל העם אשר שבה ישמעאל מן המצפה
B  v.16]   מן המצפה אחר הכה את גדליה בן אחיקם

both om. 𝕲. The occurrence of (A) and related clauses in verses 13, 16,
seems to make a very full text. It has been noted (e.g., Volz and
Rudolph) that verse 16 reads awkwardly: ויקח יוחנן`···`את כל שארית העם אשר
השיב מאת ישמעאל`···`אחר הכה את גדליה. While this is grammatically possible,
it would make a much smoother text to read, as often proposed (e.g., BH[3]),
ויקח יוחנן`···`את כל שארית העם אשר שבה אֹתם ישמעאל`···`אחר הכה את גדליה, or,
with A-106 L'[-36]-233 46 86 130 Bo Aeth Arab, `···`את כל שארית העם אשר שבו
מאת ישמעאל`···`. But another explanation seems preferable, one which at
the same time accounts for the unevenness of verse 16 and for the M plus
in verse 14. That is, that (A) in verse 14 is an old variant--probably
the original form--of verse 16. Thus, ויקח יוחנן`···`את כל העם אשר שבה
ישמעאל`···`אחר הכה את גדליה.

As for (B), admittedly this clause is om. 𝕲, and probably is to be
taken as secondary expansion from verses 2, 18, etc. But this indirectly
supports the above suggestion, as it is more easily understood as a gloss
to אשר שבה ישמעאל than to אשר השיב מאת ישמעאל. On the other hand, a text
which read אשר שבה ישמ' in verse 16, but without the following clause
(`···`אחר הכה`···`), would be easily corrupted to אשר השיב מאת ישמ' under
the influence of verse 16b אשר השיר מגבעון.[57]

We propose the following original text:

(13) ויהי כראות כל העם אשר את ישמעאל את יוחנן ואת שרי החילים אשר אתו
(14) [I(A] ויסבו/(B) וישבו] אל יוחנן (15) וישמעאל במלט בשמנה אנשים וילך
אל בני עמון (16) ויקח יוחנן וכל שרי החילים אשר אתו [II (A) את כל העם אשר
שבה ישמעאל מן מצפה/ (B) את כל שארית העם אשר השיב מאת ישמעאל] גברים[58]
(אנשי המלחמה) ונשים וטף וסרסים אשר השיב מגבעון (17) וילכו וישבו בגרות
כמוהם ···

M represents a text tradition in which the original reading II(A), early
displaced by II(B), was first marginally collated, then taken into the
text at verse 14, probably as part of the conflation there of the variants ויסבו/וישבו.

The probability of the above two conflations is increased by the
fact that chapter 41 M has been conflated in at least two other places,
verses 3 and 10 (see p. 17, nos. 31-32).[59]

57.   41.16 גברים אנשי המלחמה ונשים וטף וסרסים] δυνατους ανδρας εν
πολεμω (S* ανδρας πολεμου[-μωS^c]) και τας γυναικας και τα λοιπα και τους
ευνουχους. אנשי המלחמה is intrusive in the list, and often is taken as
a gloss to גברים, read גבורים (Hitzig, Rudolph, Ziegler, *Beiträge*, p.
101). An examination of the translation of איש (ה)מלחמה in the O.T.
suggests that the phrase originally was absent from ₵.

Outside of Jeremiah, the phrase occurs 25 times. Nineteen times
it is rendered (o) ανηρ (o) πολεμιστης (cf. Josh. 5.6, 6.3 o μαχιμος; Ex.
15.3 συντριβων πολεμους probably reflects a borrowing from Ps. 45(46).10,
where it translates *mĕbyt mlḥmwt*--see Patrick W. Skeehan, *CBQ* 25 [1963],
103-105). It is doubtful that the reading (o) ανηρ του πολεμου occurs in
old Greek contexts; where it does occur, it is probably to be taken as a
recensional replacement for the earlier rendering.[60] The data in Jeremiah point to the same conclusion: the usual rendering is o ανηρ o πολεμιστης (49.26, 50.30, 51.32, 52.7, 25; cf. 38.4);[61] o ανηρ του πολεμου
occurs only as the Hexaplaric correction in 39.4, 41.3, where the old
Greek is absent, and in 41.16.

In view, then, of general old Greek usage, and of normal usage in
Jeremiah, ανδρας εν πολεμω seems anomalous in Jer. 41.16 ₵, and we interpret it as infection from a late Greek tradition. Now, it is noteworthy
that the same chapter contains another instance (41.3) of the secondary
occurrence of אנשי המלחמה, again omitted in ₵. It is, of course, possible that the two passages have been glossed independently. But we
propose that the two readings are related, in something like the following

manner: אנשי המלחמה first appeared as a gloss on 41.3, perhaps to indicate that Ishmael did not kill *all* the Jews (verse 3a) who were with
Gedaliah;[62] subsequent copies variously absorbed the gloss (A) at 41.3
and (B) at 41.16;[63] 𝔊-*Vorlage* contained neither reading, and 𝔊 rendered
simply ...δυνατους και τας γυναικας.... Later, 𝔊 manuscripts became infected by a Greek recension corrected to (B);[64] 𝔐 represents conflation
of readings (A) and (B).

58.   44.10   לא דכאו עד היום הזה ולא יראו ולא הלכו] και ουκ επαυ-
σαντο εως της ημερας ταυτης και ουκ αντειχουτο. 𝔊 may be defective by
haplography. Or 𝔐 may represent conflation of variants יראו/דכאו which
are graphically and, in this context, semantically similar. In this
case, the unusual דכאו would have been mistaken at one point for יראו.
Ziegler interprets also the following readings as 𝔐 conflations:[65]

59.   15.5   כי מי יחמל עליך ירושלם] om. כי 𝔊 Syr.
60.   43.9   במלט במלבן] om. 𝔊. במלבן doublet of במלט.
61.   44.14   לשוב לשבת שם] om. לשבת 𝔊 Syr.
62.   49.13   לשמה לחרפה לחרב ולקללה] om. לחרב 𝔊.
63.   49.22   הנה כנשר יעלה וידאה ויפרש כפיו] om. יעלה ו' 𝔊 (= 48.40).
64.   49.30   נסו נדו מאד העמיקו לשבת] om. נדו 𝔊; cf. verse 8.
65.   50.21   חרב והחרם אחריהם] om. אחריהם 𝔊.

We consider these to be uncertain. In 59, the particle may just
be general expansion. In 60, the reading is obscure, but caution is
necessary (see p. 29, no. 30). 62 is plausible; or 𝔐 may be just expanding the series, as elsewhere. 61, 63-65 also are plausible, but
unsure.

### Double Readings in 𝔊

As Ziegler points out (*Beiträge*, pp. 87-88), the analysis of double
readings in 𝔊 is complicated by the fact that we cannot always distinguish between a doublet which existed already in 𝔊-*Vorlage*, and a doublet
which has arisen in 𝔊 subsequent to translation. Also, in the latter
case, we cannot always distinguish between the primary and the secondary
part of a doublet. However, as we shall see, neither of these complica-
tions poses serious problems for our study.

Since Ziegler has subjected the double readings in 𝔊 to close
analysis,[66] and his conclusions seem substantially correct, we will not

attempt a minute study of each reading, in the manner of the doublets
above.  Rather, we will just reproduce the data, together with comments
where we disagree with Ziegler, or where we would attempt to press further.[67]  The doublets in ₲ may be broken down into a number of types.

1.  *Doublets in which both parts = M, but one is more literal.*

    1.  8.7  *αγρου/στρουθια (עגור) (page 94).

    2.  8.16  *ιππασιας/ιππων αυτου (אביריך) (99).

    3.  10.20  *εταλαιπωρησεν/ωλετο (שדד) (94).

    4.  17.11  εφωνησε/*περδιξ (קרא) (95).

    5.  19.15  και επι (πασας) τας πολεις (αυτης)/*και επι τας *κωμας
αυτης (ועל כל עריה) (99).

    6.  26(46).21  *σιτευτοι/τρεφομενοι (מרבק) (100).

    7.  30(49).4  *εν τοις πεδιοις/εναкιμ (בעמקים) (99).

    8.  30.9(49.31)  *ου (ουδε) βαλανοι/ου (ουδε) μοχλοι (ולא בריח)
(101).

    9.  31(48).13  ελπιδος αυτων/*πεποιθοτες επ' αυτοις (מבטחם) (100).

    10.  34.12(27.15)  *? επ' αδικω (2°)/*? ψευδη[68] (₲ plus, presuppos-
ing שקר/משקר) (96).

    11.  39(32).17  *τω υψηλω/και/(τω) μετεωρω (הנטויה) (101).

    12.  39(32).35  τω Μολοχ/*βασιλει (למלך) (102).

    13.  49(42).16  *κατα (λημψεται) υμας/οπισω υμων[69] (אחריכם) (101).

    14.  50(43).6  *τους δυνατους/ανδρας (את הגברים) (101).

2.  *Doublets in which ₲-translator misread his* Vorlage, *or possessed a
non-M* Vorlage.

    15.  2.2-3  του εξακολουθησαι σε τω αγιω Ισραηλ λεγει κυριος αγιος
Ισραηλ τω κυριω (לכתך אחרי במדבר בארץ לא זרועה קדש ישראל ליהוה)
(93).
As Ziegler indicates, αγ. Ισ. τω κω  (= M)  is secondary in ₲.  He is
also correct in rejecting the suggestion (Movers, Köhler) that ₲ read
אחרי as 'אחר י (= אחר יהוה) (אחר יהוה) and translated αγιος Ισραηλ.  It is probable
that זרועה לא בארץ במדבר had dropped out of ₲-*Vorlage*, so that the translator read לכתך אחרי קדש ישראל.
    16.  3.8  *ων κατελη(μ)φθη/εν οις εμοιχατο (אשר נאפה) (93).  It is

difficult to know what $\mathcal{G}$ was translating.

17. 9.16-17(15-16) *εν αυτη/ταδε ([אמר יהוה] [כה]) (94). Ziegler comments, "Wenn man ταδε, wie es sich gehört, in den App. verweist, dann ist 'spricht Yahwe' als Schlussformel zu v. 16(15) zu setzen."[70] But in Jer., אמר יהוה is always translated ειπε κυριος, never λεγει κυριος. Unless $\mathcal{G}$-*Vorlage* read נאם יהוה, it is likely that $\mathcal{G}$ read the same text as 𝔐, and that εν αυτη is either the secondary part of the doublet, or translated בה in its *Vorlage* (developed by dittography from כה). This would eliminate the need to emend υμας...υμων 1°2° (verse 18[17]) to ημας...ημων 1°2°, against the virtually universal textual witness.[71] εν αυτη ταδε then would be the old Greek rendering of בה כה אמר יהוה.

18. 9.22(21) του πεδιου/* της γης (השדה) (98). $\mathcal{G}$-*Vorlage* read האדמה; cf. parallels in 8.2, 16.4.

19. 11.16 ανηφθη πυρ επ' αυτην/*μεγαλη η θλιψις επι σε (גדלה 3c עליה אש הצית) (100). $\mathcal{G}$-*Vorlage* read גדלה הצרה עליה.

20. 18.20 a οτι συνελαλησαν ρηματα κατα της ψυχης μου כי כרו שוחה לנפשי

.20 b ✝ και την κολασιν αυτων εκρυψαν μοι⟨ ⟩רפחם טמנו לי

.22 a οτι ενεχειρησαν λογον εις συλλημψιν μου כי כרו שיחה ללכדני

.22 b και παγιδας εκρυψαν επ' εμε ופחים טמנו לרגלי (87).

$\mathcal{G}$ presents a number of problems: (1) כרו שוחה/שיחה seems to have been understood in neither verse. συλλαλειν translates דָּבַר in Ex. 34.35 and 1 Kgs. 12.14, הקיץ(?) in Isa. 7.6, and שיח in Prv. 6.22. But ρηματα surely renders שוחה (i.e., שיחה), and we have to link the verb with כרו. Perhaps $\mathcal{G}$ reflects a reading כי דברו. ενεχειρησαν λογον is even more puzzling. The verb occurs elsewhere only in Jeremiah (28[51].12, 29.16 [49.15]; in at least the second instance, a blur-word for השיא), and in 2 Chr. (23.18 = וישם). It is odd that the same translator would render similar phrases so differently (unless he were offering alternate renderings of an obscure sentence).

(2) The variation between $\mathcal{G}$ 20b and 22b is likewise puzzling. παγις renders פח in Jer. 31(48).43, 44 (Jer. β). κολασιν renders מכשול 5 times in Ezek., and Movers proposed ואת מכשולם טמנו לי.[72] But this is unlikely; one does not *hide* a stumbling block, but place it, set it up, etc. (רום, שים, נתן).[73] The word here probably renders פחם (cf. verse 22 פחים).

(3)  As Ziegler notes, in neither verse does 𝔊 represent לרגלי,
but לי (verse 22b עלי?), as in Ps. 139(140).6, 141(142).4. 𝔐 may have
been influenced by Lam. 1.13. פרש רשׁת לרגלי.

Perhaps the above-noted differences between 𝔊 20a.b and 22a.b indicate early conflation of two Greek traditions, reflecting the position
of the couplet in verse 20 and in verse 22 respectively. 𝔐 would then
represent either partial, or subsequently defective, conflation of the
same variant traditions.

21.  21.12  *και κατευθυνατε/και εξελεσθε (והצילו) (95).  𝔊-
Vorlage read (or was misread as) והצלחו (so 13 times elsewhere in the
Septuagint and Dan. θ').

22.  23.17  *και πασι τοις πορευομενοις τοις θελημασιν αυτων/(και)
παντι τω πορευομενω πλανη καρδιας αυτου (וכל הלך בשררות לבו) (96).
Ziegler surely is correct in taking the second reading as secondary, and
the first as old Greek.  But we would question whether 𝔊-Vorlage = 𝔐.
In all other occurrences of the cliché in Jeremiah, -/לב is rendered της
καρδιας/-.[74]  It is unlikely, therefore, that τοις θελημασιν αυτων =
שררות לבו.  We propose that 𝔊-Vorlage read וכל ההלכים במצוותיהם.  Ps.
81.13 and Jer. 7.24 (cf. Mic. 6.16) illustrate the likelihood of the
secondary development of such a synonymous variant.[75]

23.  23.29  ουτως οι λογοι μου λεγει κυριος/*ουχι οι λογοι μου.
ουχ' ουτως οι λογοι μου O L  = 𝔐 (הלוא כה דברי) (100).  As Ziegler points
out, הלוא/כה already constitutes a doublet in 𝔐.  Presumably the variants were סלע יפצץ וכפטישׁ/כאשׁ כה דברי B/כאשׁ דברי הלוא A.  While 𝔐 conflated only the variant words (הלוא/כה), B-S-etc., A-etc., Q-V-etc., C'-
etc., contain conflation of 𝔊 and a Greek tradition corrected to (B) or
the like.[76]

24.  27(50).2  [βηλ] *η απτοητος η τρυφερα [παρελυθη[77] Μαρωδαχ]
(בל חת מרדך) (96).  The two readings have been--rather unusually--spliced
together.  𝔊 seems to have read בלי חת מרכבה (Cornill, followed by Ziegler).  Ziegler interprets this as a pre-Origenic doublet.

25.  29.12(49.11)  *ινα ζησηται/και/εγω ζησομαι (אני אחיה) (102).
The context shows that 𝔊 misconstrued the sense of the passage.

26.  31(48).2  *λατρεια/αγαυριαμα (תהלת) (102).  𝔊 presupposes
תעלת.

27.  36(29).32  *του ιδειν.../ουκ οφονται (ולא יראה) (101).  𝔊 presupposes לראות, which probably is original.[78]

28.  37(30).6  *καὶ περὶ φόβου, εν ω καθεξουσιν οσφυν και σωτηριαν/
δια τι εορακα παντα ανθρωπον και αι χειρες αυτου επι της οσφυος αυτου
(+ ως τικτουσης O L) (מדוע ראיתי כל גבר ידיו על חלציו כיולדה) (97). $\mathcal{C}$
represents, at least in part, inner-Greek corruption.[79]  It is noteworthy that the secondary correction does not agree exactly with 𝕸 (omitting כיולדה).

In addition to the above, Ziegler identifies two more doublets in
$\mathcal{C}$, of which we are doubtful.

29.  31(48).18  καθημενη Δαιβων εκτριβεται (ישבת בת דיבון) (102).
Ziegler takes Δαιβων as secondary (= 𝕸), and relegates it to the apparatus.  He acknowledges the difficulty of projecting the Hebrew behind
εκτριβεται and suggests that the translator had in mind שמם (cf. 43[36].
29 A Q-V-etc.), or perhaps Aramaic תבר (for שבר).  His first suggestion
is attractive.  But we need only suppose dittography in $\mathcal{C}$-Vorlage, to
give יְשֶׁבֶת יֹשֶׁבֶת דיבון, and there is no need to dispense with Δαβων as a
secondary doublet.[80]

30.  50(43).9  και κατακρυψον αυτους εν προθυροις⁺ εν πυλη˟ της
οικιας φαραω εν ταφναις (וטמנתם במלט במלבן אשר בפתח בית פרעה בתחפנחס)
(102).  As Ziegler points out, εν προθυροις cannot render במלט במלבן אשר
(BH³), as εν πυλη would then render בפתח, against Jer. $\mathcal{C}$ elsewhere (25
times πυλη = שער, 4 times προθυροις = פתח) and Septuagint generally.
But, he argues, one would expect εν προθυροις της πυλης, and "das unver-
bundene εν πυλη verrät deutlich die Dublette."  Here he follows S. R.
Driver, who designates εν πυλη as "a correction."[81]  But what would εν
πυλη be correcting toward?  It is not likely to have arisen as a later
rendering of בפתח.  Of ca. 300 occurrences (according to Hatch-Redpath),
πυλη almost always renders שער, 7 times פתח, and 3 times פתח שער (where
we may doubt that the word translates the whole phrase, or פתח).

Perhaps εν πυλη arose from a Hebrew text which read בשער in place
of בפתח, and this Greek text was conflated with a pre-Hexaplaric Greek
text reading εν προθυροις.  Or, εν προθυροις εν πυλη may represent an
old Greek translation of בפתח בשער בית פרעה, in which שער became בשער by
dittography.  It may be remarked that פתח בית פרעה is somewhat odd,
since פתח בית usually refers to the door of a building, while the general
reference of verse 9 seems to be to the courtyard, and therefore to a
courtyard gate.[82]

According to Ziegler, a couple of Greek doublets stem from inner-Greek corruption.

31. 17.26 και θυσιαν/*και θυμιαματα (וזבח) (103). Ziegler takes θυμιαματα to be a miswriting of θυματα, which he holds to be original and adopts in his text. και θυσιαν is then later correction = M.[83]

32. 31(48).36 *απωλετο/απο ανθρωπου (אבדר) (96). απο ανθρωπου originated as an erroneous development from απωλετο: ΑΠΩΛΕΤΟ > ΑΠΟΑΝΟΥ > απο ανθρωπου.

Ziegler also discusses several ¢ readings which others have taken to be doublets, but which for various reasons he would evaluate differently, or hold to be uncertain.[84] Except where I disagree with Ziegler's analysis. I will simply list the readings, together with brief comment.

33. 1.17 μη φοβηθης απο προσωπου αυτων μηδε πτοηθης εναντιον αυτων (אל תירא מפניהם פן אחתך לפניהם) (88). ¢ presupposes אל תירא מפניהם ואל תחת לפניהם, which Ziegler takes as original.

34. 1.18 εν τη σημερον ημερα (היום) (89). ¢-Vorlage = היום הזה; or pleonastic rendering; or secondary development (Ziegler).

35. 1.18 [και ως τειχος] χαλκουν οχυρον (ולחמות[נחשת) (89). Addition from 15.20 (Ziegler, following Movers and Hitzig).

36. 2.29 παντες υμεις ησεβησατε και παντες υμεις ηνομησατε εις εμε (כלכם פשעתם בי) (89). A doublet is possible. But it is as likely that ¢-Vorlage read כלכם רשעתם וכלכם פשעתם בי (so Cornill). In fact M may have suffered haplography, כלכם 1°2°. One cannot be sure (Ziegler).

37. 3.17 εν ταις ημεραις εκειναις÷ και εν τω καιρω εκεινω⸓ (בעת ההיא) (90). It may well be that ¢-Vorlage read בימים ההמה ובעת ההיא, after 27(50).4, 20, and 40(33).15 (Ziegler, following Movers).

38. 4.1 ⁺εκ στοματος αυτου και⸓ απο προσωπου μου (מפני) (90). On the one hand, the preceding verb is always followed by απο προσωπου; on the other, εκ στοματος αυτου fits the context well (cf. Hos. 2.19, Zech. 9.7). ¢ probably translates מפיך ומפני; or the first phrase stems from Hos. and Zech. (Ziegler).

39. 4.19 μαιμασσει⁺ η ψυχη μου σπαρασσεται⸓ η καρδια μου (המה לי לבי) (90). Ziegler concludes that a clear solution is not possible, though he admits the possibility that the second member may have stemmed from Symmachus. The verse is worth examination as a whole:

την κοιλιαν μου την κοιλιαν μου αλγω      מעי מעי אחולה

και τα αισθητηρια της καρδιας μου      קירות לבי

μαιμασσει η ψυχη μου/σπαρασσεται η καρδια μου　　　　המה לי לבי

ου σιωπησομαι　　　　　　　לא אחריש

οτι φωνην σαλπιγγος ηκουσεν η ψυχη μου　　כי קול שופר שָׁמָעְתִּי נפשי

κραυγην πολεμου　　　　　　　תרועת מלחמה

Line 5 is metrically overloaded in M and, as BH[3] and Ziegler suggest,
נפשי is secondary, standing originally in some relation to line three.
We propose the following *Ur*-text:

מעי מעי אחולה

קירות לבי

המה לי/A נפשי/B לבי

לא אחריש

כי קול שופר שמעתי

תרועת מלחמה

M stems from a text base with variant (B), which was glossed with נפשי
from a text with (A). The relative lateness of the gloss may be indicated by the form שָׁמָעְתִּי, wherein Ketib reflects the unglossed text. It
is peculiar that ₵ contains both the misplaced gloss in line 5 *and* the
old variants in line 3, in doublet form. If σπαρασσεται η καρδια μου
stems from Symmachus (Ziegler: "es wäre...möglich"), it may be that η
ψυχη μου 2° is also a late correction, and that ₵-*Vorlage* represents the
*Ur*-text with נפשי in line 3.

40. 4.29 εισεδυσαν εις τα σπηλαια[+] και εις τα αλση εκρυβησαν
και επι τας πετρας ανεβησαν (באו בעבים ובכפים עלו) (91). Giesebrecht,
Cornill, Streane take ₵ as a doublet; Duhm, Volz, Rudolph take M as defective. One cannot be certain, though word choice makes a doublet less
likely (Ziegler).

41. 8.2 [+]και προς παντας τους αστερας και προς πασαν την στρα-
τιαν (ולכל צבא) (91). Ziegler views και προς τους αστερας as a simple
plus from Deut. 4.19 ₵.[85]

42. 8.21 ωδινες ως τικτουσης (22) μη ρητινη (הצרי) (91).
Ziegler (following Movers) takes ωδινες ως τικτουσης as expansion from
related passages, such as 6.24, 22.23.

43. 17.8 επ' αυτω στελεχη αλσωδη (עלהו רענן) (92). Not a
doublet, but "verdeutlichende Wiedergabe" (Ziegler).

44. 20.9 δυναμαι φερειν (אוכל) (92). "Verdeutlichende Wiedergabe aus stilistischen Gründen" (Ziegler).

45. 23.6 κυριος Ιωσεδεκ (יהוה צדקנו) (92). ₵ read /יוצדק

יהוצדק. Whether κυριος is a doublet to Ιω‾ or secondarily added subject
to preceding καλεσει cannot be decided (Ziegler).

|  | | | |
|---|---|---|---|
| 46. | 24.1 | και τους αρχοντας | שׂרי |
|  |  | και τους τεχνιτας | חרשׁ |
|  |  | και τους δεσμωτας | מסגר |
|  |  | ✝και τους πλουσιους×‾ | (92) |
| 47. | 36(29).2 | και των ευνουχων | סרסים |
|  |  | (+ ✖ και αρχοντων Ιουδα O L) | שׂרי |
|  |  | και παντος ελευθερου |  |
|  |  | και δεσμωτου (τεχνιτου Q–V O L C) | חרשׁ |
|  |  | και τεχνιτου (δεσμωτου Q–V O L C) | מסגר (92) |

In each passage, $\mathcal{G}$-*Vorlage* probably contained 4 members (cf. also Baruch
1.9, 2 Kgs. 24.14, 15, 16), and πλουσιους/ελευθερον are not doublets
(Ziegler).

Seven other readings are similarly doubtful. They are of such in-
significance that they will just be cited, together with the page on
which Ziegler deals with them: 3.8 (98), 5.15 (103), 11.10 (94), 14.7
(94), 21.7 (95), 22.17 (99), 26(46).15 (96).

## Summary and Conclusions

Of the doublets in $\mathcal{G}$, 14 do not originate in the Hebrew *Vorlage*,
but arise from the conflation of earlier and later (usually more literal)
renderings, each of which agrees with 𝔐. The other 18 comprise one element which usually represents the old Greek (except where inner-Greek
corruption has occurred), and one element which normally is equivalent
to 𝔐. In a few instances, the secondary element is quite early. Of the
18, it is highly unlikely that more than a few existed in $\mathcal{G}$-*Vorlage* (numbers 20, 23; perhaps 16, 21, 30, 31). Insofar as we can use such negative evidence, the data strongly suggest the prerecensional character of
$\mathcal{G}$-*Vorlage*. This will receive further support from a study (in chapter
VI) of haplography in $\mathcal{G}$.

On the other hand, the thirty-odd doublets in our best witnesses
show that the old Greek text tradition was not immune from the influence of later Greek recensions which stood closer to 𝔐. This, together
with the occasional instance where a late 𝔐-type Greek reading has infected virtually the whole witness,[86] and the series of variants in which

the old Greek reading is very narrowly transmitted,[87] suggests that originally the Greek tradition and its Hebrew *Vorlage* may have been even more
divergent from 𝔐--at least with regard to length--than indicated by
Ziegler's eclectic text. While this further divergence would be relatively small in comparison with the attested divergence, and difficult
to discover, on occasion a careful interpretation of vocabulary usage[88]
(especially where it is cleft between Jeremiah α and β) may allow us to
get behind the united Greek witness. We would emphasize that these occa-
sions may be rare, yet methodologically one should be alert to this possibility.

The number of double readings in 𝔐 is significantly high, with at
least 45 clear cases, and probably a score more. This high number serves
to confirm, and to elaborate on, the picture to be sketched in chapters
III and IV of the character of the 𝔐 text. As we might expect, a text
tradition which suffered much change and development was further expanded
by attempts to bring divergent texts into conformity with each other.
Moreover, since we now know that the Egyptian Hebrew text tradition was
present in Palestine at least in the Hasmonaean period (4QJer[b]), it is
quite possible, if not probable, that some of the 𝔐 doublets stem from
conflation of Egyptian readings to the 𝔐 text base.[89]

III   Additions from Parallel and Related Contexts

One of the most common conditions of textual expansion is the existence in a text of two or more passages similar in wording or content, or
of stock phrases which may appear in two or more closely related forms.
Through familiarity with the text as a whole, the scribe may elaborate
one passage from the other.  This may occur unintentionally, when the
copyist's memory of the related context prevails over his attention to
the context at hand.  Or the passage may be glossed intentionally from
the parallel context, for any one of a number of reasons.  The clearest
and most dramatic example of the latter phenomenon is perhaps the series
of "quotations" from Deuteronomy secondarily inserted into the text of
Numbers in one text tradition of that book, attested primarily in the
Samaritan text, but found now also in 4QNum[b] (an exemplar of an old Palestinian text tradition),[1] and in some instances in the margin of the Syro-
hexapla and three cursive Greek manuscripts.[2]  These additions are deliberate scholarly glosses.

While additions may be made to the text of one book from parallel
passages in another book of the Old Testament (as in the example just
given), most commonly such additions are taken from parallel contexts in
the same book.  We may reasonably expect that, other things being equal,
it will be a book which is characterized by repetitiveness and series of
stock phrases which will provide the most opportunity for this type of
expansion.  For various reasons, some text traditions contain more expansions of this sort than do other traditions.[3]

In this chapter I will present those instances of expansion, both
in 𝕸 and 𝕲, which I judge to have arisen in the manner just described.
I will present the data first for the additions in 𝕸, then for those in
𝕲.  A brief section will deal with the word כל as an addition.

*Additions in M*

1.  1.10 ולהרוס [om. ∅. The infinitives belong to a recurring
series, the forms of which are worth citing in full (bracketed words are
absent in ∅).

| (a) | 24.6, 42.10, 45.4 | בנה˙˙˙הרס//נטע˙˙˙נתש |
|     | Cf. 31.40 | לא ינתש ולא יהרס |
| (b) | 12.17 | ונתשתי את הגוי ההוא נתוש ואבד |
| (c) | 1.10 | ראה הפקדתיך היום הזה על הגוים ועל הממלכות |
|     | | לנתוש ולנתוץ ולהאביד (ולהרוס) לבנות ולנטוע |
| (d) | 18.7 | רגע אדבר על גוי ועל ממלכה לנתוש (ולנתוץ) ולהאביד |
|     | 18.9 | ורגע אדבר על גוי ועל ממלכה לבנת ולנטע |
| (e) | 31.28 | כאשר שקדתי עליהם (לנתוש ולנתוץ) ולהרס (ולהאביד) ולהרע |
|     | | כן אשקד עליהם לבנות ולנטוע |

Examples (a) and (b) indicate the proper form of this series to be
contrasting pairs. In (e) M, the balance of the sentence has been disrupted by additions from (c). The same has occurred in (d) M. In (c),
ולהרוס is intrusive from (a) and (e). ולהאביד probably is also secondary,
from (b) and (d)[4] (note the general similarity between 18.7, 9, and 1.10),
in which case the expansion occurred before divergence of ∅ and M archetypes, or ∅ was revised secondarily to a partially expanded Hebrew text.
    Thus, in this saying the positive pair is constant (בנה-נטע), while
the negative pair is variable (נתש-נתץ, נתש-האביד, הרס-נתש, הרס-הרע), a
device, perhaps, for "ringing the changes" on what was the main burden of
Jeremiah's message. This variation invites filling out, especially in
1.10 which is the programmatic statement of Jeremiah's prophetic ministry
toward the nations.
    2.  1.11 ירמיהו [om. ∅. From 24.3; cf. 1.13.
    3.  1.18 לכהניה [om. ∅. Streane and Cornill see the word as M
addition, but Volz argues "es ist unentbehrlich." We have here, as elsewhere, a stereotyped list of officials. Compare:

| (a) | 2.26, 32.32 (and Neh. 9.32) | המה מלכיהם שריהם כהניהם נביאיהם |
| (b) | 4.9 | מלך˙˙˙שרים//כהנים˙˙˙נביאים |
| (c) | 26.11, 12, 16, 34.10 | שרים-כל העם    כהנים-נביאים |
| (d) | 44.21 (cf. Dan 9.6) | אתם ואבותיכם מלכיכם ושריכם ועם הארץ |

37.2                                          הוא [המלך] ועבדיו ועם הארץ ,.i.e]

מלך-שרים-עם הארץ and ,שרים-כל העם ,מלך-שרים, כהנים-נביאים While are

natural groupings,[5] it would seem from the above instances that in 1.18

לכהנים is intrusive, from 2.26 and 32.32.

4.  3.8,10 [אחותה] om. 𝄢. From verse 7. In verse 10 𝕸 is awkward,
as the pronoun has no proper antecedent.

5.  3.9 [ותחנף את הארץ] om. 𝄢. Probably a gloss on the following
phrase, based on verses 1, 2 (but possibly a conflated variant to the
following העץ).

6.  3.11 [משבה] om. 𝄢. Probably from verses 6, 8, 12.

7.  4.8 [לא שב חרון אף יהוה] om. חרון G. From 30.24, cf. also 7
times elsewhere. The form ישוב אף יהוה (לא) occurs in 23.20 (cf. 2.35).

8.  5.19 [עזבתם אותי ו' י'] om. 𝄢. Secondary from 16.11, 19.4, 22.9;
cf. 1.16. The intrusive clause spoils the balance and thrust of the prophetic word כאשר עבדתם'''כן תעבדו (so also Volz; cf. Cornill).

9.  7.1-2 הדבר אשר היה אל ירמיהו מאת יהוה לאמר עמד בשער בית יהוה
וקראת שם את הדבר הזה ואמרת שמעו דבר יהוה כל יהודה הבאים בשערים האלה
להשתחות ליהוה] Ακουσατε λογου κυριου, πασα η Ιουδαια. Volz and Rudolph
prefer 𝕸, and interpret 𝄢 as radical abbreviation. Gerstenberger argues
that 𝄢 has altered the editorial framework of Jer. 2.25, in part because
he no longer understood its meaning, and in part because he was not interested in preserving this systematization.[6] To be sure, it is doubtful
that the translator of Jeremiah (or of any other book!) was interested
in the editorial framework *per se*. But why should this lead him to muti-
late the text? The words are easily understood, and similar introductory
sentences in numerous other places are translated fully and precisely.
The fact is, as Gerstenberger acknowledges, that he *assumes* 𝕸 to be older.
But in the context of the same argument, he also acknowledges that the
editorial framwork of 𝕸 is "clearly late." Given, then, two witnesses
to the form of Jeremiah, it would seem to be more sound methodology to
proceed on the assumption that the more systematic text is *later* than
the less systematic one.

As for Volz's judgment that "es liegt kein Grund vor, von 𝕸 abzu-
gehen," just the opposite is the case. In addition to the methodological
grounds just suggested, there are other indications that 𝕸 is secondary:

(a)  הבאים בשערים האלה להשתחות ליהוה] om. 𝄢. Similar phrases
occur after the exhortation, in 17.20, 22.2, and 26.2. But the phrase

is out of place in 7.2, as the sermon was delivered, not in the gate(s),
but in the Temple *court* (26.2); moreover, the phrase properly refers, as
in chapter 17 and 22, to the city or palace gates. As often happens,
the expansion arose from a superficial similarity between two passages,
and in the process introduced a slight incongruity into the text. It
should be noted that in 19.3, ȼ adds the phrase והבאים בשערים האלה after
the exhortation, a reading generally taken (e.g., BH[3]) as secondary from
17.20, 22.2. To interpret the latter reading as expansion in ȼ, and the
former zero variant as abbreviation in ȼ, is methodologically unacceptable.

(b)  הדבר אשר היה אל ירמיהו מאת יהוה לאמר עמד בשער בית יהוה וקראת
[שם את הדבר הזה ואמרת] om. ȼ. The common content of chapters 7 and 26,
and their verbal parallels, invite secondary harmonization (see below,
nos. 10 and 11). The introduction is derived from 26.2. Hyatt's attempt
to explain שער בית יהוה (7.2) and חצר בית יהוה (26.2) serves to point up
another minor incongruity created by the expansion. Several other instances of secondary insertion in 𝕸 of introductory and concluding sentences may be cited: 2.1-2, 27.1, 46.1, 46.26, 47.1, 48.47, 49.6, 51.64
(on these see pp. 111-114).

     10.  7.10 [בבית הזה] om. הזה ȼ. From 26.6, 9, 12; cn. 7.14.

     11.  7.11 [הבית הזה] ביתי ȼ. See no. 10 above.

     12.  7.13 [השכם ודבר] om. ȼ. 𝕸 represents infection of one expres-
sion by another, closely related; cf. ואדבר אליכם ולא שמעתם ואקרא אתכם
ולא עניתם (35.17 [cf. 7.27], Isa. 65.12, 66.4) and ואדבר אליכם השכם ודבר
ולא שמעתם (35.14; cf. 7.25, 26.5 29.9, etc.).

     13.  7.26 [ויקשו את ערפם הרעו מאבותם] om. הרעו ȼ. Streane com-
ments, "the M.T. has scarcely the air of an insertion." The opposite is
suggested by the following: 2 Chr. 30.8 (ולא תקשו ערפכם כאבותיכם) and 2
Kgs. 17.14 (ויקשו את ערפם כערף אבותם) indicate that in this expression
one should expect ‑/אבות to modify ויקשו.[7] 17.23 ולא שמעו ולא הטו את אזנם
מאבותם + [אזנם ויקשו את ערפם] ȼ. The expansion clearly is from 7.26, and
indirectly supports ȼ there. Syr wqšyw qdlhwn ṭb mn ᵓbhyhwn seems to
support ȼ (cf. 16.12 Syr). 𝕸 הרעו probably is from 16.12 ואתם הרעתם לעשות
מאבותיכם (ȼ om. לעשות; cf. 1 Kgs. 14.9, 16.25, 2 Kgs. 21.11).

     14.  7.27-28  ודברת אליהם את כל הדברים האלה ולא ישמעו אליך וקראת אליהם
[ולא יענוכה ואמרת אליהם] και ερεις αυτοις του λογου τουτον. Streane's
suggestion that ȼ may be due to haplography, אליהם verse 7 to אליהם verse

8, overlooks the fact that και ερεις presupposes וְאָמַרְתָּ, so that the copyist's eye could not have jumped from וְדִבַּרְתָּ over to אֲלֵיהֶם (וְאָמַרְתָּ). Verse
27 is similar to verse 13, and probably secondary from it. This may be
supported by two observations: In 7.13, 35.17 𝔐, Isa. 65.12, 66.4, the
expression always constitutes a protasis introduced by יַעַן, the apodosis
of which expresses a judgment meted out by Yahweh. Further, it is Yahweh's speaking which falls on deaf ears. On the other hand, in 7.27 𝔐
the expression lacks יַעַן, and is not a protasis but a simple declaration.
Moreover the unheeded speaker is not Yahweh but Jeremiah. The likelihood is that the context (verses 25-28) has attracted a secondary, and
blurred, intrusion of a set expression. The parallel passage 17.23 (וְלֹא
שָׁמְעוּ וְלֹא הִטּוּ אֶת אָזְנָם וַיַּקְשׁוּ אֶת עָרְפָּם לְבִלְתִּי שְׁמוֹעַ וּלְבִלְתִּי קַחַת מוּסָר) would seem
to suggest that 7.28 follows verse 26 better than verse 27.

        The text may once have read וְאָמַרְתָּ אֲלֵיהֶם אֶת הַדָּבָר הַזֶּה זֶה הַגּוֹי.  Sec-
ondary introduction of the expression from verse 13 involved replacement
of אָמַרְתָּ by דִבַּרְתָּ, and in addition אֶת הַדָּבָר הַזֶּה became אֵת כָּל הַדְּבָרִים הָאֵלֶּה
which is frequent in Jeremiah. Or, the original text may have read
וְאָמַרְתָּ אֲלֵיהֶם זֶה הַגּוֹי.  אֶת הַדָּבָר הַזֶּה would then be expansion (before divergence of 𝔐 and 𝔊 archetypes) from 13.12, 14.17.[8]

        15.  8.3 הַנִּשְׁאָרִים] om. 𝔊 Syr. The word makes no sense here, in-
trudes upon this set expression (for references, see p. 53, no. 141), and
is secondary from verse 3a.

        16.  8.11 שֶׁבֶר בַּת עַמִּי 𝔐] אֶת שֶׁבֶר עַמִּי 𝔐] אֶת שֶׁבֶר עַמִּי 6.14 𝔐 𝔊.[9] שֶׁבֶר עַמִּי has
become שֶׁבֶר בַּת עַמִּי under the influence of 8.21 (cf. also 8.19, 22, 23).
This expansion seems in turn to have infected 6.14 in some proto-𝔐 manuscripts (+ της θυγατρος O(𝕏)-86mg(sub+) 62 613 Arm σ'-Qmg(𝕏) Syr Targ
Vulg).

        17.  9.9 מִבְּלִי אִישׁ עֹבֵר] om. 𝔊. From verse 11 (cf. verses 9,
10, 11 מִבְּלִי עֹבֵר-מִבְּלִי אִישׁ מִבְּלִי אִישׁ-מִבְּלִי יוֹשֵׁב-מִבְּלִי עֹבֵר with Zeph. 3.6
מֵאֵין יוֹשֵׁב-).

        18.  9.12 וְלֹא הָלְכוּ בָהּ] om. 𝔊. The clause probably originated as
a gloss on עַל עָזְבָם אֶת תּוֹרָתִי in verse 12a, on the basis of such passages
as 26.4, 44.10.

        19.  10.3 מַעֲשֵׂי יְדֵי חָרָשׁ] om. יְדֵי 𝔊. 𝔐 may be glossed from verse 9,
but more likely from the related passage Deut. 27.15 (מַעֲשֵׂה יְדֵי חָרָשׁ) making the idolatry a verbally precise example of the action accursed in
Deut. For similar theological glosses from Deut. see p.48f, nos. 79, 86.

20. 10.16 וישראל שבט [כי יוצר הכל הוא וישראל שבט נחלתו om. ₵ (cf.
Jer. 51.19). The addition was inspired by Deut. 32.9, Isa. 63.17, Pss.
74.2, 78.71.

21. 11.4 ועשיתם אותם] om. אותם ₵. From verse 6. The word is
impossible in this verse.

22. 11.7-8 כי העד העדתי באבותיכם ביום העלותי אותם מארץ מצרים ועד
היום הזה השכם והעד לאמר שמעו בקולי ולוא שמעו ולא חטו את אזנם וילכו איש
במשררות לבם הרע ואביא עליהם את כל דברי הברית הזאת אשר צויתי לעשות] om. ₵.
This reading is difficult to explain with certainty, and a number of explanations have been put forth. Cornill, for example, sees ₵ as due to
haplography, since ולא עשו (verse 8) lacks a proper subject and comes too
abruptly after verse 6 for ₵ to be original.[10] Others[11] prefer ₵, reading 𝔐 either as expansion from elsewhere in Jeremiah or as a doublet of
verse 4. Still others argue that ₵ deleted deliberately "wohl weil als
zu ähnlich mit 3ff. empfunden."[12]

To the last argument, it may be objected that, though there is
some repetition of phrases, the passages do not say the same thing at
all. One relates the single historical covenant event, while the other
elaborates the familiar theme of Israel's continuing rebellion and dis-
obedience in the face of Yahweh's constant exhortation to covenant
loyalty. Moreover, if ₵ were concerned to eliminate repetition here, we
might have expected him to delete verse 6, which is just as close a
parallel to verses 1-3a. A general objection may also be raised: when
a passage otherwise shows clear signs of late development and expansion
(e.g., verse 2 שמעו את דברי הברית הזאת, which surely is from verse 6,
and verse 13, which is intrusive from 2.28), we ought to take seriously
the textual evidence for a shorter text, unless its omission can be explained by scribal error.

Is ₵ then secondarily defective? The close similarity of 6b (את
את כל דברי הברית הזאת אשר צויתי) and 8b (דברי הברית הזאת ועשיתם אותם
לעשות) is perhaps indicative of haplography. If, in addition, ₵ or ₵-
Vorlage had expanded verse 8 to לעשות אותם,[13] the case for haplography
would be secure. This would not, of course, preclude the judgment on
other grounds that verses 6-8 are an early secondary addition, perhaps a
doublet of 1-5.

On the other hand, it may be argued that ₵ does attest an earlier
stage of the text, and that verses 7-8 are secondary from 7.22-24 and

Deuteronomic language elsewhere (note the parallels between chapters 7 and 11, especially 7.22-24 and 11.1-5).[14] As for the difficulty in read-ing ולא עשׂו, it may be suggested that after verse 6 was taken into the text (the text originally following from verse 5 to verse 9), ולא עשׂו was glossed to smooth the transition to the next passage, verses 9-14. Verses 7-8 were later added as an elaboration of this phrase, from simi-lar contexts. ₡ would then represent a partially developed text, earlier than 𝔐, but not itself original.

23.  13.5  וֵאֵלֵךְ] om. ₡. Probably from verse 4.

24.  13.7  הָאֵזוֹר] om. ₡. From verse 7a, etc.

25.  13.10 הַהֹלְכִים מְשֵׁרְרוּת לִבָּם] om. ₡. From 7.24, 11.8, 23.17.

26.  14.4  כִּי לֹא הָיָה גֶשֶׁם בָּאָרֶץ] בָאָרֶץ om. ₡ Syr. From 1 Kgs. 17.7.

27.  14.10 וַיִּפְקֹד חַטֹּאתָם] om. ₡. From Hos. 8.13.

28.  14.17 כִּי שֶׁבֶר גָּדוֹל נִשְׁבְּרָה בְּתוּלַת בַּת עַמִּי om. גָּדוֹל, בְּתוּלַת ₡. 𝔐 is metrically overloaded. גָּדוֹל is added after שֶׁבֶר from 4.6, 6.1, 48.3, 50.22, 51.54. בְּתוּלַת probably came into 𝔐 from related בְּתוּלַת בַּת expres-sions (cf. 2 Kgs. 19.21, Isa. 23.12, 37.22, 47.1, Jer. 46.11, Lam. 1.15, 2.13).

29.  16.10 הַגְּדוֹלָה] om. ₡. From 32.42; cf. 32.23, 40.2, 44.23.

30.  16.12 לַעֲשׂוֹת] om. ₡. See p. 37, no. 13.

31.  16.13 וְיוֹמָם וָלַיְלָה] om. ₡. The phrase probably is a wrongly absorbed marginal gloss on the following phrase אֲשֶׁר לֹא אֶתֵּן לָכֶם חֲנִינָה, from Deut. 28.66 (note also the parallel, verse 13//Deut. 28.64).

32.  17.20 וְכָל יְהוּדָה וְכֹל יֹשְׁבֵי יְרוּשָׁלַם] יֹשְׁבֵי ₡. From the ex-pression אִישׁ יְהוּדָה וְיֹשְׁבֵי יְרוּשָׁלַם, 17.25 and several other places.

33.  17.24 בָהּ כָל מְלָאכָה] לְבִלְתִּי עֲשׂוֹת בָהּ om. ₡. The word may be an expansion according to frequent usage in this general type of prohibi-tion; but more likely it reflects specifically a form of the Sabbath com-mandment which contained the word.[15]

34.  18.4  בָּחֹמֶר] om. ₡. From verse 6, after בְיַד הַיּוֹצֵר > בְיָדוֹ (see p. 74, e).

35.  18.6  בֵּית יִשְׂרָאֵל 2°]. om. ₡. From 1°.

36.  18.8  אֲשֶׁר דִּבַּרְתִּי עָלָיו] om. ₡ Syr. 𝔐 is awkward.[16] The phrase was added from such parallel contexts as 19.15, 35.17, 36.31. The expan-sion may have been facilitated by misreading מֵרָעָתִי; but the correctness of מֵרָעָתוֹ is supported by 23.14, 44.5.

37.  18.11 וְדַרְכֵיכֶם ר] om. ₡. Two versions of a set expression

have been mixed in 𝔐; cf. היטיבו דרכיכם ומעלליכם (7.3, 7.5, 26.13) and שבו נא איש מדרכו הרעה והיטיבו מעלליכם (35.15).

38.  19.1 ומזקני הכהנים [ומהכהנים‎ 𝒢. From the preceding phrase (and cf. 2 Kgs. 19.2).

39.  19.5 ולא דברתי‎ ] om. 𝒢. The words do not belong in this sentence (cf. 7.31, 32.35). Probably they are from 14.14.

40.  19.9 ומבקשי נפשם‎ ] om. 𝒢. This variant involves an expression which occurs often, with textual variants. It will be helpful to deal with all of them together (𝒢 omissions bracketed):

| | | |
|---|---|---|
| (a) | 19.7 | והפלתים בחרב לפני איביהם וביד מבקשי נפשם |
| (b) | 19.9 | במצור ובמצוק אשר יציקו להם איביהם (ומבקשי נפשם) |
| (c) | 21.7 | אתן את צדקיהו מלך יהודה ואת עבדיו ואת העם (ואת) הנשארים |
| | | בעיר הזאת מן הדבר מן החרב ומן הרעב |
| | | (ביד נבוכדראצר מלך בבל ו)ביד איביהם (וביד) מבקשי נפשם |
| (d) | 22.25 | ונתתיך ביד מבקשי נפשך (וביד) אשר אתה יגור מפניהם |
| | | (וביד נבוכדראצר מלך בבל ו)ביד הכשדים |
| (e) | 34.20 | ונתתי אותם ביד איביהם (וביד מבקשי נפשם) |
| (f) | 34.21 | ואת צדקיהו'''אתן ביד איביהם (וביד מבקשי נפשם)ו(ביד) חיל |
| | | מלך בבל |
| (g) | 38.16 | אם אמיתך ואם אתנך ביד האנשים האלה (אשר מבקשים את נפשך) |
| (h) | 44.30 | הנני נתן את פרעה חפרה מלך מצרים ביד איביו וביד מבקשי נפשו |
| | | כאשר נתתי את צדקיהו מלך יהודה ביד נב' מ' ב' איבו ומבקש נפשו |
| (i) | 46.26 | (ונתתים ביד מבקשי נפשם וביד נב' מ' ב' וביד עבדיו ואחרי כן תשכן |
| | | כימי קדם נאם יהוה) |
| (j) | 49.37 | והחתתי את עילם לפני איביהם (ולפני) מבקשי נפשם |

(a')  No variants, so far as the expression is concerned.

(b')  From (a), (c), (h), (j). The correspondence of 𝒢 to Deut. 28.57 (of which 19.9b is a quotation) supports its superiority.

(c')  ואת 3° from the preceding phrases (the correctness of העם הנשארים is obvious). וביד 2° from, e.g., (a), (h). ביד נב' מלך בבל may be missing in 𝒢 due to haplography. But the likelihood that 𝔐 is secondary is indicated by the tendency of 𝔐 to insert (נבוכדראצר) מלך בבל (cf. 21.4, 27.12), even where the passage is not specifically concerned with him (cf. 25.9, 11, 12, 26). The insertion probably is from (h).

(d')  וביד 1° from the preceding and following; 𝔐 is awkward. וביד נב' מלך בבל is secondary (see the preceding note). In 21.4 also, 𝔐

fills in בבל מלך before הׁמׁשׁדים (once these two insertions have been made,
ו 4° is necessary to smooth out the sentence).

(e')   20.5 shows that the idiom ונתתי''''ביד איביהם is at home in
Jeremiah. ᴍ is secondary from (a). Note that for ביד איביהם 𝔊 reads
τους εχθροις αυτων; the usual translation of ביד is εις χειρας or εν
χερσι.

(f')   Again, ᴍ probably is expanded from (c). It would be unlikely
to have two such inadvertent omissions in succession, and no cogent reason can be advanced for deliberate omission by the translator. For וביד
חיל מלך בבל העלים מעליכם, 𝔊 reads και δυναμις βασιλεως Βαβυλωνος τους·
αποτρεχουσιν απ αυτων, which makes no sense. The *Vorlage* may have read
וחיל מלך בבל לעלים מעליהם, with dittography of ל before עלים. In this
case, the corruption might reflect an original text in which verse 21a
ביד איביהם ended one sentence, and the next began וחיל מלך בבל העלים
מעליכם הנני מצוה נאם יהוה והשבתים אל העיר. As Giesebrecht points out,
such a text makes sense out of the suffix in הׁשׁבׁתים, which otherwise
hangs awkwardly in the air with no antecedent. We would have in ᴍ, then,
an example of multiplication of prepositional phrases, as in (c), (d),
(j).

(g')   Secondary from 11.21.

(h')   No variants relating to the expression.

(i')   Cornill advances two arguments for the superiority of 46.26
ᴍ:   verse 26a "können nur vor dem Zuge Nebukadnezars geschrieben sein,
der in Wirklichkeit ganz anders verlief, als hier angenommen wird"; verse
26b "sieht nicht nach einem jüngeren Zusatze aus:  ein Ergänzer würde
nicht כן ואחרי gesagt haben, sondern mit unfehlbarer Sicherheit ובאחרית
הימים." To the second argument, it is sufficient to point out that in
fact we have another such secondary "comforting conclusion" with ואחרי כן
in 49.6. As for 26a, the combined explicit statements of context (verses
2, 13, 24, and cf. 44.30) would certainly be suggestive enough to a
scribe whose knowledge of the outcome of Carchemish was not so precise as
that of the modern historian.

(j')   Again, ולפני filled out from the preceding phrase.

To sum up, while the expression אׁיׁב//מבקש נפׁש occur 6 times in ᴍ-𝔊,
3 times ᴍ expands to this formula by adding the second member (for use
of only one member in ᴍ-𝔊, cf. 20.5, 22.25, 46.26 ᴍ. Moreover, ᴍ tends
to level through with the prepositional phrase.  That the idiom is less

constant than 𝕸 would suggest, is seen from 19.7, 44.30. This series of
passages illustrates well the tendency of 𝕸 to level recurrent expressions which originally were not rigidly uniform.

41.  19.11  ובתפת יקברו מאין מקום לקבור]  om. 𝕲.  The intrusive
character of these words at this point is generally recognized. Volz
suggests that they fell out of their original place at the end of verse
6 (cf. the identical passage, 7.31–33), and that the marginal correction
was taken into the text at the wrong point, near בתפת in verse 12.
Rudolph argues that the clause is not original in chapter 19, but was
glossed beside verse 6 from 7.32, then wrongly taken into the text by
verse 12. The most likely explanation is that the clause was intended
as a clarifying gloss on בתפת verse 12 (cf. כמקום חפת, verse 13) to
elucidate the point of the analogy, and thus was taken into the text at
approximately the intended spot.[17] This expansion would be not simply
due to parallel context, but would be a typical "scholarly footnote,"
similar to those in 28.16 and 29.32 (see p. 48f, nos. 79 and 86).

42.  20.5  אתן]  om. 𝕲.  The verb is not necessary in this sentence
(cf. 21.7), and probably has been inserted before ביד from 22.25, 34.20,
21.

43.  21.4  In this verse, 𝕸 and 𝕲 differ at four points, with 𝕲
omitting (a) אלהי ישראל, (b) אשר בידכם, (c) 'ו' את מלך בבל and (d) ואספתי
אותם.  Rudolph comments, "𝕲 kürzt den ungefügen Satz." This will not
stand up to close examination. (a) is a typical expansion of the prophetic cliché (see chapter IV), (b) is a simple case of haplography in 𝕲
or its *Vorlage*, while (c) is again a typical expansion (cf. similar expansion in verse 7, and 22.25), probably on the basis of verse 2. Only
(d) is a serious possibility. However, it is difficult to see what is
"ungefügen" about 𝕸. If anything, 𝕸's reading breaks up the long sentence of 𝕲 into two shorter and grammatically simpler ones. Most likely,
𝕸 has been expanded secondarily to make explicit the import of the construction  הנני מסב את כלי המלחמה''''אל תוך העיר  which, though grammatical,[18] is somewhat elliptical, especially with the interposed אשר clauses.

44.  21.5  ובאף]  om. 𝕲.  𝕸 elsewhere fills out אף secondarily behind חמה (42.18), and may be doing the same here. However, the whole
verse comprises stock Deuteronomic clichés (cf. Deut. 29.27, Jer. 32.37),
and 𝕸 may be original. We cannot be certain.

45.  21.9  בחרב וברעב ובדבר]  om. ובדבר 𝕲.  The series (חרב רעב (דבר

occurs 25 times in Jer. 𝕸: (a) 15 times in full, (b) 10 times with only
the first two terms.[19]  One of the latter series is om. 𝕲 and secondary
(44.12 2°). Of the former, 𝕲 is minus the last member (דבר) 7 times
(bracketed references in note 19). Thus, while in 𝕸 the proportion (a) :
(b) is 15 : 10, in 𝕲 it is 8 : 16.[20]  Giesebrecht comments, "ובדבר fehlt
...aus Bequemlichkeit in LXX" (p. 118), and "in LXX fehlt unrechtmässig
ובדבר, das sonst vorhanden" (p. 149). With the exception of Streane,
others assume the correctness of 𝕸. But arguments such as Giesebrecht's
start from 𝕸, conclude that the three-member series is a genuine characteristic expression in the book,[21] and judge 𝕲 accordingly. But in
that case, 𝕲 has translated the full series almost as often as it has
been shortened. The possibility that 𝕲 is original and 𝕸 secondary from
the full occurrences is at least as strong, and, in view of the general
tendency of the latter tradition, more likely.

   46.  21.12  מפני רע מעלליהם] om. 𝕲. Secondary from the doublet in
4.4; cf. also 26.3, 7.20, 17.27.

   47.  21.14  ופקדתי עליכם כפרי מעלליכם נאם יהוה] om. 𝕲. From 23.2,
perhaps by attraction to the expansion in 21.12.

   48.  22.8  רבים] om. 𝕲. From 25.14, cf. 27.7.

   49.  23.15  צבאות על הנביאים] om. 𝕲. On צבאות see chapter IV. The
rest is secondary from context and verse 9 (cf. 9.14).

   50.  23.16  הנבאים לכם] om. 𝕲. From 27.15, 16; cf. also 14.14, 15,
23.25, et al.

   51.  23.39  מעל פני] om. 𝕲. The phrase makes no sense following
ונמשתי, which does not mean to cast away,[22] but to abandon, forsake,
desert, or otherwise withdraw former support, in either a literal or
figurative sense (cf. Ex. 23.11, Num. 11.31, 1 Sam. 10.2, 17.20, 22, 28).
The superiority of 𝕲 is supported by 23.33. Confusion with נתש (often
followed by a phrase with מעל) allowed a gloss from related contexts
7.15, 32.31, also 1 Kgs. 9.7, 2 Kgs. 13.23, 17.18, etc.

   52.  24.10  ולאבותיהם] om. 𝕲. From 23.39, 25.5.

   53.  25.3  ולא שמעתם] om. 𝕲. From 7.13, 25.4, 35.14. Similarly
Giesebrecht, Streane, Volz, et al.

   54.  25.4  לשמע] om. G. Expanding from context; cf. 7.26.

   55.  25.9  נאם יהוה ואל נבוכדראצר מלך בבל עבדי] om. 𝕲. Generally
acknowledged to be secondary from 43.10. The אל is grammatically harsh
after לקחתי, but would make sense as the first word of a marginal gloss
on שלח.

56. 25.11 הזאת] om. 𝔊. From verse 9.

57. 25.11 לחרבה] om. 𝔊. From verse 18.

58. 25.18 ולקללה כיום הזה] om. 𝔊. ולקללה is from the related series in 24.9 and elsewhere. On כיום הזה as a gloss, see nos. 117, 163, 173, and Brevard S. Childs, "A Study of the Formula, 'Until This Day'," *JBL* 82 (1963), 279-292.

59. 25.33 לא יספדו ולא יאספר רי'] om. 𝔊. Compare 8.2, 16.4. This is a good example of 𝔐 filling from parallel passages. See also 16.6 where, as part of a longer plus, 𝔐 adds לא יקברו before לא יספדו.

60. 26.6 הזאתה] om. 𝔊. In view of the preceding הבית הזה we ought perhaps to expect the demonstrative here (cf. also verses 9, 11, 12). However, the Ketib הזאתה is unique, and intrudes into the orthographic tradition of Jer. 𝔐, suggesting conflation from a manuscript tradition in which the odd form was not anomalous.[23]

61. 27.1 Om. 𝔊. It is generally recognized that verse 1 is impossible here, and that it is secondary from 26.1, perhaps after an original introduction to chapters 27-29 was lost.

62. 27.9 אליכם לאמר] om. 𝔊. Probably from verse 14.

63. 27.10 והדחתי אתכם ואבדתם] om. 𝔊. From verse 15.

In 27.16-22, 𝔊 is much shorter than 𝔐, and though not all readings belong to the category discussed in this chapter, they are treated together for convenience.

64. 27.16 עתה מהרה] om. 𝔊. A gloss (perhaps assisted by 28.3) to harmonize the disagreement between Jeremiah and the false prophets with the secondary additions of 𝔐 in verse 22. The disagreement is thus changed from a matter of *whether* the vessels will return, to *when* they will return.[24] It is highly doubtful that Jeremiah spoke positively of the future of the Temple cultus; cf., e.g., 7.12-14.

65. 27.16 כי שקר המה נבאים לכם] + ουκ απεστειλα αυτους. 𝔊 secondary from verse 15, cf. also 29.9.

66. 27.17-18 אל תשמעו אליהם עבדו את מלך בבל וחיו למה תהיה העיר הזאת לחרבה רי'] om. 𝔊. Streane suggests that "M.T. harmonizes both in substance and style with the rest of the passage, and is therefore probably to be accepted." However, verses 16-22 do not belong with verses 1-15 (as verse 17 implies), but have to do with a completely different problem concerning false prophecy, namely the fate of the temple vessels,[25] so that Streane's literary argument does not stand up. With Rudolph, we

take the sentence as secondary from verses 12-14.

67.   27.18   בי [ביהוה צבאות $\cancel{\emptyset}$.   Against Volz's comment, "die Über-
setzung des $\cancel{\emptyset}$ entstand durch Missverständnis der Abkürzung בי," is the
difficulty of seeing abbreviations so early.   Moreover, Volz's suggestion
requires that the whole phrase יהוה צבאות was represented by the abbreviation י (which is unlikely), or that צבאות is a late addition in $\text{M}$.   If
יהוה צבאות were original, the presence of the epithet צבאות (either in
full or in abbreviated form) would have kept the translator from mistaking a supposed בי (צבאות) for the first person pronoun with ב.

68.   27.18   לבלתי באו הכלים הנותרים בבית יהוה ובית מלך יהודה
ובישראל בבלה [ om. $\cancel{\emptyset}$.   Conceivably, $\cancel{\emptyset}$-*Vorlage* could have been defective
by passing from בי to כי[26] (cf. Cornill).   But more likely the sentence
is an explanatory gloss on יפגעו נא בי, based on verse 21 (cf. Streane,
Cornill).   If $\cancel{\emptyset}$ were abbreviating in this section (Rudolph), it would
seem likely that he would translate this sentence at least once; or, if
verse 21 is original--and missing in $\cancel{\emptyset}$ by haplography--that he would
translate the *first* occurrence (verse 18) and delete the *second* (verse
21), according to the principle invoked elsewhere by Rudolph and others.[27]

69.   27.19   צבאות] אל העמדים ועל חים ועל המכנות ועל יתר הכלים και
των επιλοιπων σκευων.   On the epithet, see chapter IV.   אל obviously is
corrupt from על.   As for the rest, it is not clear what Hebrew text the
Greek represents.   The sense of the Greek[28] would seem to suggest ומיתר
הכלים'''בבלה יובא.   $\text{M}$ would then be glossing from 52.17 (so, e.g.,
Rudolph).   But $\cancel{\emptyset}$-*Vorlage* may have suffered haplography, ועל 3°-על 1°,
with mistranslation.[29]   The latter is most likely if we take $\text{M}$ as original in verses 20-21, while if $\text{M}$ there is secondary, the question remains
open (see no. 72).

70.   27.19   הנותרים בעיר הזאת] om. $\cancel{\emptyset}$.   Perhaps a summarizing gloss
based on verse 21.

71.   27.20   נבוכדנאצר, בן יהויקים מלך יהודה] om. $\cancel{\emptyset}$.   On $\text{M}$'s expansion of names, see chapter IV.

72.   27.20-21   בבלה ואת כל חרי יהודה וירושלם כי כה אמר יהוה צבאות
אלהי ישראל על הכלים הנותרים בית יהודה ובית מלך יהודה וירושלם] om. $\cancel{\emptyset}$.   The
most obvious, and most likely, explanation is that $\cancel{\emptyset}$-*Vorlage* (not $\cancel{\emptyset}$, for
syntactic reasons; see no. 69) suffered haplography: מלך יהודה מירושלם
בבלה'''מלך יהודה וירושלם בבלה.   However, the passage $\text{M}$ 19-22 is so awkward and overloaded with repetition that it cannot be original.   In

particular: The recurrence of כֹּה אמר יהוה כִּי in verse 21, following upon
the unfinished sentence in verses 19-20, is highly unlikely.[30] The repetition of בֵית הנותרים הכלים, after לקחם לא אשר יתר הכלים, is
altogether redundant. To lay these at the feet of Baruch, however prolix
his general style may be, would be to augment with literary evidence the
textual evidence (see p. 72) that originally he had no claim to the
title סופר. The divine name יהוה צבאות אלהי ישראל never occurs in original or stable formula contexts (see pp. 76-79).

We strongly suspect that verses 19-20 and 21 are old variants, and
that 𝕸 is conflate.[31] In this case, וירושלם יהודה חרי כל ואת is to be
taken as a gloss (based on 2 Kgs. 24.12, 15, Jer. 24.1, 28.4, 29.2) intended to follow יכניה but wrongly, and awkwardly, taken into the text
after מירושלם.[32] Finally, verse 20 בבלה may be taken either as secondary
in 𝕸 from the following verses, or deleted from ¢ by haplography.

73. 27.22 המקום אל והשיבתים והעליתים אתם פקדי יום עד יהיו ושמה
הזה] om. ¢. There is no indication of scribal lapse in ¢ or ¢-*Vorlage*.
On the other hand, it is pointless to attribute to ¢ dogmatic grounds for
the deletion (cf. Giesebrecht), unless these grounds are specified, and
the specific dogmatic bias supported with other evidence. The simplest
explanation (with Rudolph) is that the words are expansion on the basis
of Ezra 1.7ff. Ehrlich, however, correctly notes that פקד used in this
sense applies to persons, not to things. He proposes emending אתם to
אתכם (and, presumably, altering to והשיבתיכם והעליתיכם). But another possibility exists. If, as I suggest, verse 21 is an old variant of verses
19-20, the words in question once would have followed directly upon verse
20, and would constitute a gloss on the fate, not of the vessels, but of
those people taken into exile, inspired by 24.6, 29.10, 14, 32.5.

The original form of 27.16-22 may have been something like this:
דברי אל תשמעו אל יהוה אמר כה לאמר דברתי הזה העם כל ואל הכהנים ואל
נבאים המה שקר כי מבבלה מושבים יהוה בית כלי הנה לכם לאמר הנבאים נביאיכם
על יהוה אמר כה כי] בי נא יפגעו אתם יהוה דבר יש ואם הם נבאיאים אם לכם
ומיתר/יתר על] יהוה אמר כה כי /הכלים יתר ועל המכנות ועל הים ועל העמדים
יהוה נאם יובא בבלה מירושלם יכניה את בגלותו בבל מלך לקחם לא אשר [הכלים

A final word is in order concerning the attempt to attribute some
(Rudolph) or most (Graf, Giesebrecht) of these readings to a deliberate
abbreviating tendency on the part of ¢. If the translator was so intent
on abbreviating as to shorten his text by over one-half, it is remarkable

that he never once translated in summary fashion, but translated exactly
the text which he did choose to reproduce, skipping wholesale over sentences and then carefully picking up certain connecting words and phrases.
The notion that a translator who handled his text so loosely *at the same
time* was careful to reproduce part of that text precisely cannot be seriously entertained.

74.   28.3  אשר לקח נבוכדנאצר מלך בבל מן המקום הזה ויביאם בבל] om.
₲. From the previous chapter, especially verse 20; and cf. 2 Chr. 36.7.
Note also the late spelling נבוכדנאצר, and my comment on its significance,
p. 70.

75.   28.4  הבאים בבלה אני משיב אל המקום הזה נאם יהוה] om. ₲. From
verse 3.

76.   28.11  בעוד שנתים ימים] om. ₲. The temporal phrase here is
not parallel in usage to the same phrase in verse 3. In verse 11 it
modifies אשבר and refers to the breaking of Nebuchadrezzer's grip over
the nations, whereas in verse 3 it modifies משיב and refers to the return
to Jerusalem of the deported temple vessels. The phrase in verse 11 M
is secondary from verse 3, arising out of the superficial similarity of
the clauses שברתי/אשבר את על מלך בבל.

77.   28.14  האלה] om. ₲. From 25.9, 11; cf. 27.6.

78.   28.14  ועבדהו וגם חית השדה נתתי לו] om. ₲. From 27.6.

79.   28.16  כי סרה דברת אל יהוה] om. ₲. Against most commentators,
Volz and Weiser maintain the primary character of M. But they give no
explanation of the omission in ₲. This reading and the similar one in
29.32, are based on Deut. 13.6, and are as clear examples of scholarly
glossing as one could with to find.

80.   28.17  בשנה ההיא]om. ₲. From verse 16. Note that in verse
16, ₲ and Eb 22 add הזאת to השנה.

81.   29.1  אשר הגלה נבוכדנאצר מירושלם בבלה] om. ₲. From 24.1,
52.28-30.

82.   29.4  בבלה] om. ₲. From 27.20, etc.

83.   29.14  נאם יהוה ושבתי את שבותכם···אתכם משם] om. ₲. This passage is secondary from numerous other contexts; cf. especially 16.15,
23.3, 32.37, also 12.15, 24.6-7, 30.3, 31.8, 33.7. Moreover, the passage
does not fit the context of this letter, as it alludes to exiles who are
"scattered among all nations and places." (So also most commentators.)
The addition may have arisen to enhance the fate of the exiles in contrast

to 29.18.

84. 29.21 הנבאים לכם בשמי שקר] om. ₡. From 29.9; cf. also 14.14, 15, 23.25, 27.15, 29.23.

85. 29.23 שקר] om. ₡. From verse 21, 27.15, 29.9, 33.

86. 29.32 נאם יהוה כי סרה דבר על יהוה] om. ₡. Scholarly gloss from Deut. 13.6 (see no. 79).

87. 30.6 כירלדה] om. ₡. From 6.24, 50.43. The late character of the plus is indicated by the fact that, in the ₡ doublet, the word is missing even in the part of the doublet which otherwise corresponds to M, and is restored only in O L.[33]

88. 30.10-11 Om. ₡. From 46.27-28. See pp. 93-94.

89. 30.22 והייתם לי לעם ואנכי אהיה לכם לאלהים] om. ₡. From 7.23, 11.4, 24.7, 31.33, cf. also 31.1. As Volz points out, the second person (והייתם/לכם) does not fit the context.

90. 31.35 חקת] om. ₡. From verse 36, and 33.25. The word over-loads the meter, while ₡ gives good balance. The suggestion of Rudolph, Volz, and others to read originally חֹקֵק (or מֵחֹקֵק), leaves unexplained the omission in ₡.

91. 32.9 אשר בענתות] om. ₡. In verse 7 the phrase refers to the field, and clearly also in verse 9 where, however, its position is awk-ward. Probably it is a marginal gloss taken into the text at the wrong place.

92. 32.9 את הכסף] om. ₡. From verse 10.

93. 32.19 וכפרי מעלליו] om. ₡. From 17.10 (so also Streane).

94. 32.22 לתת להם] om. ₡. From 11.5, and often in O.T.

95. 32.36 הזאת] om. ₡. From verses 28, 29, 31.

96. 32.40 להיטיבי אותם] om. ₡. From verse 41.

97. 32.43 הזאת] om. ₡. From verse 15, and verse 41.

98. 33.5 מהעיר הזאת] απ' αυτων (= מהם) ₡. M is developed sec-ondarily from the similar sentence in 32.31.

99. 33.10 (a) מאין אדם ובהמה [מאין אדם ומאין בהמה] ₡. (b) מאין ₡. מאין אדם ובהמה [אדם ומאין ירשב ומאין בהמה] ₡. That ₡ preserves the cor-rect form of the cliché is indicated by 32.43. (a) M adds מאין (note that in 33.12, for ועד בהמה, Eb 22 similarly expands to ומאין בהמה). (b) M expands similarly, and in addition inserts the related cliché מאין ירשב (cf. 4.7, 26.9, 34.22, etc.). ₡ thus preserves a fixed form, מאין אדם ובהמה, parallelling the fixed forms מאין מקום, מבלי ירשב, מבלי עובר.

מאין יושב.

100. 33.12 מאין אדם ועד בהמה] om. ₵ (that is, V-26-86'-106'-239-534-538 Co Arab, which Ziegler surely is correct in identifying as old Greek)/+ (ᚷO-Q) παρα το μη ειναι ανθρωπον και κτηνος (-νη A Q-130-613 C') rel.: cf. M̶. Only α'(86mg) και εως κτηνους agrees exactly with M̶, while to the above weighty Hexaplaric evidence for ובהמה is added the identical reading of π' (Qtxt) οι γ' (86mg). This underlines the above observation on the fixed form of the cliché. M̶ ועד (note Eb 22 ומאין, which indirectly supports rel.) probably arises from the similar set idiom (ו)עד בהמה מאדם, Gen. 6.7, 7.23, Ex. 9.25, 12.12, Num. 3.13, Ps. 135.8, Jer. 50.3, 51.62. The entire cliché in 33.12 probably is secondary from verse 10.

101. 34.2 ואמרת] om. ₵. From 28.13, 35.13, 39.16.

102. 34.3 ופיהו את פיך ידבר] om. B-S-106'-538 Bo Aeth Arab; rel. = M̶. M̶ may be secondary from 32.4 (the parallel sentences are in other respects not exactly identical). On the other hand, B-S-etc. may represent an early Greek haplography, while A-etc. Q-V-etc. O L' may contain the old Greek text.

103. 34.8 אשר בירושלם] om. ₵. From verses 1, 6, 7.

104. 34.8 להם] om. ₵ Syr. From verse 17b.

105. 34.9 איש 2°] om. Eb 22/ᚷO/om. S* V-26-86'-233'-534-544 Bo/ εκαστον rel. = M̶. Ziegler includes εκαστον in his text, but in view of the support of Eb 22,[34] we ought perhaps to take S*-etc. as the old Greek (cf. no. 102). See also verses 10 (איש 2° om. B-410 239 Bo Arab) and 16 (איש 2° om. 534 Co).

106. 34.10-11 (a) וישובו [וישמעו] ₵. (b) הפשים verse 10 to הפשים verse 11] om. ₵. The original reading is not easy to decide. Giesebrecht and Streane suggest haplography in ₵ for (b), with subsequent alteration of (a) to make sense. However, haplography should not overleap *both* occurrences of הפשים. Moreover, verses 9-11 are suspiciously repetitious. It may be (cf., e.g., Cornill) that the process went in the other direction, starting with confusion in verse 10, וישמעו ⟩ וישובו 1°, which then would require an addition to indicate that the people reneged the covenant. This would have been drawn from verse 16. הפשים לבלתי עבד בם עוד וישמעו וישלחו would also be secondary, from verses 9-10a.

Rudolph defends M̶ on the ground that in source C we expect "Weitschweifigkeit (vgl. 10 f. 16. 18-21), die schon ₵ zu Kürzungen und neuere

Erklärer zu allerlei Streichungen veranlasst hat" (p. 203). But the style
of C does not of itself ensure the superiority of the longer reading (the
relative brevity of verses 8-11 fits well their function as prologue to
verses 12-22), and such a position can lead to absurd textual conclusions
(see next paragraph).

107. 34.12 מאת יהוה] om. ∅ Syr. 𝔐 has crossed two formulas, verse
8 (and elsewhere) הדבר אשר היה אל ירמיהו מאת יהוה, and verse 12 ∅ (and
elsewhere 𝔐 ∅) ויהי דבר יהוה אל ירמיהו. Rudolph's comment, "beim Stil
der Quelle C sind Streichungen nicht ratsam,"[35] cannot be taken seriously;
the secondary character of 𝔐 could not be clearer.

108. 34.14 מעמך] om. ∅. 𝔐 has filled out from Deut. 15.12-13 (cf.
also 15.18). That the passage is not quoting Deuteronomy precisely is
suggested by another reading in this verse: איש את אחיו העברי] ∅ = Deut.
15.12 את אחיך העברי. In the latter instance, ∅ (or its *Vorlage*) may be
secondarily attracted to Deut. 15.12, while 𝔐 probably is the original,
slightly paraphrased citation of this law.

109. 34.14 אבותיכם] om. ∅. From verse 13. Giesebrecht's argument that 𝔐 "ist nothwendig wegen des Übergangs zur Generation Jeremias
in 15," is not compelling. Shift of subject without the use of nouns is
common Biblical usage. אבותיכם, and אתם in verse 15, are typical glosses
intended to clarify the subject, much in the same way that proper nouns
often are added.

110. 34.15 אתם] om. ∅. ∅-*Vorlage* must have been minus the pronoun, otherwise the confusion ונשבו] וישבו would not have been possible.

111. 34.16 ותכבשו אתם להיות] om. ∅. From verse 11 (so also
Streane; cf. Rudolph, p. 203).

112. 34.17 איש לאחיו ו'] om. ∅ Syr. Haplography may have occurred
in both ∅ and Syr; or, more likely, 𝔐 may be secondary (cf. verse 15)
from 23.35, 31.34 (also Deut. 15.2).

113. 34.18 דברי] om. ∅. From 11.2, 3, 6, 8, and especially 2
Kgs. 23.3.

114. 35.7 לא חמעו ו'] om. ∅, perhaps by haplography, לא 3° 4°.
However, verse 9 וכרם···לא יהיה לנו (describing fulfilment of the com-
mand) may support ∅ in verse 7, in which case 𝔐 has expanded with נטע
after כרם (as about 90 per cent of the time in the O.T.).

115. 35.8 לכל אשר צונו] om. ∅. From verses 10, 14.

116. 35.14 עד היום הזה כי שמעו את מצות אביהם] om. ∅. The clause

is from verses 8, 10, 16, perhaps to reinforce the contrast between the
Rechabites (verse 14a) and Jeremiah's hearers (verse 14b). Verse 18 𝖌
would provide the perfect source for the expansion: επειδη ηκουσαν υιοι
Ιωναδαβ υιου Ρηχαβ την εντολην του πατρος αυτων = יען אשר שמעו בני יהונדב
בן רכב את מצות אביהם.[36] On עד היום הזה as a secondary gloss, see the
article by B. S. Childs cited in no. 58.

117.   35.15  השכים ושלח] om. 𝖌. From 25.4 (cf. Streane).

118.   35.16  אשר צום] om. 𝖌. From verses 10, 14.

119.   35.17  ויען דברתי אליהם ולא שמעו ואקרא להם ולא ענו] om. 𝖌.
From 7.13.

120.   36.9  וכל העם הבאים מערי יהודה בירושלם] ובית יהודה] 𝖌. From
verse 6 (so also Streane; cf. Giesebrecht); cf. 26.2.

121.   36.13  בספר] om. 𝖌. From verses 8, 10.

122.   36.14  בידו] om. 𝖌. From verse 14a.

123.   36.15  באזניהם] om. 𝖌. From verse 15a, cf. verses 13, 14.

124.   36.16  אל ברוך] om. 𝖌. From verses 15, 19 (so also Giesebrecht, Rudolph; cf. Volz).

125.   36.17  מפיו] om. 𝖌. From verse 18 (so also Giesebrecht,
Streane, Rudolph, *et al.*).

126.   36.22  בחדש התשיעי] om. 𝖌. From verse 9.

127.   36.29  על יהויקים מלך יהודה] om. 𝖌. From verse 30.

128.   36.32  באש] om. 𝖌. It is striking that, while שרף otherwise
virtually always occurs with באש in Jeremiah,[37] with reference to the
burning of the scroll in chapter 36 the verb occurs four times *without*
the adverb, and with it only here in 𝕸. Whatever the nuance, we seem to
have a special usage, which 𝕸 blurs in verse 32 by filling to otherwise
normal idiom.

129.   37.5  הצרים על ירושלם] om. 𝖌. 𝕸 has filled out from 21.4,
9.

130.   38.9  לירמיהו הנביא את אשר השליכו אל הבור] om. 𝖌. From verse
6.

131.   38.11  בידו] om. 𝖌. From verse 10.

132.   38.11  בחבלים] om. 𝖌. From verse 6,[38] cf. verses 12, 13.
Note that for וישלחם 𝖌 reads ερριψεν αυτα = וישליכם (F. M. Cross has
drawn my attention to the resemblance of כי to ח in the fifth and fourth
centuries).[39] It is probable that 𝕸 is an error of reading, ישלחם for
ישליכם, later expanded.

133. 38.12 [האלה] בלואי הסחבות והמלחים תחת אצלות ידיך $\emptyset$. A clarifying gloss which includes expansion from verse 11 (so also Streane).

134. 38.16 [בסתר] om. $\emptyset$. From 37.17.

135. 38.18 [אל שרי מלך בבל] om. $\emptyset$. From verse 17.

136. 38.18, 23 [מידם] om. $\emptyset$. From 34.3 (cf. 32.4; in these instances, מיד/- is translated by $\emptyset$).

137. 40.1 [גלות יהודה] כל גלות ירושלם ויהודה $\emptyset$. From 29.1, 4, 20; cf. 24.5, 28.4, 29.22.

138. 40.3 [ליהוה] לו $\emptyset$. $\mathfrak{M}$ fills out the proper name under the influence of 44.23.

139. 40.6 [ואתו] om. $\emptyset$. From verse 5.

140. 40.7 [רטף ומדלת הארץ] om. $\emptyset$. From 43.6 (cf. 41.16) and 52.15-16. Giesebrecht comments, "ומדלת הארץ scheint aus 52.16 eingedrungen, doch nicht רטף, cf. 41.16, 43.6, LXX haben auch gekürzt." Methodologically it is not clear why one-half of the reading should be labeled an abbreviation by $\emptyset$ and the other half an expansion by $\mathfrak{M}$. It is evident that G-*Vorlage* was minus רטף, from the fact that $\emptyset$ reads και γυναικας αυτων, ους... (= ונשיהם אשר which developed, partly by wrong word division, from ונשים מאשר).

141. 40.12 [וישבו כל היהודים מכל המקמת אשר נדחו שם] om. $\emptyset$. This sentence occurs 12 times in $\mathfrak{M}$, 8.3, 16.15//23.8, 23.3, 24.9//29.18, 29.14, 30.11//46.28, 32.37, 40.12, 43.5. Of these seven appear in $\emptyset$. 29.18 probably is missing in $\emptyset$ by haplography.[40] 30.11 is part of a large doublet secondary in $\mathfrak{M}$.[41] In all these instances, the sentence refers to the dispersion proper, whether the connotation is return or punishment.[42] The occurrences in 40.12 and 43.5 are out of place, for here the reference is only to those who temporarily took refuge in the hills when danger struck, and who filtered back once the fighting was over.[43] (For further discussion of 43.5, in connection with the Qumrân manuscript 4QJer[b], see below, pp. 180-181.) The same holds for 29.14 (see discussion of no. 83).

142. 41.1 [במצפה] om. $\emptyset$. From verse 3.

143. 41.7 תוך 2°] om. $\emptyset$. From תוך 1°.

144. 41.10 [וישבם ישמעאל בן נתניה] om. $\emptyset$. The verb may be repetition from verse 10a. The name is a characteristic addition.

145. 41.13-14 [וישמחו ויסבו כל העם אשר שבה ישמעאל מן המצפה] om. $\emptyset$. $\emptyset$ could be the result of homoioarchon, וישמחו וישבו. But the כל העם

····אשר seems over-full after verse 13. M probably is secondary, partly
from verse 10, partly by embellishing gloss. See further p. 22, no. 56.

146.  41.16  בן נתניה מן המצפה אחר הכה את גדליה בן אחיקם] om. ₵.
The awkwardness of verse 16 is generally recognized, and is sometimes
resolved by reading שבה אתם (so, e.g., Volz, Rudolph). An alternate
solution is to take the above words as a secondary gloss, initiated by
the superficial similarity of וכל שרי החילים אשר אתו את את כל שארית העם אשר
השיב מאת ישמעאל to verses 13-14 M, and extended on the basis of verses
1-3 (see further, pp. 22-24).

147.  41.17  לבוא] om. ₵. Perhaps from 42.17, cf. 42.18, 19, 43.2,
7.

148.  42.8  אשר אתו] om. ₵. From 41.11, 16.

149.  42.9  אלהי ישראל אשר שלחתם אתי אליו להפיל תחנתכם לפניו = 2QJer]
om. ₵. A typical expansion of the prophetic formula, together with an
expansion from verses 2, 6, 20.

150.  42.15  שארית יהודה] om. ₵. From verse 19.

151.  42.15  לבא] om. ₵. cf. no. 147 above.

152.  42.17  לבא מצרים] εις γην Αιγυπτου. Probably both M and ₵
are secondary, and we should read שמו את מניהם מצרים (so also verse 15 ₵).

153.  42.18  אפי ר'] om. ₵. M spoils the symmetry between verse 18
a and b, and is from 33.5, 44.6, etc.

154.  42.20  אל יהוה אלהיכם] om. ₵. From context, especially
verses 2-4.

155.  42.20  ואלהינו כן הגד לנו ר'] om. ₵. From verses 3, 5.

156.  42.21  ואגיד לכם היום] om. ₵. From verse 20.

157.  42.22  ידע תדעו כי] om. ₵. From verse 19.

158.  43.5  מכל הגוים אשר נדחו שם] om. ₵. See no. 141.

159.  43.5  יהודה] om. ₵. From verse 4.

160.  43.10  עבדי] om. ₵. This title is applied to Nebuchadrezzar
three times in M, 25.9, 27.6, 43.10, but does not occur at all in ₵,
according to most commentators because of ₵'s dogmatic bias.[44]

(a)  *25.9*  The whole name clearly is secondary, as is frequently
recognized. Note the similarity of the sentence opening in 25.9 and
43.10, the general tendency of M to make more explicit the identity of
Judah's impending foe (especially in chapters 21-22, 25), and the syntactic awkwardness of M (see also no. 55).

(b)  *27.6*  עבדי] om. S Bo Aeth /τω δουλω μου O-233 θ'-Q α'σ'θ'-86

(= לְעָבְדִי)[45] / του δουλου μου L' Arm Tht 86° = M̶/ δουλευειν αυτω (= לְעָבְדוֹ)
rel. (pr. του 26 198). At first glance ₵ seems to rest upon a *Vorlage*
which was either original, with M̶ > עבדי by haplography of ל and וי, or
secondary by dittography of ל and וי. S Bo Aeth might then simply be
due to scribal lapse. In this case it would be difficult to be certain
of the original reading, though the superiority of ₵ is suggested by the
parallel verse, 28.14, which reads וְעָבְדֻהוּ in the slot where 27.6 reads
לְעָבְדוֹ/עבדי.

     But it is highly probable that δουλευειν αυτω does not represent
the old Greek text. Werner E. Lemke observes that "in every other instance where the text speaks of serving the King of Babylon, the Greek
translator uses the verb *ergazesthai* rather than *douleuein* to render '*bd*
.... This would suggest that *douleuein autō* in 34.6a is from another
hand."[46] This point may be sharpened by the observations that the verb
עבד is in fact translated differently in Jer. α and β: α renders δουλευειν 11 times, εργαζειν once; β renders εργαζειν 11 times, δουλευειν
twice;[47] and that when the old Greek text of Jer. has a zero variant to
M̶ עבד, in either Jer. α or β, Origen and precursors regularly correct
with δουλευειν. Now, it would be most peculiar for Jer. β to render עבד
once with δουλευειν (against normal usage), and then five times in succession in the following verses with εργαζειν. More likely, S Bo Aeth
are old Greek, and δουλευειν αυτω is a later infection in the large majority of Greek witnesses (see further below). The question then becomes:
did the translator delete the title on dogmatic grounds, as most scholars
argue? Or is M̶ עבדי secondary, and if so, where did the title come from?

     At this point, it will be helpful to examine the parallel passage
in 28.14 (bracketed words are omitted in ₵):

עֹל בַּרְזֶל נָתַתִּי עַל צַוַּאר כָּל הַגּוֹיִם (הָאֵלֶּה) לַעֲבֹד אֶת (נְבֻכַדְנֶאצַּר) מֶלֶךְ בָּבֶל
(וַעֲבָדֻהוּ וְגַם אֶת חַיַּת הַשָּׂדֶה נָתַתִּי לוֹ)

To be sure, the clause which parallels 27.6 is omitted in ₵, and probably
is an expansion from 27.6. Even so it is important, as a reflection of
the form of the clause in the latter place. Two features are noteworthy:
there is no לְעָבְדוֹ at the end of the clause; the verb וַעֲבָדֻהוּ stands where
M̶ reads עבדי.[48] In view of the pronounced tendency toward filling out
names and titles in M̶ (see below, Chapter IV), we might have expected that
if 27.6 had read עֲבְדִי, this would have reappeared in 28.14.

     The data of 27.6 M̶ and ₵, and 28.14 M̶,[49] combine now to arouse the strong suspicion that we have to do with two earlier variant forms:

(א)        נבוכדנאצר מלך בבל וגם את חית השדה [50](נתתי לו) לעבדו

(ב)        נבוכדנאצר מלך בבל לעבדו וגם את חית השדה נתתי לו

These variants would have risen in something like the following manner:

(α)  The verse originally read נתתי [51]ואת הארץ ביד נ' מ' בבל לעבדו.

(β)  Verse 6 was marginally glossed with וגם את חית השדה, from the content of verse 5.[52]

(γ)  This gloss was received into the text differently in subsequent copies: (א) before לעבדו, (ב) after לעבדו. Either at this time, or later, נתתי לו was inserted into (ב) to smooth the reading. Also, sometime between here and stage δ, 28.14 was expanded from 27.6.

(δ)  (א)--minus נתתי לו--was the archetype of the text tradition taken to Egypt, and represented in S Bo Aeth. (ב) was the archetype of the text tradition which became proto-M̞, reflected in the reading in 28.14.

($\varepsilon^1$)  While (א) and (ב) existed side by side, they were conflated in (ב) to give נ' מ' בבל לעבדו וגם את חית השדה נתתי לו לעבדו.

(ζ)  At some time after stage γ, proto-M̞ suffered haplography of ל and ו/י confusion, producing the text of M̞.[53]

($\varepsilon^2$)  The Greek translation of Jeremiah was based on a Hebrew manuscript which contained the text represented by (א) minus נתתי לו. At some later point, most old Greek manuscripts were infected with the reading (του) δουλευειν αυτω, which may represent either late Greek correction to a Hebrew tradition still reading לעבדו,[54] or (less likely) a misplaced doublet of εργαζεσθαι αυτω, conflated from those Greek recensions which had replaced the latter phrase with δουλευειν αυτω in their text.[55]

This reconstruction of 27.6 is admittedly more complex than one which adopts B-(etc.) as the old Greek text and explains the ₵/M̞ divergence by simple עבדי/לעבדו confusion.[56]  But we believe that it accounts adequately for a number of data which the latter reconstruction leaves unexplained.  Moreover, it receives additional support from the following reading in 27.6: τω Ναβ. βασ. Βαβ.] ✷O; τω βασ. Βαβ. S Bo Aeth; τω βασ. Ναβ. Βαβ. 534 Tht^cit; τω βασ. Ναβ. 26; τω Ναβ. Βαβ. 62; τω Ναβ. C'-239. The Greek tradition is suspiciously complex. The presence of Ναβ. is dubious, because eight occurrences of this proper name in chapters 27-29 are spelled נבוכדנאצר, almost uniquely in this book, and the other seven are all omitted in ₵; and in the same verse, the old Greek reading is contained in just those witnesses which omit the proper name here (see above),[57] so that the name entered the majority Greek tradition probably at the same time as the nearby late correction (or revision) του δου-λευειν αυτω. For several other examples of old Greek readings narrowly transmitted, see Ziegler, *Ieremias*, pp. 42-43, and for examples of old Greek readings preserved in S and one or two other witnesses, see Ziegler, *Ieremias*, pp. 50-51.[58] It becomes, then, virtually certain that in chapters 27-29 (which may have existed independently before incorporation with the other Jeremianic materials) the king of Babylon was referred to only as such, and never by name. Furthermore, the frequent references to "serving the king of Babylon" make the reading מלך בבל לעבדו in 27.6 all the more likely.

(c)  *43.10* 𝔐 is to be taken as secondary expansion from 27.6[59] Since both passages have in common the theme of judgment of the nations at the hand of Nebuchadrezzar, the conditions were ideal for such an expansion.

The evidence for the title עבדי is therefore extremely tenuous, resting ultimately on the problem in 27.6, and ought not to be made the basis for comment on Jeremiah's conception of the role of the Babylonian king.[60]

161.  44.1  ובנף] om. 𝒢. Probably from 2.16, 46.14.

162.  44.2  הירם הזה] om. 𝒢. From verse 22.

163.  44.2  מאין יושב = απο ενοικων [ואין בהם יושב.[61] Compare 2QJer, which the editor, M. Baillet, reconstructs ה[ירם הזה מפ̇]ני רעתם and comments, "après הירם הזה, omission de quelques mots, contre TM et versions."[62] However, this unique variant is based upon a misreading of the broken letter after מ, which cannot be read פ, but clearly is א.[63] We reconstruct ה[ירם הזה מא̇]ין.[64] One of Baillet's two unique readings is thereby eliminated from 2QJer, and we have recovered a reading in at least partial agreement with 𝒢 against 𝔐. Note that the idiom מאין יושב/מקום/אדם occurs fifteen times in Jeremiah (מאין יושב nine times). Only in 4.29 do we have ואין יושב בהן איש = ου κατοικει εν αυταις ανθρωπος, and it is this to which 44.2 may be attracted secondarily (cf. also 48.9). Note also verse 22 𝔐 מאין יושב (om. 𝒢) which, as expansion from verse 2, indirectly may lend support to 𝒢 in verse 2.

164.  44.10  בתורתי ו'] om. 𝒢. From 44.23 (cf. 26.4, 32.23). The construction הלך בחקות occurs several times in various other books.

165.   44.10   לפני אבותיכם ולפני לפניכם M [ ולאבהיהון להרן Syr/ לפני

אבותיהם ¢. 'ו   לפניכם probably is secondary; cf. 7.14, 23.39, also 9.12,
26.4. As well, the third person suffixes of ¢ Syr are original, while M
is attracted to the suffixes of verses 3, 9, 21.

166.   44.11-12

M לכן כה אמר יהוה צבאות אלהי ישראל[a]   ¢ לכן כה אמר יהוה

הנני שם פני בכם לרע[b] ולהכרית את כל   הנני שם פני

יהודה[c]

ולקחתי[d] את שארית יהודה[e]   להכרית את כל השארית אשר במצרים

אשר שמו פניהם לבוא ארץ מצרים לגור שם

ותמו כל בארץ[f] מצרים

יפלו בחרב ברעב יתמו מקטן ועד גדול   ויפלו בחרב וברעב יתמו מקטן ועד
גדול

בחרב וברעב ימתו[g]

והיו לאלה[h] ולשמה ולקללה ולחרפה   והיו לשמה ולקללה ולחרפה

(a)  Characteristic expansion of the formula (see chapter IV).  (b)  Probably from 21.10, cf. 44.27.  (c)  Cf. 44.27. The oracle is not, however, concerned with כל יהודה.[65]  (d)  This verb can only have arisen,
by way of further embellishment, after the (secondary) distinction between
כל יהודה and שארית (יהודה).  (e)  From 44.14, 28, and often.  (f)  From
the parallel oracle, 42.19, 22, especially verses 15, 17.  In chapter 42
the remnant has only *decided* to go to Egypt; in chapter 44 they are already
there, and כל השארית אשר במצרים (cf. verse 27) accordingly is to be preferred.  (g)  The cliché may be a doublet of the similar one early in the
verse, reflecting old variants יתמו/ימתו.[66]  We can hardly have both
here, especially with the repetition of the cliché again in verse 13.
(h)  From 42.18, a typical filling out of the pejorative series.

167.   44.14   הבאים לגור שם בארץ מצרים] των παροικουντων εν γη
Αιγυπτω. Perhaps it is impossible to decide whether ¢ is reading הגרים
בא' מצ' or בא' מצ' הירשבים (cf. 44.28, M and B-etc.). In any case, שם
doubtless is secondary, from 42.15, 17, 22, 43.2, 44.8, 12, 28.

168.   44.22   מאין יושב] om. ¢. From verse 2 (cf. no. 163 above).

169.   44.23   כיום הזה] om. ¢. From verses 6, 22.

170.   44.24   כל יהודה אשר בארץ מצרים] om. ¢. From verse 26.

171.   44.25   את נדריכם] om. ¢. Probably secondary from the same
verse.

172.   46.6   נהר] om. ¢. From verses 2, 10, and frequently.

173. 46.8 עיר ו'] om. ℭ. From 8.16, 47.2, where however the
cliché (properly) is ארץ ומלואה//עיר וישבי בה. For 46.8 ℭ, see the similar usage in Am. 8.8, 9.5.

174. 46.14 במצרים והשמיעו, ובתחפנחס] om. ℭ. Probably secondary
from 44.1.

175. 47.4 כי שדד יהוה את פלשתים שארית אי כפתור] כי שדד יהוה
שארית איים ℭ. M is secondary with פלשתים את from verse 4a,[67] and
(subsequently) from Gen. 10.14, Deut. 2.23, Am. 9.7, 1 Chr. 1.12. On
שארית איים cf. verse 5: שארית (ℭ) ענקים/(M) עמקם.

176. 48.1 הבישה] om. ℭ. Probably secondary from verse 1b.

177. 48.15 עלה] om. ℭ. From verse 18.

178. 48.33 מכרמל ו'] om. ℭ. From Isa. 16.10 (so also Duhm and
Volz; cf. Giesebrecht and Streane).

179. 48.40 הנה כנשר ידאה ופרש כנפיר אל מואב] om. ℭ.

41. והיה לב גבורי מואב ביום ההוא כלב אשה מצרה] om. ℭ.
Hitzig, Scholz (Comm.), Duhm, Giesebrecht, Streane, Cornill, Nötscher,
and Rudolph take these lines as secondary from 49.22; Graf, Volz, and
Weiser hold them to belong here. While 41a.42 (so ℭ) follow quite
smoothly, 40b.41b cannot really be said to disrupt the context. On the
other hand, it is difficult to account for the omission in ℭ.[68] Perhaps
the couplet arose as a gloss on בצרה in 48.24 (49.22 has בצרה where
48.40 has (מואב[69] and was taken into the wrong column of the manuscript,
with appropriate change of names.

180. 48.45-47 Om. ℭ. It is generally agreed that the original
content of the Oracles against Foreign Nations has been heavily reworked,
and expanded in patchwork fashion from other places in the O.T. (compare,
for example, the Oracle against Moab in Jeremiah and Isaiah). In these
verses we have a good example of secondary addition, in this instance
after the separation of the Egyptian archetype. Verses 45-46 are taken
from Num. 21.28-29 (cf. also Num. 24.17), perhaps as a gloss on חשבון in
verse 34 or 49.3. Verse 47a probably has developed from 49.39. Verse
47b is a late editorial rubric, similar to the one in 51.64.

181. 49.2 בני עמון] om. ℭ. רבה (eight times in O.T.; cf. 49.3)
expanded to רבת בני עמון (Ezek. 21.25 and 3 times), overloading the
meter.

182. 49.13 לחרב] om. ℭ. Typical filling out of this series.

183. 49.17 ישם וישרק על כל מכותה] om. ישם and מכותה כל על ℭ.

From 19.8, 50.13, cf. 1 Kgs. 9.8. That the cliché כל עובר עליה ישם וישרק
may occur with only one of the verbs is shown by 18.16, Zeph. 2.15.

184.  49.30 עליהם] om. ₵ (B-S-538 Co Aeth; εφ'υμας rell. = plus
100 mss. M^Kenn. Targ Vulg). The word probably is secondary from the preceding clause.

185.  50.1 אל ארץ כשדים is om. ₵. אל ארץ כשדים ביד ירמיהו הנביא]
secondary from 50.8, 51.54 (cf. also 50.25, 35, 51.4, 24, 35). ביד
ירמיהו הנביא probably is a gloss from 51.59 (and cf. 46.13 ₵).

186.  50.3 נדו הלכו] om. ₵. From 9.9.

187.  50.7 יהוה] om. ₵. From 17.13 (cf. 14.7 ₵).

188.  50.9 גדלים] om. ₵. From verse 41.

189.  50.28 נקמת היכלו] om. ₵. From 51.11 (so also Rudolph).

190.  50.39 ולא תשכון עוד דור ודור] om. ₵. Commentators generally
prefer M.[70] However, it is to be noted that Jer. 50.39-40 and Isa.
13.19-22 are not precise parallels (bracketed words in common):

| Isa. 13 | | Jer. 50 |
|---|---|---|
| 19 היתה בבל צבי ממלכות תפארת גאון כשדים | | 39 לכן ישבו (ציים) את (איים) |
| (כמהפכת אלהים את סדם ואת עמרה) | | וישבו בה (בנות יענה) |
| 20 (לא תשב לנצח) (ולא תשכון עד דור ודור) | | (ולא תשב) עוד (לנצח) |
| ולא יהל שם ערבי ורעים לא ירבצו שם | | (ולא תשכון עד דור ודור) |
| 21 ורבצו שם (ציים) ומלאו בתיהם אחים (כמהפכת אלהים את סדם ואת עמרה) | | ואת שכניה נאם יהוה |
| ושכנו שם (בנות יענה) ושעירים ירקדו שם | | לא ישב שם איש |
| 22 וענה (איים) באלמנותיו ותנים בהיכלי ענג | | ולא יגור בה בן אדם |
| וקרוב לבוא עתה וימיה לא ימשכו | | |

Jer. contains only disjointed segments of Isa. Specifically: Jer.
verse 39a summarizes Isa. verses 20-22, utilizing just the first member
of the pairs ציים//אחים, שעירים//בנות יענה, תנים//איים. In Isa., 19b is
related syntactically to 19a, while its explication follows in 20-22.
In Jer., 40a is syntactically related to its primary explication in 40b
(as also in 49.18).

We have in Jer. 50.39-40, then, selection and reshaping of some of
the Isa. material,[71] while other material is discarded (or rather, left
unused). Therefore, it is not necessarily the case that the text most
closely resembling Isa. 13 is the earliest. Given the general similarity
between Isa. 13 and Jer. 50-51 and the slightly different way in which
common words and phrases appear in the latter, it is more likely, a pri-
ori, that the text least like Isa. 13 (discounting obvious corruption)

is the earlier one. If Jer. chapter 50 were written stichometrically, the line ולא תשכון עד דור ודור could have been dropped by homoioarchon. But since we cannot be sure the chapter was so written, 𝔊 seems the preferable text, with 𝔐 secondary from Isa. 13.

191. 51.19 ושבט] om. 𝔊. Expansion from 10.16.

192. 51.28 ממשלתו] om. 𝔊. There are a number of variants in this verse, which should be dealt with together:

(a) מלך [מלכי 𝔊 Syr (similarly, 51.11).

(b) פחותיו [פחותיה 𝔊 Syr.

(c) סגניו [סגניה 𝔊 Syr.

(d) ואת כל ארץ ממשלתו] precedes את פחותיו 𝔊; om. Syr.

(e) ממשלתו] om. 𝔊.

Before discussing these variants, it will be worthwhile to give some attention to the variants in the apparatus to 𝔊, as they shed light on the development of both the Greek and the Hebrew text types. The following readings are found (minor, and we believe insignificant, divergences are indicated in footnotes):

I. B-130-538 S Q-V-(omn.) C'[72]

και πασης της γης τους ηγουμενους αυτου και παντας τους στρατηγους αυτου

II. 106'-239[73]

και πασης της γης τους ηγουμενους αυτου και παντας ⟨τους⟩ στρατηγους αυτου και πασης της γης

III. A

και πασης της γης τους ηγεμονας [sic!] αυτου και παντας τ. στρατ. αυτου και πασης της γης εξουσιας αυτου

IV. Aeth Arab[74]

και τους ηγουμενους αυτου πασης της γης και π. τ. στρατ. αυτου και πασης της γης της εξουσιας αυτου

V. O L'

| τους (O) | αυτης (O) | αυτης (O) | της (O) |
|---|---|---|---|

και ηγουμενους αυτου και παντας τους στρατ αυτου και πασης της γης (της) εξουσιας αυτου

VI. fin.] οι γ' ο' +※ 86mg.

και πασαν την γην της εξουσιας αυτου [καιγε]

These variants provoke the following questions: Why are O and L' minus the old Greek reading, when in the great majority of instances they just obelize the old Greek plus (which is then often omitted in 233) or the old Greek half of a doublet? Why do O and L' read (with 2° A 106'-239) και πασης της γης when, in this position, they ought to have read (with ου γ' ο') και πασαν την γην? Why do 106'-239 read only *part* of the correction toward 𝔐 (cf. also A and 62-407 [Lucianic sub-group], which omit της 2° of this correction)?

The following reconstruction of the development of the text is proposed to account for the above data.[75]

(α)  The old Greek reading, contained in B-S Q-V-(omn.) C':
και πασης της γης  τ.η.α.  κ.π.τ.σ.α.

(β)  The old Greek text was corrected to a proto-𝔐 text which did not yet read ממשלתו, simply by transposing the phrase to accord with its position in proto-𝔐. The resulting impossible syntax of the genitives went unnoticed:
τ.η.α.  κ.π.τ.σ.α.  και πασης της γης

(γ)  Some old Greek manuscript(s) (underlying A and 106'-239, and cf. Aeth Arab and (ε) below) underwent conflation of (α) and (β):
και πασης της γης  τ.η.α.  κ.π.τ.σ.α.  και πασης της γης

(δ)  The revised text (β) was the base text which Origen corrected to 𝔐[76] by adding της εξουσιας αυτου (from ου γ' ο' or the like). Again, a relatively larger correction distracted attention from the need for a minor one, and the syntax of the phrase escaped notice:
τ.η.α.  κ.π.τ.σ.α.  και πασης της γης της εξουσιας αυτου

(ε)  The Hexaplaric correction της εξουσιας αυτου infected the tradition represented by A Arab Aeth,[77] and of course was adopted in L', which previously probably contained the text of stage (β).

We may now turn to the variants between 𝔐 and 𝔊 (Syr) listed on p. 61. (e) ממשלתו is a late addition in 𝔐, perhaps from 1 Kgs. 9.19 (cf. also Jer. 34.1). (d) The phrase ואת כל (ה)ארץ probably is original in 𝔊 position, was dropped from proto-𝔐 by haplography (ואת 1° את 2°), and the marginal restoration, as often, was absorbed into the text at the end of the series. The superiority of 𝔊 is indicated by the poetic structure of verses 27-28 (verse 28 cannot be read as poetry in 𝔐): bicolon : tricolon : bicolon : tricolon. Verse 28 then corresponds nicely to verse 27a:

| | |
|---|---|
| קדשו עליה גוים | קדשו עליה גוים |
| מלך מדי וכל הארץ | השמיעו עליה ממלכות |
| פחותיו וכל סגניו | אררט מני ואשכנז |

(a-c) 𝔊 and Syr are superior. The shift to plural מלכי may have been made on the basis of 25.25 (cf. also 51.11, and note (a), p. 61). The rise of the third feminine singular suffixes (referring now to מדי) occurred perhaps after the shift of מלך to מלכי, which rendered third masculine suffixes unintelligible.

193. 51.33 עֹה] om. 𝔊 Syr. From 50.16.

194. 51.37 גלים מעון תנים] om. 𝔊. From 9.10. ושרקה] om. 𝔊. From 18.16, 19.8, etc. The couplet then reads והיתה בבל לשמה מאין יושב; cf. verse 41b.

195. 51.43 לשמה] om. 𝔊. From verses 37, 41.

196. 51.43 ארץ 2°] om. 𝔊. 𝔐 intrudes on the syntax: בהן = עריה (so also Rudolph); cf. 2.6.

197. 52.9 בארץ חמת] om. 𝔊 2 Kgs. 𝔐 𝔊. From 52.27.

*Additions in 𝔊*

1. 1.18 נחשת] + οχυρον = בצורה. From 15.20.

2. 3.17 בעת ההיא] prec. εν ταις ημεραις εκειναις και = בימים ההמה ו'. From 33.15, 50.4, cf. also 3.16, 18.

3. 3.18 מארץ צפון] + και απο πασων των χωρων = ומכל הארצות. From 16.15.

4. 6.16 ושאלו לנתבות עולם] + και ιδετε = וראה (= Syr). From verse 16a.

5. 7.4 דברי השקר] + οτι το παραπαν ουκ ωφελησουσιν υμας = לבלתי הועיל or the like.[78] From verse 8.

6. 7.9 אשר לא ידעתם] + του κακως ειναι υμιν = לרע לכם. From 7.6.

7. 7.11 אשר נקרא שמי עליו] + εκει = שם. From verse 12.

8. 7.32 התפת] prec. βωνος = במת. From verse 31.

9. 8.21 החזקתני] + ωδινες ως τικτουσης = חיל כיולידה. From 6.24.

10. 9.13 וילכו אחרי שררות לבם] + της κακης = הרע. From 3.17, 7.24.

11. 13.13 ואת כל ישבי ירושלם] prec. και τον ιουδα = ואת יהודה. Cf. 11.12, 18.11, etc.

12. 14.7 מקוה ישראל] + κυριε = יהוה. From 17.13.

13. 14.13 הנביאים] + προφητευουσι και = נבאים ו'. From verses 14, 15.

14. 14.15 הנבאים בשמי] + ψευδη = שקר. From 23.15, 27.15.

15.   14.15 ‏בחרב] εν θανατω νοσερω αποθανουνται. Secondary from
16.4, where the same clause translates ‏ממותי תחלאים ימתו. (The two passages are somewhat similar, and in each one the relevant clause or term
follows ‏בארץ הזאת/επι της γης ταυτης or εν τη γη ταυτη.)

16.   17.23 ‏וריקשו את ערפם] + υπερ τους πατερας αυτων = ‏מאבותם.
From 7.26; cf. 19.15.

17.   19.3 ‏וישבי ירושלם] prec. και ανδρας Ιουδα = ‏ואיש יהודה. From
11.2, 18.11, etc.

18.   19.3 ‏וישבי ירושלם] + και οι εισπορευομενοι εν ταις πυλαις
ταυταις = ‏והבאים בשערים האלה. From 17.20, 22.2.

19.   19.7 ‏ירושלם] prec. την βουλην = ‏את עצת. From the preceding
phrase.

20.   20.16 ‏אשר הפך יהוה] + εν θυμω = ‏באף (or ‏באפו). From Deut.
29.22, cf. Job 9.5.

21.   21.9 ‏והיתה לו נפשו לשלל] + και ζησεται = ‏וחי. From 38.2.

22.   22.1 ‏כה אמר יהוה] + πορευου και = ‏הלך ר'. From 3.12, 13.1,
etc.

23.   23.14 ‏מרעתו] απο της οδου αυτου της πονηρας = ‏מדרכו הרעה.
From 18.11, 25.5, 26.3, etc. For ‏M, cf. 18.8, and 1 Kgs. 13.33 (‏מדרכו
‏הרעה/απο της κακιας αυτου!).

24.   27.15 ‏אתם והנביאים הנבאים לכם] + επ᾿αδικω ψευδη (an inner-
Greek doublet) = ‏לשקר. From verse 15a, and 23.25, etc.

25.   27.16 ‏כי שקר המה נבאים לכם] + ουκ απεστειλα αυτους = ‏לא
‏שלחתים. From verse 15, and 29.9.

26.   28.10 ‏ויקח חנניה הנביא] om. ‏הנביא ₵ (see Chapter IV); + εν
οφθαλμοις παντος του λαου ₊ O–Q–86; om. 233; κατ᾿ οφθαλμους π.τ.λ. 407
106; εναντι π.τ.λ. Chr. While the phrase clearly is pre-Origenic, it is
doubtful that it is old Greek (cf. verses 1, 5, 11 κατ᾿ οφθαλμους). In
any case, a gloss suggested by verses 5, 11.

27.   29.8 ‏קסמיכם] prec. μη αναπειθετωσαν υμας = ‏אל ישיאו לכם.
From the preceding phrase.

28.   29.26 ‏מתנבא] prec. παντι ανθρωπω = ‏לכל איש. From the preceding phrase.

29.   32.25 ‏והעד עדים] και εγραψα βιβλιον και εσφραγισαμην και
επεμαρτυραμην μαρτυρας = ‏ואכתב בספר ואחתם ואעד עדים. The brevity of ‏M
accords well with what may originally have been a very terse prayer.[79]
₵-*Vorlage* probably expanded from verse 10 (cf. also verse 44), in the

process changing הֵעִד to אָעִד[80] (or the latter shift may have encouraged the expansion; cf. 25.3).

30. 32.43 ‏ונקנה‎] + ετι = עוד. From verse 15.

31. 34.1 ‏עריה‎] τας πολεις Ιουδα = עָרֵי יְהוּדָה. Probably from verse 7.

32. 34.2 ‏ושרפה באש‎] prec. και συλλημψεται αυτην = וּלְכָדָהּ. From 34.22, etc.

33. 35.19 ‏ליונדב‎] των υιων Ιωναδαβ = לִבְנֵי יוֹנָדָב. From verse 16, and verse 18 ℊ.

34. 35.19 ‏כל הימים‎] πασας τας ημερας της γης = כָּל יְמֵי הָאָרֶץ. As Rudolph suggests, this may be expansion from Gen. 8.22.

35. 38.27 ‏הדבר‎] λογος κυριου = דְּבַר יהוה. From frequent occurrence. M clearly is superior.

36. 42.17 ‏כל האנשים‎] + και παντες οι αλλογενεις = וְכָל הַזָּרִים. Probably corrupt from הַזֵּדִים, 43.2 (which, however, is om. ℊ). It is probable that the latter word was an early marginal gloss on הָאֲנָשִׁים in 42.17, and that while ℊ-*Vorlage* archetype received it into the text there, it was taken in by M-archetype at 43.2 (which may well have stood opposite 42.17, in the next column of the manuscript).

37. 46.17 ‏פרעה‎] + Νεχαω = נְכֹה. From 46.2.

38. 50.22 ‏ושבר גדול‎] + εν γη χαλδαιων = בְּאֶרֶץ כַּשְׂדִּים. From 51.54.

39. 52.17 ‏בבלה‎] prec. και απηνεγκαν = וַיְבִיאוּ(ם).. Probably from 20.5, 24.1, 52.11.

## *The Addition of* ‏כל‎/πας

This rather insignificant word provides useful evidence for the character of the various text traditions. Though such a small word is easily dropped, it is often added as a gloss, to clarify, emphasize, make more explicit, or otherwise nuance the text. The word occurs over 500 times in Jeremiah M ℊ. In addition, it occurs as a plus 62 times in M and 11 times in ℊ. In most cases it is difficult to say whether the zero variant in ℊ represents a zero variant in its *Vorlage*, and if it does, whether the minus or the plus is original. The following passages, however, merit individual attention:

1. 9.3 ‏כל‎ 1°] om. ℊ. Secondary from the following line; it disrupts the poetic structure ‏רֵעַ : אָח : : אָח : כֹּל : רֵעַ‎.

2.  25.4  כל] om. 𝔊.  The phrase הנביאים עבדי-\עבדיו occurs 6 times in
Jeremiah, 11 times elsewhere in the O.T.  Of the latter, it occurs 10
times without כל, with כל only once in 2 Kgs. 17.23.  In Jeremiah the
phrase occurs twice without כל, and 4 times in 𝔐 with כל.  Of the latter, 3 times 𝔊 solidly omits (25.4, 35.15, 44.4), and 7.25 106 Bo, which
are good members of B family and here may possibly represent the old
Greek text.[81]  The data strongly suggest that the phrase in Jer. orig-
nally was without כל, and that in 4 instances the Jer. 𝔐 plus is secondary.

3.  25.2  כל 2° and 35.17 כל 1°] om. 𝔊.  The phrase ישבי ירושלם
occurs without כל otherwise in Jer. 12 times, in the rest of the O.T. 21
times; with כל it occurs otherwise once in Jer., and twice in the rest
of the O.T.[82]  The phrase thus is normally without כל, and in 25.2, 35.17
it is probably secondary from context.

4.  25.9  את כל משפחות צפון] πατριαν απο βορρα.  The presence of
כל in 𝔊-Vorlage would have indicated that משפחת was to be read as a
defectively written plural, instead of a singular.  כל is from 1.15.

5.  27.6  את כל הארצות האלה] την γην.  In my judgment, 𝔊 makes better sense: אנכי עשיתי את הארץ''ונתתיה לאשר ישר בעיני'''ועתה אנכי נתתי
את הארץ ביד נב' מ' ב'.  It is the whole created earth, comprising man and
beast,  which has decided to give (cf. ונתתיה) into the hand of Nebuchadrezzar.  Had the reference in verse 6 originally been to nations, we
might have expected את כל הגוים האלה (cf. verses 8, 11, and the parallel
passage 28.14).  𝔐 is a secondary development, misinterpreting את הארץ
because of preceding and following references to individual states.  The
development may have been aided by the parallel in 28.14.

6.  31.1  לכל משפחות ישראל] τω γενει Ισραηλ.  See comment on reading no. 4 above.  כל is from 2.4.

7.  33.8  כול 2°] om. 𝔊.  Perhaps from the same verse.  The plene
spelling, which is unique in construct form in Jeremiah, suggests that
the word is a late intrusion from a manuscript written with plene spelling.

8.  34.7  כל] om. 𝔊.  𝔐 manifestly is out of place here, as ערי
יהודה is immediately qualified by אל לכיש ואל עזקה, which at this time
are the only fortified cities left.  The inconcinnity of 𝔐 (probably
added from 26.2, 2 Kgs. 18.13; cf. Jer. 25.18) was sensed by a scribe
who then inserted הנותרות.  It may be remarked that the use of כל to
refer to *two* cities would be rather curious!

9.  42.21 ‏ולכל‎] om. ∅, which clearly is superior: ‏ולא שמעתם בקול‎
‏יהוה אשר שלחני אליכם‎. 𝔐 is secondary from verse 20.

10.  52.2 ‏ככל‎] Verses 2-3 are absent in ∅; om. ‏כל‎ O-Qmg L' Arm ϑ'-
86.  The absence of ‏כל‎ from the late pre-Hexaplaric and Hexaplaric re-
visors is noteworthy.  This formulaic sentence occurs 11 other times in
Kings, 8 times with ‏ככל אשר‎, 3 times with ‏כאשר‎.  It is likely that Jer.
52.2 𝔐 is filling to the long form.

11.  52.17 ‏כל‎] om. ∅ and 2 Kgs. 25.13.

12.  7.20 ‏על השדה‎] prec. παν.  Out of place, as each item is
generic and therefore already inclusive.  From frequent O.T. usage.

13.  23.8 ‏את זרע בית ישראל‎] απαν το σπερμα Ισραηλ.  απαν is secondary (cf. //16.15); cf. 2 Kgs. 17.20, Isa. 45.25, Ps. 22.24.

14.  26.6 ‏לכל גויי הארץ‎] πασης prec. ‏הארץ‎.  ∅ is secondary; cf.
Gen. 18.18, 22.18, 26.4, Deut. 28.1, Jer. 33.9, 44.8, Zech. 12.3.

Close examination of the other variants involving ‏כל‎ would seem to
indicate that in most instances the plus (whether in 𝔐 or ∅) is secondary,
and has arisen from adjacent or parallel context.

## Summary and Conclusions

In number of expansions from parallel passages, 𝔐 exceeds ∅ by a
ratio of just under 6 : 1.[83]  This contrast extends to the size of the
additions.  In ∅, they are quite small, with 18 of one word, 13 of two
words, 4 of three words, and 1 of four words.  On the other hand, 𝔐 contains, in addition to a good number of similar short additions, a great
many in the form of long clauses or sentences, sometimes comprising several lines.[84]

The contrast may further be described in terms of the character of
the additions.  In ∅, with the exception perhaps of number 31, all are
innocuous, and of the sort that one might expect to find in any text
tradition.  Of the 36, 18 spring from the immediate context (the same
chapter).  Most, if not all, may be attributed to scribal memory of
(slightly different) parallel passages prevailing over attention to the
text at hand.

In 𝔐, while many additions are from the immediate context, a great
many are drawn from chapters some distance away.  In several instances
the expansion results in a slight distortion of syntax, stylistic usage,

normal connotation of clichés, or other unevenness.  For example, two
closely related clichés or expressions have been mixed, in nos. 3, 12,
36, 37 (cf. also 8, 15, 128).  Syntactical awkwardness has been introduced, in nos. 21, 36, 55, 89, 91, 146.[85]  Intrusion into a new context
has given a phrase a nuance different from that which it bears in textually solid occurrences, in nos 9, 14, 76, 83, 141, 158.

Furthermore, while many of the additions in 𝔐 were the result of
subconscious or mechanical scribal processes, a good many of them, especially the larger ones, presuppose something more than this.  Here, we
probably have to do with scholarly marginal notation, and clarifying
"cross-reference" (e.g., nos. 41, 79, 86).  We also catch the tail end
of the development of the editorial framework (nos. 9 and 21, and the
instances cited along with no. 9 in the preceding paragraph), and of the
production of extended doublets (see pp. 91-96, 134).

Another interesting characteristic of 𝔐 is the number of expansions
drawn from outside the book of Jeremiah, 14,[86] as compared with 2 in 𝔊.
The large expansions, numbers 79, 86, and 180, are especially reminiscent
of the large synoptic additions in the Samaritan Pentateuch.

The variants involving כל/πας are harder to control, as this small
word may be overlooked in transmission (or translation) more easily than
most words.  But the basic correctness of our interpretation of these
readings as expansions is suggested by the rough correspondence between
the ratio of these plusses (5.5 : 1) and the ratio of the other expansions considered in this chapter (just under 6 : 1); the occurrence elsewhere of similar constructions from which these would have been expanded;
and the general tendency to add small particles such as this to embellish
the text.

Final interpretation of the data of this chapter must be left to
the Conclusion, but a few preliminary conclusions may be sketched here:

The Hebrew text underlying 𝔊 was very conservative, and probably
had been transmitted through a very small number of manuscript generations
before its translation into Greek.

The Hebrew text tradition underlying 𝔐 was highly developed, and
undoubtedly had been transmitted through a great many manuscript generations.  It received much study and notation, resulting especially in the
large glosses, doublets, and editorial-type expansions which we have
identified above.

IV   The Proper Names in Jeremiah

*Human Names*

The divergence between 𝔐 and 𝔊 with respect to human names follows
the general pattern of divergence in other types of readings. Now, one
might expect occasional omission of a name by simple scribal error; but
the divergence of 𝔊 from 𝔐 is so wide that it cannot be accounted for by
inadvertent omission. We must suppose either that the names were shortened (by 𝔊-translator, or already in 𝔊-*Vorlage*), or that 𝔐 has undergone
extensive filling out. The latter process is indicated, in my judgment
conclusively, by the following considerations:

1.   Jer. 40.7-9, 41.1-4, and 52.1-34, are contained also in 2 Kgs.
25.22-24, 25.25, and 24.18-21, 26-30; also, Jer. 52.7-11, 13-16 are paralleled in Jer. 39.4-10. Here we have a *Hebrew* text against which we may
cross-check some of the zero variants in 𝔊. As shown in Appendix A, 𝔊
is supported against 𝔐 in readings A56, B56, K4, 6, 14, 15, M1, N13 (cf.
also B46, N2), while 𝔐 is supported against 𝔊 in S5, BB2.[1] That 2 Kgs.
should support Jer. 𝔊 against 𝔐 by a ratio of 5 to 1 is remarkable, in
view of the undoubted tendency of the two Hebrew passages toward harmonization.

2.   As 𝔐 stands, there are several passages in which the repeated
full name renders the narrative unwieldy and stylistically grotesque.
Long after persons have been introduced, they continue to receive their
full name or *nomen opificum*.[2] This is especially true of chapters 28,
36-38, 40-41 (see, for example, H25-31, I1-9, K2-22, M3-14, O2-21, and
P1-5). It is hard to imagine anyone writing narrative Hebrew in this
fashion, while the secondary process of filling out names to their long
forms is a common type of textual embellishment which can be illustrated[3]
(albeit to a much smaller degree) in any of the versions as well as in
the Masoretic text of the rest of the Old Testament. On the other hand,

we have no real analogy for extensive abbreviation of names, anywhere
else in the Septuagint.

3.   There is some evidence within Jer. 𝕸 itself of the secondary
character of at least some of the instances of נבוכדראצר as an 𝕸 plus.
This name occurs with original spelling (= nabu-kudurri-uṣur) only in
Ezek. (4 out of 4 times) and in Jer., the two biblical books which stem
from the Nebuchadrezzar period and mention his name.  In the rest of the
O.T. it occurs without exception in the later form resulting from dis-
similation of the first ר to נ.  Now, the later spelling does occur in
Jer. eight times (according to BH[3]), all within the passage 27.6–29.3
(see A13–29).  Strikingly, all eight are missing in 𝕲.  The combination
of late orthography and omission in 𝕲 strongly suggests the secondary
character of 𝕸 in these eight instances.  The other fifteen occurrences
of the name in 𝕸, where 𝕲 omits name or context, and which have the
earlier spelling, are scattered through the book.  We may have in 27.6–
29.3 a late, wholesale insertion of the name,[4] while in the other instances the filling may have been more sporadic, perhaps earlier, con-
forming to original usage in Jer.

One other reading is of interest in this connection:  39.5 (A56).
Whereas 52.9 and 2 Kgs. 25.6 (parallel passages) read מלך בבל, 39.5 reads
נבוכדראצר מלך בבל, but the name is spelled with נ in BH[2] (the only instance of divergence between BH[2] and BH[3] in spelling this name).  It may
well be that BH[2] here attests the "original" spelling of the secondarily
introduced proper name (מלך בבל clearly is the earliest reading, while
נב' מלך בבל arose at a tertiary stage of development, *after* 39.4–10 had
arisen from chapter 52), and that BH[3] in this instance reverted back to
standard (for this book) spelling.  Thus, if the usage of BH[2] be preferable to that of BH[3], this reading gives further hint of the lateness of
the intrusion of the name in 27.6–29.3.[5]

4.   F. M. Cross has generously allowed me to publish a transcription of the fragmentary manuscript 4QJer[b] (below, Appendix D).  In the
space of three short verses, 4QJer[b] agrees with 𝕲 *several times* against
𝕸 on short-name readings, and *never* sides with 𝕸 against 𝕲.  This evidence removes all doubt from the issue, refuting once and for all the
notion that 𝕲's short-name readings are the result of a desire to condense names in translation.  It is clear that, as in other types of readings, the long names in 𝕸 are the result of extensive addition and

filling-out to related occurrences.

*Detailed Comments*

1. In K15, M אתו את גדליהו clearly is a conflation of two traditions, one agreeing with ₵ and 2 Kgs. (and original), the other secondary
according to a tendency (see below) to specify the pronoun.[6]

2. The filling out of the name יוחנן בן קדח (series M) is virtually complete in M, which reads the short name only in 41.15. But here
₵ lacks the phrase מפני יוחנן, which probably is a gloss coming into M
after the otherwise complete filling out of this name.

3. The treatment of צדקיהו in chapters 37-38 M is remarkable (B22,
23, 25, 27, (31), 33, 34, 35, 36, 37, 38). The original text read simply
המלך throughout, similar to the situation in chapter 36 (C13-22). In
B34, 38, the glossed name replaced the title, instead of being absorbed
after it in the text.

4. 32.2. B11 בית מלך יהודה] om. יהודה ₵. M probably was filled
out to the long form (cf. 21.11 and 5 other times; for ₵ cf. 26.10 and
6 other times).

5. 52.24. BB2 שריה כהן הראש = 2 Kgs. 25.18] om. שריה ₵; S5, צפניה
כהן המשנה = 2 Kgs. 25.18] om. צפניה ₵. It would appear at first glance
that the ₵ omission is secondary. Yet, it is unlikely that *two* such
accidental omissions should occur in the same verse; and we have seen
that there are no grounds for the supposition that ₵ is deliberately
shortening names--in any case, this is not shortening, but outright omission. On the other hand, M צפניה is easily explained as secondary from
S1-4. While שריה is otherwise not mentioned in Jer., the name was available to scribes who would wish to make more specific the narrative (cf.
1 Chr. 5.40, which is in the context of a historical note on the events
of Jer. 52). Note also that in the rest of Jer. 52.24-27 the officials
taken and slain are listed only by office. It may well be that Jer. M
is secondary, and that 2 Kgs. 25.18 has been harmonized with it.

6. 29.21. Y1 צדקיהו בן מעשיה] om. בן קוליה ₵; Z1, אחאב בן קוליה]
om. בן מעשיה ₵. Again, it is odd that ₵ omits two consecutive name elements. Even more curious is the coincidence that the only other occurrence of the name קוליה in the O.T. is in Neh. 11.7 (a genealogy), in
the phrase סלא'''בן קוליה בן מעשיה! On the other hand, the possibility
of a prophetic play on the name קוליה in 29.22 קללה and קלם would argue

for the originality of the patronyms. We cannot be certain.

о 7. 36.28-29. C23-24 ויהויקים מלך יהודה ועל יהויקים מלך יהודה[
βασιλευς Ιωακιμ. In BH[3] Rudolph tentatively suggests that $\mathbb{C}$ omits by
haplography. But for the name in verse 28, $\mathbb{C}$ reads המלך יהויקים (cf. C5,
12, B2, 10, 12, 17, 18, 21, 54), and the conditions for haplography
vanish. The name in verse 29 $\mathbb{M}$ probably is to be explained as secondary
from verse 30.

8. The filling-out process is particularly rich with the name
Nebuchadrezzar. As well as filling out מלך בבל with the proper name, $\mathbb{M}$
often inserts the whole phrase, either from parallel passages, or along-
side הכשדים as Judah's enemy or the agent of Yhwh's judgment. Of the
nine times that $\mathbb{C}$ concurs with $\mathbb{M}$ in reading נבוכדראצר מלך בבל, five are
in oracular introductions (24.1, 34.1, 43.10, 46.2, 49.28, one is at the
end of an oracle against Egypt (44.30) in parallel construction with the
kings of Judah and Egypt (who are also mentioned by name), two are in historical notes about the fall of Jerusalem (39.1[7]//52.4), and another is
in the middle of the Oracle against Babylon (51.34). Thus we see again
the tendency of $\mathbb{M}$ to fill out, in mid-narrative contexts, the name which,
in its full form, originally stood mainly in introductory position.

9. 36.32 וירמיהו לקח מגלה אחרת ויתנה אל ברוך בן נריהו הספר ויכתב
ויעליה מפי ירמיהו[και ελαβη βαρουχ χαρτιον ετερον και εγραψεν επ'αυτω απο
στοματος ιερεμιον. Rudolph comments, "$\mathbb{C}$ lässt Baruch selbstandig handeln,
aber der Anstoss zur Erneuerung der Rolle konnte nur von Jeremia selbst
ausgehen, vgl. 28." But it is entirely possible that Rudolph was antici-
pated by a proto-Masoretic scribe. It is easy to see verse 32 being harmonized to accord literally with verse 28 (while the elliptical form of
$\mathbb{C}$ is perfectly acceptable); a reason for the secondary development of $\mathbb{C}$
is hard to discover. Note that this is one of two places in $\mathbb{M}$ where
Baruch is called סופר; the other is 36.26, where $\mathbb{C}$ again lacks the *nomen
opificum*. The title probably is a gloss, suggested by Baruch's steno-
graphic function described in chapter 36 (note also the mention of other
scribes in this chapter: Q, CC5, 8, 9), and may have first entered the
text when the clause ויתנה···הספר was added to facilitate harmonization
of verse 32 with verse 28. Baruch's activity and relationship to Jeremiah went beyond that of a scribe. He invites comparison with other
prophets' disciples in the O.T., and his literary activity probably is
to be seen more in the context of the בני הנביאים than that of the סופרים
strictly so called.

10.  38.7.  P1 עבד מלך הכושי איש סריס] om. איש סריס 𝔊.  The fact
that עבד מלך is a foreigner serving in the house of the king (cf. 2 Kgs.
20.18),[8] and that he is named with reference to the king (cf. 2 Kgs.
23.11 נתן מלך הסריס,), makes it clear that he is a eunuch. 𝔐 may well be
a gloss to make this status explicit. We cannot be sure. To see the
title as esthetically offensive to the translator (Graf) is nonsense;
the ancient equivalents of the term "eunuch" were as common--and inoffen-
sive--in the ancient world (including Egypt) as the word "steer" to a
Texas cattleman.

11.  20.3.  R6 מגור מסביב] om. מסביב 𝔊.  The phrase מגור מסביב
occurs four times elsewhere in Jer., as an expression of doom, and each
time is rendered fully by 𝔊.  In 20.3 there is no clear cause of deletion by 𝔊, and 𝔐 probably is filling in from the other passages, especially 20.10 (so also Rudolph).

12.  32.8.  U2 חנמאל בן דדי = Syr] αναμεηλ υιος σαλωμ αδελφου
πατρος μου. 𝔊 probably is secondary from verse 7. In 32.12 (U4 חנמאל
דדי] αναμεηλ υιου αδελφου πατρος μου = Syr), 𝔐 is secondarily defective,
as the man clearly is not Jeremiah's uncle.

13.  𝔊 contains a few secondary name-expansions: A32 (but note,
Syr = 𝔊), B3, E5, H57 (again, Syr = 𝔊 which may be original), J10, U2.

14.  36.14.  J10-11. The closeness of these two zero variants in
𝔐 and 𝔊 looks suspicious, especially when it is noted that, after the
introductory use of ברוך בן נריה in 36.4, the passage elsewhere originally used only ברוך (cf. J5-9, 12-19). I suspect that in verse 14 בן
נריה is an early gloss, variously absorbed in the archetypes of 𝔐 and 𝔊.

15.  𝔐 shows a tendency to supply secondarily a proper name as
subject of the verb: C6, H70, 74, 75, 82, 106, J5, O9, P2, 5, R2; as
object of the verb: C24, J13, M8; and as vocative before address: B31
(probably from 37.20; similarly 32.25 אדני יהוה] om 𝔊), H2, R5.[9]

16.  An original pronoun has been expanded to the corresponding
name, in A40, B36, 56, H10, 30, 40, 49, 51, 77, 81, (cf. 84), 85, 89, 91,
92, 94, 98, 105,[10] K15, O16, V3. The following readings are of the same
type:

(a)  6.11.  חמת יהוה] חמתי 𝔊.  The context is in the first person;
דבר יהוה in verse 10 has influenced 𝔐.

(b)  8.14.  לו] ליהוה 𝔊.

(c)  15.1.  אל העם הזה] אליהם 𝔊.  The whole sentence must be considered:

М    אם יעמד משה ושמואל לפני אין נפשי אל העם הזה שלח מעל פני ויצאו

𝒢    אם יעמד משה ושמואל לפני אין נפשי אליהם שלח את העם הזה ויצאו

If we restore שלחם in М, following Syr Vulg, then it becomes difficult
to choose between М and 𝒢. We may have here ancient variants, or in 𝒢-
*Vorlage* perhaps אל העם הזה became אליהם and then a marginal correction
was wrongly taken into the text after שלח(ם). On the other hand, one
might prefer 𝒢 as the harsher reading, with אליהם referring to the two
intercessors (this would give even greater force to the statement being
made).

  (d)  18.4.  ביד הירצר [בידו 𝒢.

  (e)  18.4.  בעיני הירצר [בעיניו 𝒢.  In (d), М clearly is secondary,
probably from verse 6; in (e), М probably is secondary as well.

  (f)  20.13.  את יהוה [אתו 𝒢.

  (g)  26.23.  את נבלתו [אתו 𝒢.  Cf. 41.9:  את כל פגרי האנשים אשר]
את כל אשר 𝒢.  In both of these instances (very similar in form), М probably is glossed for explicitness.

  (h)  26.23.  ממצרים [משם 𝒢.  М perhaps is secondary from verse 22.
Note that 26.23 contains three readings (including V3) of the type noun/
pronoun, and that 26.20-23 contains a good number of expansions.

  (i)  27.8.  על הגוי ההוא [עליהם 𝒢.  М possibly is from 25.12.

  (j)  27.18.  בי [ביהוה צבאות 𝒢.  Cf. (a) above, and p. 46, no. 67.
The context is first person, with М influenced by the preceding דבר יהוה,
plus the addition of צבאות.

  (k)  29.32.  בתוככם [בתוך העם הזה 𝒢.

  (l)  29.32.  לכם [לעמי 𝒢.  In both (k) and (l), М moves away from
the specific reference of 𝒢 (cf. לכם in verse 31).  (k) possibly is influenced by 39.14, 40.5, 6 העם בתוך וישב.

  (m)  32.12.  את הספר המקנה [אתו 𝒢.  М may be understood as a clarifying expansion, to avoid ambiguity.

  (n)  35.5.  לפני בני בית הרכבים [לפניהם 𝒢.

  (o)  35.11.  בירושלם [שם 𝒢.

  (p)  36.6.  אשר כתבת מפי את דברי יהוה [הזאת 𝒢.  М is secondary from
verse 4:  מפי ירמיהו את כל דברי יהוה (om. 𝒢) ויכתב ברוך.

  (q)  40.3.  ליהוה [לו 𝒢.  For М, cf. 44.23.

  (r)  43.12.  אלהי מצרים [אלהיהם 𝒢.

  (s)  43.13.  בתי אלהי מצרים [בתיהם 𝒢.

  (t)  47.4.  איי כפתור [איים 𝒢.

In the majority of the above readings, 𝕸 moves toward explicitness,
a common secondary phenomenon in textual transmission. Sometimes the
development is influenced by parallel or neighboring context.[11]

## Divine Names

The great majority of the readings to be discussed in this section
involve epithets which follow upon the name Yahweh. For example, צבאות
occurs 82 times in Jer. 𝕸, but only 10 times in 𝕲. Again, אלהי ישראל is
attached to Yahweh 49 times in Jer. 𝕸, but only 14 times in 𝕲. The point
which we made in introducing the variants in human names pertains here
also: one might expect an occasional omission of a name by scribal
error; but the divergence of 𝕲 from 𝕸 is so wide that it cannot be
accounted for by inadvertent omission. We must suppose either that the
names were shortened by 𝕲-translator, or already in 𝕲-*Vorlage*, or that
𝕸 has undergone extensive filling out.

If one wishes to argue that the names were shortened by 𝕲-translator, one must attribute such a practice to the eccentricity of the
translator himself, and not to any discoverable motive of the Alexandrian
community as a whole. For the epithet צבאות is rendered with great regu-
larity outside the book of Jeremiah.[12] One cannot, therefore, see behind
the shorter readings of Jer. 𝕲 a supposed synagogue lectionary custom[13]
or general community-wide theological bias. But if the translator of
Jer. had some specific objection to the word צבאות, why did he render
it 10 times by παντοκρατωρ (thereby revealing his familiarity with this
rendering of the term elsewhere in the Greek Bible), and not eliminate
the term altogether?[14]

But perhaps צבאות and אלהי ישראל were omitted simply *ex industria*,
either by the translator or at some stage in 𝕲-*Vorlage*. The pattern of
readings is as follows (𝕲 minuses in brackets):

(a)  16 times                          כה אמר יהוה (צבאות)
(b)  8 times                           כה אמר יהוה (אלהי ישראל)
(c)  17 times                          כה אמר יהוה (צבאות אלהי ישראל)
(d)  2 times                           כה אמר יהוה (אלהי צבאות אלהי ישראל)

One could take these readings as evidence for abbreviation; but the rest
of the data militate against this:

(d)  9 times                           כה אמר יהוה (צבאות) אלהי ישראל

(f)   2 times                          כה אמר יהוה צבאות (אלהי ישראל)

(g)   1 time                           כה אמר יהוה (אלהי) צבאות

(h)   1 time                           כה אמר יהוה (אלהי) צבאות (אלהי ישראל)

(i)   5 times          $\phi = M$      כה אמר יהוה אלהי ישראל

If the examples in (a)-(d) represent abbreviation *ex industria*, how do
we explain the failure to delete one or other of the epithets in over
one-quarter of the occurrences (e)-(i)? It will not do to attribute
these mixed data to inconsistent or fluctuating translation procedure.[15]
Why would the translator (or, alternately, a copyist in the Hebrew tradition behind $\phi$) sometimes omit both clichés after Yahweh, sometimes
only צבאות, sometimes only אלהי ישראל, and once (f) carefully strip away
elements on both sides of צבאות but leave *it* in the text?[16]

         These considerations, together with the clear evidence that in its
frequent zero variants to human names $\phi$ was following a shorter, superior
Hebrew text (see pp. 69-70), point most naturally to the conclusion that
with respect to the divine names the short text of $\phi$ represents a corresponding *Vorlage*. We maintain, further, that in its plusses to the
divine name $M$ reflects the same sort of expansionist activity as occurred
with the human names. The development of these expansions, in my judgment, is connected with the fact that the great majority of these readings are linked with the prophetic clichés כה אמר יהוה and נאם יהוה.
Thus, of the 82 occurrences of the epithet צבאות in Jer. $M$, 65 are in
the prophetic clichés. Similarly, and more strikingly, all 49 occurrences
of the epithet אלהי ישראל in Jer. $M$ are in the cliché כה אמר יהוה.[17]
This can hardly be coincidental, and invites an examination of the forms
of the divine name in the prophetic clichés throughout the O.T. The data
are gathered in the tables in Appendix B, which form the basis for a
large part of the following discussion.

*The Divine Names in the formula* כה אמר יהוה *(Appendix B, Tables B.1 and
B.2)*

         1. Outside of Jeremiah, Ezekiel, and Haggai-I Zechariah-Malachi
(hereafter HZM), the formula occurs predominantly without divine epithets
(Table B.1, total 4). To the extent that epithets occur in this formula,
their literary grouping is as follows:

         (a) The formula with אדני, while rare elsewhere, constitutes a
special usage in Ezek. While אדני may be secondary, it is odd that the

epithet occurs almost exclusively in the prophetic clichés and a few other set phrases. The problem needs further study.

(b) The formula with צבאות also has a special literary setting. Outside of Jer. and HZM, it occurs just twice in the Deuteronomic History (out of 44), twice, in the form כה אמר אדני יהוה צבאות, in I Isa. (out of 12), and once, in the form כה אמר יהוה אלהי צבאות אדני, in Amos (out of 13). However, in the three post-exilic prophets HZM, כה אמר יהוה צבאות occurs no less than 23 times. When it is noted that these 23 are out of a total of 25 occurrences of the formula in these three books (peculiarly, in the two instances without צבאות in Zechariah, 1.16, 8.3, the formula is followed by almost identical clauses, which occur nowhere else in the O.T.), the conclusion seems inescapable that here we have a striking instance of special usage.

(c) The formula with אלהי ישראל seems to have a special literary setting, though here the statistics admittedly are less striking. Outside Jer., this form occurs almost exclusively in the Deuteronomic History.[18] The proportion of its use in the latter material is noteworthy: כה אמר יהוה 28 times, כה אמר יהוה אלהי ישראל 13 times, כה אמר יהוה צבאות twice, כה אמר יהוה אלהי דוד אביך once. Further, in Josh. and Jud. all three occurrences of the formula are in this longer form. Such a special usage would be natural in this literary context, since the great majority of the occurrences of אלהי ישראל *outside* the formula are found in Josh.-Kgs. and parallels in Chron. By contrast, the prophetic books outside of Jer. (which contain אלהי ישראל much less often) never use this epithet in the formula.

(d) In a few books, the formula contains epithets (Table B.1: "Other") which are not significant for our study, except to indicate further that כה אמר יהוה and its variations were not rigidly exclusive alternatives.

2. In Jer., textually stable forms of the cliché are כה אמר יהוה and כה אמר יהוה אלהי ישראל (Table B.2, types [a] and [b]; cf. [q] and [r]). כה אמר יהוה צבאות also occurs in both M and ₵, but in different places (Table B.2, types [d], [e], [i], [j], and [s]). The variety of forms is not surprising. The usage with צבאות does appear occasionally in pre-Jer. contexts; and the usage with אלהי ישראל, common to the prose sections of Jer. and the Deuteronomistic literature, parallels other stylistic elements common to these two literatures.

The 𝕸 pluses in types (c)-(k) are to be interpreted as expansions.
Readings in (c) are expanded from (b). Those in (d) are expanded from
(s), heavily reinforced by the influence of the special usage in HZM
(that is, scribal familiarity with the striking usage in HZM would tend
to reproduce the usage in a text with expansionist tendencies). 𝕸 readings in (e)-(g) are unparalleled in Jer.-₵, or in 𝕸 outside Jer., suggesting that this form is a secondary hybrid, created under the combined
influence of the expansionist tendencies seen in types (c) and (d). The
form in (h)-(i) is a hyper-hybrid development, with a form of the divine
name paralleled nowhere else, in or out of the clichés.[19]  𝕸 (j) and (k)
likewise are secondary, the former probably a reflex of this form of the
name elsewhere in free contexts, the latter a reflex of the special
usage in Ezekiel. (1) may be inner-Greek expansion, or it may reflect
an expanded *Vorlage*, perhaps with כה אמר אדני יהוה. Readings (m)-(p)
are discussed below, pp. 84-86.

    In short, we interpret the above data as showing that, with respect
to the formula כה אמר יהוה, ₵ generally preserves the superior text,
while Jer. 𝕸 has undergone heavy expansion, during which it has moved in
the direction of special usages elsewhere in the Old Testament, and has
developed forms of the formula which never existed in the primary form
of any text.

*The Divine Names in the formulas* נאם יהוה *and* אמר יהוה *(Appendix B,
Tables B.3, B.4, and B.5.*

    These two formulas are virtually identical in usage, though in
their origin אמר יהוה probably stands closer to כה אמר יהוה than does
נאם יהוה. Again, the formulas occur predominantly without divine epithets. HZM again seem to have a special usage with צבאות. While for
נאם יהוה this special usage appears only 48 per cent of the time, for
אמר יהוה it is the usual form. Ezekiel also has the special usage נאם
אדני יהוה.

    The divergence in Jer. between 𝕸 and ₵ is not so wide as that shown
in Table B.2. Nevertheless, the same tendency can be seen. The nine
occurrences of נאם יהוה צבאות, etc., in 𝕸 which are either absent from ₵
or present without צבאות, and the one occurrence of אמר יהוה צבאות אלהי
ישראל[20] which is absent from ₵, represent secondary expansion in the
direction of special usages in HZM. The presence of אדני in 𝕸 in the

formulas probably is a reflex of the special usage in Ezek.

Zero variants involving the whole cliché are discussed below, pp. 82-84.

*The Divine Names in the Phrase* יהוה'''שמו

In the rest of the O.T., the phrase occurs in three forms: יהוה
שמו Ex. 15.3, Am. 5.8, 9.6; יהוה צבאות שמו Isa. 47.4, 48.2, 51.15, 54.5;
יהוה אלהי צבאות שמו Am. 4.13, 5.27.[21] The occurrences in Jer. are as
follows:

(a)  33.2  יהוה שמו = ₵.

(b)  10.16//51.19  יהוה צבאות שמו] om. צבאות ₵.

(c)  31.35  יהוה צבאות שמו = ₵.

(d)  32.18  יהוה צבאות שמו] om. צבאות שמו ₵.

(e)  46.18  חי אני נאם המלך יהוה צבאות שמו] ζω εγω λεγει κυριος ο
θεος ₵.

(f)  48.15  נאם המלך יהוה צבאות שמו] om. ₵.

(g)  50.34  יהוה צבאות שמו = ₵.

(h)  51.57  נאם המלך יהוה צבאות שמו = ₵.

Examples (c), (g), and (h) are all in late, non-Jer. contexts, and
the form יהוה צבאות שמו may therefore be literarily affiliated to the
similar usage in 2 Isa. (cf. Jer. 31.35 רגע הים ויהמו גליו = Isa. 51.15;
Jer. 50.34 גאלם חזק יהוה צבאות שמו, cf. Isa. 47.4, 54.5); thus, the
textual stability of these three examples. Once both forms, יהוה שמו
and יהוה צבאות שמו, are in the text, the longer infects the shorter (b),
and the phrase itself intrudes upon new contexts (d, e, f).[22]

*The Epithet* צבאות *in free contexts*

11.17  יהוה צבאות] om. צבאות ₵.

11.20//20.12  יהוה צבאות] om. צבאות ₵.

15.16  יהוה אלהי צבאות] om. אלהי ₵.

23.36  יהוה צבאות אלהינו'''] context om. ₵ and probably secondary;
see, p. 99, no. 8.

27.18  ביהוה צבאות] μοι (= בי) ₵.

33.11  יהוה צבאות = ₵.

46.10  לאדני יהוה צבאות] τω κθριω θεω ημων.[23]

46.10  לאדני יהוה צבאות] τω κυριω.

50.25  לאדני יהוה צבאות] τω κυριω θεω.

51.5　יהוה צבאות = ∅.

51.14　יהוה צבאות] om. צבאות ∅.

We have already seen that the term צבאות is textually secondary in most of its occurrences in the prophetic formulas in Jer. M, according to a consistent pattern of expansion to usage elsewhere in the O.T. The above nine occurrences with zero variants are in "free" contexts. In the light of the general tendency of M to expand with צבאות, we would interpret these nine M pluses also as secondary.

Thus, of the 82 occurrences of (יהוה) צבאות in Jer. M, only 10 are textually sound:

(a)　כה אמר יהוה צבאות - 5.14, 25.27, 32.14, 44.7.

(b)　יהוה צבאות - 15.16, 33.11, 51.5.

(c)　יהוה צבאות שמו - 31.35, 50.34, 51.57.

As noted above (p. 79), the occurrences of (c) are in secondary literary contexts. In (b), this is true of 51.5. We may conclude, then, that the epithet צבאות is not a genuine characteristic of the book of Jer. (occurring only six times originally), let alone a theologoumenon as it seems to be in 1 Isa.

*Readings involving* יהוה *or* -/אלהי *versus* -/אלהי יהוה

(a)　3.25.　כי ליהוה אלהינו חטאנו] διοτι εναντι του θεου ημων ημαρτομεν = כי לאלהינו חטאנו. יהוה may be secondary in M from 16.10, 50.7, etc. But a Greek text written κου του θεου may have dropped κου accidentally.

(b)　7.28.　לא שמעו בקול יהוה אלהיו] om. אלהיו ∅.

(c)　26.13.　שמעו בקול יהוה אלהיכם] om. אלהיכם ∅.

(d)　42.13.　לבלתי שמע בקול יהוה אלהיכם] om. אלהיכם ∅.

(e)　42.21.　לא שמעתם בקול יהוה אלהיכם] om. אלהיכם ∅.

This sentence in (b), (c), (d), and (e) occurs elsewhere in the O.T., both with and without -/אלהי (especially in Deut. 11 times, of which 10 are with -/אלהי, and in 1 Sam. 4 times, all without -/אלהי). We take Jer. M as expanding to the more frequent form (16 : 9 outside Jer.). Note also that near 26.13, 42.13, and 42.21 occur instances of -/יהוה אלהי in which M and ∅ agree.

(f)　37.3.　התפללנא בעדנו אל יהוה אלהינו] om. אלהינו ∅.

(g)　42.20.　התפלל בעדנו אל יהוה אלהינו] om. אלהינו ∅.

This sentence (f, g) appears elsewhere in the O.T., in both forms, as it does in Jer. where 𝔐 = 𝔊 (long, 42.4; short, 29.7). We take 𝔐 as expanding to the long version.

(h)  42.5.  אלהיך 𝔊. om. [ככל אשר ישלחך יהוה אלהיך אלינו

(i)  42.20.  אלהינו 𝔊. om. [ככל אשר יאמר יהוה אלהינו

(j)  43.1.  אלהיהם 𝔊. om. [את כל דברי יהוה אלהיהם

(k)  43.1.  אלהיהם 𝔊. om. [אשר שלחו יהוה אלהיהם אליהם

In (h) and (k), 𝔊-*Vorlage* may have suffered haplography. In (i) and (j) 𝔐 is expanded, in line with similar development described above, and under the influence of six other textually stable occurrences of יהוה/(-) אלהי nearby (40.2, 42.2, 3, 4, 6, 6). Note that of the eleven (יהוה)/(-) אלהי variants treated so far, seven occur in 42.1-43.1. There remain only two other variants involving אלהי/(-):

(1)  8.14.  [יהוה אלהינו o θεος. It is difficult to decide which reading is original, and the question is left open.

(m)  15.16.  אלהי 𝔊. om. [יהוה אלהי צבאות. 𝔐 is expanded to a secondary form of the name (see 5.14, and elsewhere outside Jer.).

*The Divine Names with* אדני

I   (a)  7.20.  [כה אמר אדני יהוה ταδε λεγει κυριος.

II  (b)  2.19.  [נאם אדני יהוה צבאות λεγει κυριος ο θεος σου.

(c)  2.22.  [נאם אדני יהוה λεγει κυριος.

(d)  49.5.  [נאם אדני יהוה צבאות ειπε κυριος; Syr ʾmr mryʾ ḥyltnʾ.

(e)  50.31.  [נאם אדני יהוה צבאות λεγει κυριος.

III (f)  1.6.  [אהה אדני יהוה o ων δεσποτα κυριε.

(g)  4.10.  [אהה אדני יהוה o ων δεσποτα κυριε.

(h)  14.13.  [אהה אדני יהוה o ων κυριε; δεσποτα pr. κυριε A L'-499-538 Arab Chr.(comm.) Cyr. IV993; + κυριε O Arm.

(i)  32.17.  [אהה אדני יהוה o ων κυριε B-S-106' Co Aeth Arab PsAmbr. Ps.Vig.c.Var. 1,11; δεσποτα pr. κυριε 36-407; + κυριε rel.

IV  (j)  46.10.  [לאדני יהוה צבאות τω κυριω θεω ημων; Syr ʾmryʾ ḥyltnʾ.

(k)  46.10.  [לאדני יהוה צבאות τω κυριω; Syr ʾmryʾ ḥyltnʾ.

(l)  50.25.  [לאדני יהוה צבאות τω κυριω θεω.

V   (m)  44.26.  [חי אדני יהוה ζη κυριος.

VI  (n)  32.25.  [אדני יהוה om. 𝔊.

It is difficult to interpret the textual evidence. As Ziegler says, of similar readings in Isa., "der griech. Übersetzer hatte ja bereits die Schwierigkeit, אדני mit einem entsprechenden Wort wiederzugeben, nachdem κυριος für יהוה festgelegt war."[24]  Baumgärtel would go so far

as to argue that, because of this difficulty, 𝔊 originally let κυριος

serve as the translation for אדני יהוה, and that therefore 𝔊 is of no

use for textual study at this point.[25]  According to his argument, the

renderings in various Greek text traditions, such as δεσποτα κυριος,

κυριος ο θεος, κυριος (μου) κυριος, κυριος πιπι, all are secondary cor-

rections toward 𝔐.  Now, it need not be doubted that in some contexts

(especially that of direct address) the name אדני יהוה is original.  But

it is clear from even a cursory survey that in a number of instances the

אדני of the name is secondary, and that 𝔊 provides evidence for this.

Moreover, in his above-mentioned article, Ziegler uses 1QIs[a] to demon-

strate the usefulness of 𝔊 in this type of variant.

In Jer., I suggest that here too the Greek evidence must be taken

seriously, especially when it is supported by Syr (d, j, k, on p. 81).

In I, II, and V, we see 𝔐 אדני as secondary under the influence of the

usage in Ezek. (see Appendix B, Tables B.1 and B.3).  Jer. 𝔐 and Isa.

both have undergone infection from Ezek. 𝔐 in the prophetic formulas.

In VI the whole phrase probably is a gloss, making more explicit the one

who is being addressed (similarly in 38.9, אדני המלך] om. 𝔊).

In IV (k), אדני is absent in 𝔊 Syr, and secondary in 𝔐.  In (j)

and (1), κυριω θεω (υμων) may represent אדני יהוה, or perhaps יהוה

אלהים\נו.  On the other hand, in (j) Syr om. אדני may mean that θεω ημων

is an inner-Greek addition, as may be indicated also for (1) by omission

of θεω by A Q*-V-26-46-86'-233 C Arab CyrIII953.

III:  As Baumgärtel has pointed out,[26] אחה אדני יהוה is a fixed

phrase in its 10 occurrences in the O.T.,[27] and this may indicate its

original form.  In (f) and (g), then, 𝔊 = 𝔐, while in (h) and (i) 𝔊 om.

אדני would be secondary omission.

*The formulas* כה אמר יהוה, אמר יהוה, נאם יהוה *and*

Though the readings to be discussed here do not turn on the form

of the divine name itself, they are included in this chapter in order to

group them with the related readings above.

נאם יהוה.  This cliché occurs 175 times in 𝔐, with 𝔊 agreeing in 102 of

the occurrences.  In addition, 𝔊 reads the phrase 8 times where 𝔐 does

not have it.  The variants are as follows:

(a)  𝔐 נאם יהוה alone omitted in 𝔊.  3.10, 5.11, 7.13, 8.3, 17,

9.2, 5, 21, 12.17, 13.11, 15.9, 20, 18.6, 21.10, 13, 23.1, 2, 11, 12, 24, 28, 29, 31, 32, 32, 25.7, 29, 27.11, 29.9, 11, 31.14, 16, 34, 32.44, 34.17, 35.13, 39.17, 44.29, 48.15, 25, 30, 43, 44, 49.16, 30, 31. 37, 38, 50.4, 10, 20, 35, 51.25. = 53 times

(b) יהוה נאם in an 𝕸 context which is omitted in 𝕲. In each instance, as is argued in chapter III, the 𝕸 context is secondary from parallel context, as a gloss or the like. 16.5, 21.14, 25.9, 12, 28.4, 29.14, 14, 32, 30.10, 11, 31.17, 32.5, 30, 33.14, 46.26, 48.47, 49.6. = 17 times.

(c) יהוה נאם in an 𝕸 context which is absent in 𝕲 by haplography. 29.19, 19, 51.48 = 3 times.

(d) יהוה נאם alone in 𝕲, absent in 𝕸 (or a variant reading). 1.17, 2.2, 17 (v.r.), 19 (v.r.), 5.1 (v.r.), 16.1 (v.r.), 31.35, 50.20. = 4 + 4 times.

The readings in (c) need no discussion, and those in (b) fall within readings discussed in another chapter. Concerning (a), many scholars have taken 𝕸 as secondary. For example, Scholz suggested that the frequent occurrence of the phrase in Jeremiah was due to synagogue homiletical practice:

> Nicht weniger als hundertsiebenundsiebzigmal wird im masorethischen Texte die Phrase Ne'um Adunai wiederholt, und zwar in zahlreichen Stellen, wo sie fast nur den Sinn haben kann, w i e d e r h o l t zu  v e r s i c h e r n, dass das Gesagte gewiss wahr sei, weil Gottes Wort, etwa wie ein Prediger sich auf Bibelstellen als auf Gottes Wort beruft.[28]

Volz, commenting on 5.11, judges that "es ist wie so oft Beiwort des Schreibers." Streane and Cornill similarly on the whole consider 𝕸 plus נאם יהוה as secondary (though at times metrical considerations lead Cornill and others to retain the 𝕸 reading, or to reject an occurrence which is textually stable).

It is difficult to base one's judgment on more than general grounds. Because נאם יהוה is not related to its context in any necessary way, it can enter the text or drop out without disturbing the context. Moreover, the phrase seems normally to stand outside the metrical structure of poetic contexts,[29] so that meter is no criterion of authenticity. Evaluation of the divergence between 𝕸 and 𝕲 on this phrase usually depends upon one's explanation of the general divergence between these two text traditions. There are some clues, however, which point to the most likely interpretation of the data.

The introductory phrase הִנֵּה יָמִים בָּאִים is characteristic of the book of Jeremiah, occurring there 15 times compared with only 15 times in the rest of the O.T. Further, while in the latter instances it occurs only twice with נְאֻם יְהוָה following, in Jer. the regular form is הִנֵּה יָמִים בָּאִים נְאֻם יְהוָה (14 out of 15 times).[30] Now, it is striking that, in every instance where the context is present in both texts (13 out of 15 times),[31] ₵ agrees with 𝕸. This agreement precisely where נְאֻם יְהוָה is a fixed element, as contrasted with the wide divergence in free contexts, strongly suggests that in the latter instance נְאֻם יְהוָה was not wilfully deleted in ₵ or ₵-*Vorlage*. Another, more general observation may be made. Rendtorff says, "das Fehlen der Formel in LXX ist so häufig und dabei so unregelmässig, dass es vorläufig ausser Betracht bleiben muss."[32] It is true that, if we were to look for a principle by which ₵ supposedly deleted the cliché, we would look in vain--unless we were to conclude that for some reason he was careful not to delete it when it occurred after הִנֵּה יָמִים בָּאִים! But if he deleted the phrase elsewhere *ex industria*, for example in chapters 23 (10 out of 17 occurrences), 48 (6 out of 9), and 49 (6 out of 12), why did he translate the phrase in other congested areas such as chapters 2 (6 out of 6 occurrences), 3 (7 out of 8), and 31.20-38 (9 out of 10)? If we turn the question around, and consider the occurrences of 𝕸 + נְאֻם יְהוָה as secondary additions (in line with Scholz's, or more simply Volz's, judgment), then the *unregelmässig* character of the 𝕸 pluses is easily understood. Scribal glosses of this sort are not governed by strict rules. They enter the text sporadically and at random, and at times--owing perhaps to a particularly enthusiastic glossator--they are added wholesale, to produce a congested text at that point.[33]

אָמַר יְהוָה. There are only 9 occurrences of this formula in Jer. 𝕸, 2 of which are missing in ₵, 46.25 and 49.2. The phrase is synonymous with נְאֻם יְהוָה (cf., e.g., 49.18 אָמַר יְהוָה // 50.40 נְאֻם יְהוָה), and the likelihood is that the 𝕸 plus in 49.2 is a reflex of the frequent addition of the latter cliché. On 46.25, see p. 76, n. 17.

כֹּה אָמַר יְהוָה. Of 154 occurrences in Jer. 𝕸, 7 occur in larger contexts missing in ₵ (33.17, 20, 25 are in a passage secondary in 𝕸. The contexts 17.5, 29.16, 17 are missing in ₵ by haplography. On 27.21, see

p. 118, while in the following 8 instances the formula alone is missing:

(a)  11.22.  [לכן כה אמר יהוה צבאות] om. ₵. The introductory formula occurs already in verse 21, and is out of place here. M is secondary from frequent occurrence of the formula elsewhere before הנני +
participle, and especially with הנני פקד (23.2, 29.32, 50.18, cf. 46.25).
הנני + participle also occurs often without this formula.

(b)  13.12.  [כה אמר יהוה אלהי ישראל] om. ₵. M is secondary from
frequent occurrence in Jer. of the formula after ואמרתי אל'''', e.g.,
13.13.

(c)  18.11.  [כה אמר יהוה] om. ₵. For secondary insertion of the
formula before הנה אנכי + participle, see (a) above.

(d)  22.30.  [כה. אמר יהוה] om. ₵. For the formula after שמע דבר יהוה
cf. 34.4 (also 22.2). M is secondary.

(e)  23.16.  [כה אמר יהוה צבאות] om. S La$^W$ Bo Aeth$^P$; ουτως λεγει
κυριος παντοκρατωρ rel. The majority Greek reading does contain the old
rendering παντοκρατωρ, and Ziegler relegates the minority reading to the
apparatus. We consider the latter to be original, and the former an
early revision (note the partially atypical form ουτως λεγει). For other
early readings transmitted only by S and versions, see p. 56, no. 160,
and n. 58.

(f)  29.25.  [כה אמר יהוה צבאות אלהי ישראל] om. ₵. M is secondary
after ואל''''תאמר (cf. (b) above).

(g)  31.37.  [כה אמר יהוה] om. ₵. The formula has occurred already
at the head of this oracle, and seems intrusive in M.

(h)  35.19.  [לכן כה אמר יהוה צבאות אלהי ישראל] om. ₵. M is secondary, cf. verses 13, 17, 18. The whole of ₵ verses 17-19 is different
from M and will be discussed more fully below, p. 105, no. 19. For now,
it is sufficient to note the preferable structure of ₵ in verses 18-19:
Introduction – לכן כה אמר יהוה; Protasis – יען אשר שמעו; Apodosis – לא
יכרת איש. The formula probably came into verse 19 M along with the
other reworking of this passage.

In one instance, ₵ contains the formula where M does not:  2.31
[הדור אתם ראו דבר יהוה] και ουκ εφοβηθητε. ακουσατε λογον κυριου ταδε
λεγει κυριος = כה אמר יהוה. ולא יראתם שמעו דבר יהוה כה אמר יהוה. In ₵-*Vorlage*, לא
יראתם probably was corrupt from הדור אתם, perhaps suggested by verse 30a
(מוסר) ולא לקחו, which in ₵ is incorrectly לא לקחתם. Poetically, מוסר
לא לקחו is balanced by כאריה משחית, indicating the correctness of the

verse division in 𝔐.  In ακουσατε (for ראו) 𝔊 probably obscures an unusual but acceptable expression (ראו דבר יהוה; cf. Am. 1.1), leveling
to customary usage.  In דבר יהוה] + ταδε λεγει κυριος 𝔊 is secondary
(cf. p. 85, d).

*Summary*

The readings examined in this chapter are a special form of the
type examined in chapter III.  The analysis has shown that in the over-
whelming majority of instances the shorter Greek text is superior, while
the longer Masoretic text is to be explained as being due to secondary
expansion toward usages elsewhere in Jer. or in the O.T. generally.  The
evidence from the proper names joins the evidence in chapters II and III
in pointing to the received text of Jer. as the product of a long tradition of intense scribal activity, during which the text was reworked,
clarified, and embellished.

V   Supposed Abridgement in ȼ

There is a consensus--shared by scholars who recognize that the 𝕸
plusses in Jer. at least to some degree are expansions--that a number of
ȼ minuses represent neither a superior text nor accidental omission (in
ȼ or its *Vorlage*), but intentional deletion by the translator. Rudolph's
summary statement is characteristic: "Dass ȼ nach Kürzung strebt, ist
unverkennbar und bei der Breite der Quellen B und C wohl begreiflich."[1]
If this consensus is correct, the text-critical use of ȼ becomes more
complicated by the fact that, in many places, it will be exceedingly
difficult to decide between a superior short reading and an abridgement
or tendentious omission. Accordingly, the identification in the preceding chapters of 𝕸 plusses as expansions becomes, at least in some instances, less sure. It is necessary, therefore, to re-examine the view
which attributes to the Greek translator a tendency to abridge or to
delete part of his *Vorlage* for one reason or another.

In the following discussion, I shall examine the argument from
translation technique, the argument that the translator omitted the second occurrence of doublets, and *ad hoc* attribution of deliberate omission. The last systematic presentation of the case for deliberate abridgement in ȼ is Giesebrecht's discussion of "die alexandrinische Überset-
zung," in the introduction to his commentary.[2] In dealing with translation technique I shall confine myself to a consideration of Giesebrecht's argument (while some earlier discussions may differ in a few
cited examples, the argument is basically the same). The passages involved in omission of second occurrences of doublets are not many and,
though their number is not entirely agreed upon, those will be discussed
which are commonly so explained. Since almost every ȼ minus at some time
or another has been attributed to the intention of the translator, we
must be selective in the passages to be considered under deliberate omission. Nevertheless, an attempt will be made to deal with most of those

passages which are commonly so analyzed, and which are of prime significance for the point at issue.

### *The Argument from Translation Technique*

Giesebrecht's argument from translation technique to abridging
tendency may be summarized as follows:

A close examination of minute details reveals that the translator
"nicht mit peinlicher Akribie wie Aquila sondern mit einer gewissen
Freiheit seiner Vorlage gegenüberstand."[3]  To begin with, one finds that
certain Hebrew expressions are paraphrased, especially awkward abstract
concepts; abstract expressions are rendered concretely, and vice versa;
remote (or unfamiliar) proper nouns are replaced by more familiar ones;
and a number of renderings display unwarranted liberty in translating
(pp. xxvi-xxviii).

If the translator's liberty often conveyed the right effect, yet
often the effect was achieved not without violence.  One may fairly find
fault in him for proceeding without due circumspection (*der nötigen
Umsicht*, p. xxix).  A number of instances display a hasty, now and then
bold, grasping after the sense, rather than a careful study of the content.  For example, only *geringer Sorgfalt* can explain the treatment of
כלה/כלו (where context demands כל) as כָּלָה *vergehen*, the latter meaning
often being pressed with great violence into the context (pp. xxviii-
xxix).

The translator stands accused of inadequacy of linguistic (especially lexical) knowledge.  His inadequate equipment is shown above all
in the rendering of less familiar expressions.  Frequently in such
cases the translation gives the impression that it was achieved only
from the context, or that it intended only a free paraphrase (pp. xxix-
xxxi).

Free rendering is also manifested in a few instances where 𝔊 has a
small addition.

The preceding observations may now be used in evaluating a number
of variants in which the longer text of 𝔐 is to be considered superior.
Since the translator undertook his task with insufficient equipment, and
since he often contented himself with a paraphrase of his *Vorlage*, we
must reckon with the definite possibility that unclear words or phrases

would be deleted, and if individual words, so also smaller and greater
verse parts, which seemed to him not of significance for the essential
meaning of various passages. Thus, the omission of words like וְעַתָּה,
הִנֵּה, שָׁם, אָז, עוֹד, and הַזֹּאת. Moreover, given the diffuseness and prolix
style of the Hebrew text, it is easy to understand how the translator
would delete what seemed superfluous (pp. xxxiv-xxxviii).

Finally, at the other end of the scale, such freedom in deleting
material is seen in the tendency to omit the second occurrence of
doublets (pp. xxxviii-xxxix).

Giesebrecht's procedure is clear. He begins with the character of
the translation as revealed in minutiae. He uses evidence for freedom
in translation, and incompetence, to interpret omissions small and large
as resulting from the translator's free attitude toward his *Vorlage*. On
the other end of the scale, the translator's method can be seen in his
practice of omitting second occurrences of some doublets.

Giesebrecht adduces over two hundred examples to support his argument. An exhaustive analysis of all of them underlies the following remarks.

Giesebrecht's examples do not support his claim that ₵ is a free,
paraphrastic translation. For example:

7.29: נֵזֶר-κεφαλη (p. xxvi). But the whole phrase is גָּזִּי נִזְרֵךְ
which involves a highly idiomatic use of the term נֵזֶר. For this idiom
₵ renders κειραι την κεφαλην σου which, as usage in Herodotus shows, is
good Greek idiom paralleling ₥ in its general, if not technical, sense.[4]
15.17: זַעַם-πικρια (p. xxvii). The context is כִּי זַעַם מִלֵּאתָנִי, where
πικρια, while not identical with זַעַם, certainly falls within the latter's
range of meaning as it is used here and is vividly appropriate. 33.5:
הִסְתַּרְתִּי-απεστρεφα (p. xxvii). But the idiom הִסְתַּרְתִּי פָנַי *regularly* is translated απεστρεφα το προσωπου μου at widely scattered points throughout
the Septuagint![5] Similarly, the title αρχιμαγειρος for רַב טַבָּחִים is the
standard rendering in the Septuagint. In like manner, a great many of
Giesebrecht's examples of "free translation" vanish under close examination.

The charge that the translation often rides carelessly over the
meaning of the text cannot be sustained from the examples cited. For
example, Giesebrecht says, "nur aus geringer Sorgfalt erklärt es sich,
dass dem Übers. bei Formen wie כְלוּ oder כָלָה, auch wo es der Kontext
fordert, כֹל nicht einfällt, sondern כָלָה 'vergehen,' dessen Sinn er oft

mit grösster Gewaltsamkeit in den Zusammenhang presst, vgl. 8.6, 13.19,
15.10. Dasselbe Versehen hat...6.13 συνετελεσαντο verschuldet" (p. xxix).
But 𝔊 does *not* have trouble with כלו in 6.13; it is rendered παντας,
while συνετελεσαντο renders בֹצֲע. The form כָלֹה was misunderstood in
almost all of its occurrences outside of Jeremiah as well.[6] And indeed,
it is not surprising to find such misunderstanding of an archaic form.
That the translator did violence to the context by such a translation
argues just the opposite of Giesebrecht's conclusion. That is, a translator who was willing to violate the context for the sake of faithful
rendering (according to *his* understanding) of כלה, rather than deal
freely with כלה in the interest of the context, may be accused of lack of
knowledge of archaic orghography, or of imagination, but hardly of a
lack of conscientiousness.

To treat one more example: In 18.22, ενεχειρησαν λογον does not
constitute free paraphrase of כרו שוחה (p. xxvii), but an attempt to make
sense out of an obscure passage.[7] It is significant that most examples
of this sort are from poetic contexts, where it is notoriously easy to
misunderstand syntax and sense, and where even if a passage is understood
it is often difficult to give a word-for-word translation which results
in intelligible Greek. Even so, most of the examples show that the translator was attempting to make sense out of what was, to him, an obscure
text.

It is not clear how the argument from inadequacy of linguistic
knowledge supports the case for deliberate deletion. In fact, the number of times the translator guessed at and missed, or transliterated,
rare words and obscure or difficult constructions, tells heavily against
the view that he occasionally omitted such words and passages. Such
evidence should rather make one hesitate to attribute odd renderings to
caprice or carelessness.

Most or all of the 𝔊 additions cited (p. xxxii) can be explained
as owing to a different, secondarily expanded *Vorlage*, or to subsequent
inner-Greek expansion.

In short, the argument from translation technique to abridgement
depends for its validity upon the cogency of each stage of the argument.
It is our contention that if each of Giesebrecht's examples are weighed
closely, in the above manner, they will be found wanting. Moreover, if
one were to start on an opposite tack, and list the passages which are

translated literally and exactly, one would have a body of evidence which far outweighs Giesebrecht's data, and which would be difficult to account for if his thesis were correct. It is unnecessary to provide such a list here; our point may be verified from almost any page of the Septuagint of Jeremiah.

## The Second Occurrence of Doublets

A number of the larger omissions in $\mathcal{C}$ have been explained by the theory that "LXX habitually omits doublets on their second occurrence."[8] Not all who take this position agree on which omissions are to be explained in this way, but the passages usually discussed[9] are: (1) 6.13-15//8.10b-12,[10] (2) 7.24-26 (or alternately 11.3ff)//11.7-8, (3) 15.13-14//17.3-4, (4) 16.14-15//23.7-8, (5) 24.8-10//29.16-20, (6) 46.27-28//30.10-11, (7) 49.22//48.40b, 41b. Since (3) and (5) can be explained satisfactorily as owing to haplography in $\mathcal{C}$ or $\mathcal{C}$-Vorlage (17.3-4 is part of a larger $\mathcal{C}$ omission, verses 1-4), they should be dropped from this list, and need no further discussion here.

The argument in general runs as follows: The Greek translator did not wish to take the trouble to translate the same passage twice. This is suggested by the observations that it is the *second* occurrence of the doublet which is omitted, and that in a number of instances, as Giesebrecht says, "grade die in LXX fehlenden vv. stehen in gutem Zusammenhang, während die von ihnen gebotenen nicht übler plaziert sein könnten" (p. xxxix).

But how are we to understand such an approach to the translator's task? If he were concerned to save space and labor, why did he reproduce both occurrences of the doublets 5.9//5.29//9.8, 6.22-24//50.41-43, 10.12-16//51.15-19, 11.20//20.12, 23.19-20//30.23-24, 21.9//38.2, 49.18 // 50.40, 49.19-21//50.44-46? In view of the number of doublets translated both times, it is incorrect to say, as Bright does, that $\mathcal{C}$ is "habitually" (p. cxxiii) or "normally" (p. lxxv, n. 23) minus such material on its second occurrence. We reject out of hand Graf's statement that "wenn dagegen die gleichlautenden Stellen 49.19-21 u. 50.44-46 beide in LXX vorhanden sind, so folgt daraus nur die Inconsequenz und Willkür dieses abkürzenden Verfahrens, welches wahrscheinlich aus Mangel an Aufmerksamkeit hier nicht in Anwendung gebracht wurde, wie sich auch aus

der Verschiedenheit der Uebersetzung ergibt."[11] The suggestion that the
deletions were *ad hoc* (when the translator remembered that he had already
translated such a passage) and that the instances of double translation
represent either inattention or carelessness is totally unacceptable.
We cannot believe that the translator came to his task withouth a thorough acquaintance with his base text, and in particular with the frequent
occurrence of doublets.  As Volz suggests, the practice would have to
have been based on conscious reflection.[12]  But the fact that more than
half of the time the large doublets were rendered both times poses a
serious problem for this theory, one which cannot be dismissed by appeal
to inconsistency.[13]

The assertion that $\mathcal{G}$ several times is minus a passage where it is
primary, but contains it where it is secondary, seems a strong argument
against the originality of $\mathcal{G}$.  But we question the possibility of deter-
mining with sufficient confidence which position is original, in the
cases at issue.  Examples (4) and (6) are both self-contained oracles,
which probably existed independently before their collocation with other
materials.  They are therefore secondary to both of their contexts, in
the sense that wherever they were *first* placed, their relationship to
their new context is redactoral and not integral.  This means that recog-
nition of the primary context will depend upon a correct understanding
of the canons or motives which guided the redactors--a difficult task,
to say the least.  The point here is that, unless it can be shown clearly
and convincingly that the passage omitted in $\mathcal{G}$ is redactorally primary
there while the commonly transmitted passage is intrusive, this argument
falls to the ground.  We will examine (4) and (6) from this point of
view, and then move on to discuss (2), (7), and (1).

(4)  16.14-15//23.7-8 (in $\mathcal{G}$, after verse 40).  The argument is
that the translator deleted the passage, which was later entered in the
margin by a corrector of the Greek text, and subsequently wrongly taken
into the text.[14]  The appropriateness of verses 7-8 to verse 3 (according
to content) and verses 5-6 (according to structure) clearly contrasts
with the manner in which 16.14-15 intrude into the judgment motifs of
16.1-13, 16-18.

Now, chapter 16 may well have moved directly from verse 13 to verse
16 at an earlier literary stage.  But is it really so that verses 14-15
"nicht übler plaziert sein könnten" (Giesebrecht, p. xxxix)?  Redactoral

insertion of oracles of hope after judgment materials is by no means
unique to this passage in the O.T.! Moreover, the striking similarity
of 16.10-13 to Deut. 29.23-28, and the likewise similar hope-motif in
Deut. 30.1-5, indicate that the oracle would have been not at all out of
place in chapter 16, in the view of an exilic or early post-Exilic re-
dactor.

Moreover, the integral connection of 23.7-8 to 23.1-6 is not so
obvious as appears at first. For the dominant motif of verses 1-6 is
that in place of bad shepherds Yahweh will appoint for the people good
shepherds, yes, even a descendant of David, the shepherd *par excellence*.
In this context, the theme of return (verse 3) is only ancillary. Verses
7-8, relating exclusively to the sub-theme, are definitely anti-climactic,
and we are entitled to ask whether they are original where they now stand.
One could argue that they are a secondary gloss on verses 1-6, drawn by
similarity of content (verse 3) and of structure (verses 4-5). But an
alternative explanation suggests itself, one which satisfies those who
wish to see the passage as primary here (either in an original or a redactoral sense), removes the awkwardness of its present position, and uses
the Septuagint as an aid to the recovery of the original text, rather
than of the supposed editorial method of the translator.

We propose that at one time[15] the order of 23.1-8 was 1-4, 7-8, 5-6.
The order of the last two sections would then correspond both in logic
and importance to the order of verses 3-4. This text suffered haplography, הנה ימים באים verse 5 ⁀ verse 6.[16] The subsequent marginal restoration, however, was received into the text at different points in the
archetypes of 𝔐 and 𝔊.[17]

One further point of detail clinches the fact that 𝔊 did not delete
a passage which was present in his Hebrew *Vorlage*. If verses 7-8 were
in his text, after verses 5-6 and before לנביאים, how could he possibly
mistake the latter superscription as an adverbial phrase belonging to
verse 6, and translate it καὶ ταυτο το ονομα ο καλεσει αυτον [κυριος]
Ιωσεδεκ εν τοις προφηταις?

(6) 46.27-28//30.10-11 Again we have to do with a self-contained
oracle which probably existed independently before its inclusion in
either context. Here, it would seem, there is no question about its
proper place, for 46.27-28 stand in no discoverable relation to their
context in 𝔐.[18] However, it is highly suggestive that in the Greek order

of the Oracles against Foreign Nations this oracle, which contains the
motifs of Israel's return from Exile and Yahweh's judgment on her captors,
is followed by the Oracle against Babylon, which opens with Babylon's
doom (verses 2-3) and Israel's return from captivity (verses 4-5; cf.
also 17-20, 33-34)! If the Greek order of these Oracles against Foreign
Nations is original, the presence of 46.27-28 is not strange after all.
They probably stood as a marginal gloss on verses 2-5 of the Oracle
against Babylon,[19] and later were taken into the text before the Oracle.[20]
Subsequently, when the order of the Oracles was shifted to the order in
M̵, these verses were taken as connected with the preceding rather than
the following material. Once this happened, any clue as to how they
came to be present among these Oracles vanished.

Moreover, it is difficult to prove conclusively that the oracle is
integral to the original form of chapter 30. Bright, for example, acknowledges that "it is probable that a Jeremianic nucleus (verses 5-7), perhaps uttered just prior to 587, has by means of a conventional priestly
oracle (verses 10f.) been made to apply to the situation of the exiles."[21]
Indeed it is quite possible that, once this oracle entered the text of
Jeremiah in chapter 46 (26 in ȼ), it was secondarily drawn into chapter
30 as a gloss on verses 7-9, to reinforce the motifs of comfort for Israel
(so Cornill) and of judgment upon her captors—the same function which,
we have suggested, it served in glossing 50.2-5 (27.2-5 in ȼ).

(2)   7.24-26 (or 11.3ff.)//11.7-8  On the argument that ȼ deleted
11.7-8 because they repeat 11.3ff.,[22] see the discussion above, pp. 39-40,
no. 22. Against the argument that ȼ deleted the verses because they
repeat 7.24-26 (Graf. p. xlviii), it may be noted that the two passages
are not strictly doublets, but only substantially similar prose sentences.
If we are to take such "parallels" into consideration, then we are at a
loss to explain the scores of such so-called "doublets" which were doubly
rendered in ȼ.

(7)   49.22//48.40b, 41b  The point made in the preceding paragraph
can only be reiterated here. We cannot believe that the translator, having translated the couplet already in 49.22, was so concerned to avoid
repetition of doublets that he would go to the trouble to ferret the
parallel lines from their interwoven context and excise them, only to
translate several large doublets and scores of smaller ones, too indif-
ferent or careless in his method to notice that he had already translated

*them* once before.  For further discussion, see p. 59, no. 179.

(1)  6.13-15//8.10b-12  As the text stands in M, verse 13a (אֹסֵף
אֲסִיפֵם נְאֻם יהוה) clearly is to be read with what follows.  Now, if the
translator had verses 10b-12 in the text before him, and omitted them
deliberately, how could he suppose that verse 13a belonged with the preceding lines (καὶ τους αγρους αυτων[δωσω] τοις κληρονομοις και συναξουσι
τα γενηματα αυτων λεγει κυριος)?  He could have connected 10b with 13a
as he did only if the latter followed directly upon the former in his
*Vorlage*.  As we shall show in a moment, 8.10b-12 are secondary from 6.13-
16.  But first, it is worth considering whether 𝔊 may not be correct in
reading 13a with 10a.

No one is happy with verse 13a as it reads in M, and several emen-
dations have been proposed.  Bright summarizes the most likely possibilities thus:  אֲסֵף אֹסִיפֵם ("I will gather their harvest," cf. LXX); אֹסֵף
אֹסְפֵם ("I will thoroughly harvest them"); or possibly אֹסֵף אֹסִיפֵם ("Gather
their harvest!").  Incorrect interpretation of the 𝔊 omission of 10b-12
has prevented the proposal that 𝔊's reading may be correct: וְאֹסְפוּ אֲסִיפֵם.
Verses 10a-13 would constitute two tri-cola (omitting the last line in
verse 13, with 𝔊 and many commentators):  "Therefore I will give their
wives to others / and their fields to new owners / and they shall gather
their fruits, says Yahweh // no grapes on the vine / no figs on the trees /
only withered leaves."

As for the M doublet, its development may be traced with reasonable
confidence.  Our point of departure is the observation that the two passages differ strikingly in orthography:

Chapter 6                 פקדתים הכלים יבושׁו הבישׁו כלו בוצע כלו
Chapter 8                 פקדתם הכלם ימשׁו הבשׁר כלה בצע כלה

What is noteworthy is that, whereas in other parallel passages in Jeremiah
orthographic variants are random,[23] the orthography of 6.13-15 is consistently fuller than that of 8.10b-12, which stands much closer to the
generally conservative orthography of Jeremiah M.[24]  This contrast calls
for an explanation, preferably one which can also account for the absence
of the passage in 𝔊 chapter 8.

We propose that Jeremiah M is a conflation of two text traditions
which contained the passage in different places.  The development of the
two traditions, A and B, and their subsequent conflation, was as follows.

The passage originally was situated in chapter 6 (text type A).
At one point in transmission, it dropped out by *homoioteleuton*, verse 12
נאם יהוה to verse 15 אמר יהוה.[25] The subsequent correction was wrongly
executed, owing to the similarity of 6.12 and 8.10a,[26] producing a variant text tradition with the passage in chapter 8 (text type B). Now, as
our analysis has shown, the passage in chapter 8 is orthographically "at
home" in Jeremiah 𝔐, while the passage in chapter 6 contains uncharacter-
istic orthography and is intrusive in 𝔐. This would indicate that the
text tradition behind 𝔐 was type B, and that the collator, whose type B
base text was orthographically conservative, inserted the passage into
chapter 6 as a conflation from a type A manuscript which was written with
full orthography.[27] As for 𝔊, it is superior to 𝔐 not only in containing
the passage only once, but in containing it where it belongs in chapter 6.

Our conclusions in this section may be summarized as follows: The
theory that 𝔊 purposely deleted the second occurrence of doublets is
based on a narrow and selective group of passages, proceeds with insufficient attention to text-critical and literary-critical detail, and ends
by creating more problems than it solves. In the absence of clear evidence that 𝔊 delected purposely, and in view of the abundant evidence for
the expansionist character of 𝔐, we contend that the readings considered
in this section represent further expansion from parallel contexts.

### *Ad Hoc Attribution of Deliberate Omission*

1.   1.17   אל תחת מפניהם פן אחתך לפניהם] μη φοβηθης απο προσωπου
αυτων μηδε πτοηθης εναντιον αυτων.  Volz (p. 4): "𝔊 änderte allem nach,
weil er den sprachlichen Unterschied der Sätze nicht recht erkannte, oder
was noch wahrscheinlicher ist, aus dogmatischen Gründen." It is unlikely
that 𝔊 misunderstood the text, as it is straightforward. Ziegler has
argued persuasively that 𝔊 represents a variant *Vorlage*, אל תירא מפניהם
ואל תחת לפניהם, and this is the original text, while 𝔐 is corrupt.[28]
There is no reason to doubt his first point. His second contention is
not certain, as 𝔊 may represent a secondary change from an unusual expression to a closely-related, more common cliché. But this would be more
likely to occur in the course of transmission than at the point of translation. That is, harmonization or trivialization is a textual development
more characteristic of transmission than of translation.

2. 3.17 לשם יהוה לירושלם] om. ₵. Rudolph (p. 23): "Die in einem einheitlichen Satz lästige (und deshalb von ₵ weggelassene) Wiederholung von 'in Jerusalem' (mit dem Zusatz 'beim Namen, d.h. bei der Offenbarungs- stätte Jahwes') beweist ja deutlich den Nachtragscharakter von 17aβ.b." We would agree with Rudolph that verse 17 in its present form contains primary and secondary elements.[29] But his supporting argument is not entirely satisfactory. One cannot use the *lästigkeit* of לשם יהוה לירושלם as proof of the secondary character of anything but the phrase itself. Since this phrase is absent in ₵ and stylistically intrusive in the verse, the clear probability is that 𝔐 is a glossed text and that ₵ preserves an earlier reading.[30]

3. 5.15-17 Volz (p. 38): "Auch die Septuaginta verrät, dass der Spruch Jeremia nicht angehört; sie behandelt ihn mit einer gewissen Gleichgültigkeit und lässt manches weg." The major variants in this pas- sage are:

(a) verse 15  גוי איתן הוא גוי מעולם הוא] om. ₵.

(b) verse 15  גוי לא תדע לשנו ולא תשמע מה ידבר]  εθνος ου ουκ ακουση [της φωνης] της γλωσσης αυτου.

(c) verse 16  אשפתו כקבר פתוח] om. ₵.

For the rest, ₵ has one plus (v. 17, ותאנתך] + και τους ελαιωνας υμων), and in verse 17 reads plural forms for 𝔐 singular forms, 5 times with verbs and 10 times with pronouns.

Since 𝔐 itself fluctuates arbitrarily between singular and plural (e.g., verse 15 עליכם but verse 17 קצירך, verse 17 יאכלו but יאכל *bis*), ₵ variants in number simply reflect leveling at some point in the tradi- tion and cannot be ascribed with certainty to the indifference of the translator. The ₵ plus probably is inner-Greek expansion, from Ex. 23.11, Deut. 6.11, Josh. 24.13, 2 Kgs. 5.26, 1 Chr. 27.28, Neh. 5.11, 9.25.

Of the major variants, (a) surely is due to haplography, גוי (or εθνος) 2°⌢4°. In (b) ₵ is not simply minus one member. Rather, it pro- bably reflects haplography (לא/ουκ 1°⌢2°) in a text which, under the influence of Deut. 28.49 (גוי אשר לא תשמע לשנו), had been transposed to read גוי לא תדע מה ידבר ולא תשמע לשנו. (c) The phrase looks suspiciously like a gloss on verse 17, inspired partly by Ps. 5.10 קבר פתוח גרונם.[31] But perhaps the phrase has an original connection with verse 17, was acci- dentally omitted (by stichometric haplography?), and was restored in 𝔐 at the wrong place, after the divergence of the ₵ archetype. In any case,

it is doubtful in the extreme that the translator would display an indif-
ferent attitude in his translation of non-Jeremianic materials, even if
he were concerned (or equipped!) to distinguish authentic from secondary
material.[32]

4.  16.4  ממותי תחלאים ימתו לא יספדו ולא יקברו לדמן על פני האדמה
εν θανατω [ויהיו ובחרב וברעב יכלו והיתה נבלתמ למאכל לעוף השמים ולבהמת הארץ
νοσερω αποθανουνται ου κοπησονται και ου ταφησονται εις παραδειγμα επι
προσωπου της γης εσονται και τοις θηριοις της γης και τοις πετεινοις του
ουρανου εν μαχαιρα πεσουνται και εν λιμω συντελεσθησονται. Rudolph (p.
98): "Der (an sich unlogische) Pleonasmus entspricht dem Stil dieser
Quelle und ist zu belassen; ₵ sucht zu glätten." While the verse multi-
plies images of destruction, there is nothing illogical about it: some
people will die of fatal diseases and be left to rot on the ground,
others will perish by sword and famine, and will become food for birds
and beasts. The two are separate images. The mere removal of והיתה
נבלתמ למאכל would not alleviate the supposed illogicality of the bodies
being at the same time dung and food. If this were the translator's
intent, he would have to omit also the reference to bird and beast. It
is not clear that ₵, with its different order, is any smoother than the
neat two-figure sequence of 𝔐; if anything, it is inferior. It is not
impossible that in ₵-*Vorlage* one whole line dropped out, from ובחרב to
הארץ (the half-verse contains 48 letters, about the length of an average
line), and that the subsequent correction was imperfectly received into
the text. In any case, ₵ rendered the final image (והיתה'''') adequately
in 7.33, 19.7, 34.20, and it is unlikely that considerations of style or
logic would have led him to do otherwise here.

5.  16.5-6  נאם יהוה'''לא יקברו] om. ₵. Volz (p. 139): "₵ hat in
v. 5b 6a gekürzt." The superior reading is disputed (Duhm and Cornill,
for example, favor ₵; Giesebrecht, Volz, and Rudolph favor 𝔐). The
omitted part of verse 5 looks suspiciously like a gloss on שלומי. On the
other hand, verse 6a seems necessary to what follows. But for this very
reason, it is unlikely that the translator would omit it. If he were
concerned to save labor, or space, one would think it more likely for him
to delete some of the following multiplied negative statements. Possibly
a line (of about 52 letters) fell out of ₵-*Vorlage*.

6.  18.4  ביד היוצר'''בעיני היוצר בידו'''בעיניו] om. ₵.  בחמר] ₵.
Volz (pp. 154, 155): "Die Versionen kürzen....Die Verss. eine willkürliche

Kürzung darstellen." Volz at great length elaborates the different
import given to the verse by these readings, and by the difference in
verbal aspect. According to him, 𝔊 conceives the proceedings to be a
single happening, which Jeremiah saw (διεπεσε...εποιησεν). On the other
hand, 𝔐 depicts what *frequently happens* in the potter's house (ושחת
ושב···עשה הוא אשר הכלי). Moreover, the omissions shift the emphasis of
the parable. In 𝔐, it is the freedom of the potter which is of central
importance, as emphasized by the repeated היוצר ביד, היוצר בעיני, and
the whole concluding sentence לעשות היוצר בעיני ישר כאשר. In 𝔊, the
*vessel* becomes central (the suffix in ויעשהו is made to refer to the
*vessel*--αυτο--rather than to the clay), and the point of the parable
becomes the final completion of the once-flawed form.

We fail to see the force of Volz's argument.[33] His point about the
translator's misunderstanding of the verbal aspect is well taken, but it
has no bearing on the readings at issue. His second point cannot be
made to turn on the difference between the nouns and the pronouns; and
the supposed shift in antecedent, between כלי and חמר, is likewise ques-
tionable. The most natural antecedent of the pronoun is the *main* object
of the preceding clause, which is כלי. Moreover, 𝔊 text carries the
same emphasis upon the potter's freedom which Volz finds only in 𝔐.
Finally, 𝔐 contains a very congested and awkwardly balanced text, with
two consecutive sentences beginning with a pronoun (or understood) subject, and ending with the noun equivalent. We hold the two occurrences
of היוצר to be expansions from verses 3, 6, according to a pattern familiar in M,[34] with בחמר likewise expanded from verse 6.

7. 21.4 Rudolph (p. 124): "𝔊 kürzt den ungefügen Satz." For our
treatment of this verse, see p. 43, no. 43.

8. 23.34-40 Volz (p. 197): "Wenn 𝔊 kürzt, so beweist das eben
nur, dass ihm wie den neueren Exegeten die Abhandlung zu lang war." The
relevant readings are (a) verses 36-37 יהוה ענך מה···והפכתם] om. 𝔊; (b)
verse 38 האמרו יהוה משא ואם] om. 𝔊; (c) verse 39 נשא אתכם] om. 𝔊; (d)
verse 39 פני מעל] om. 𝔊. Also, for verse 37 יהוה, and for verse 38 יהוה
2°, 𝔊 reads κυριος οθεος ημων and κυριος ο θεος.

On 𝔐 as secondary in (d), see p. 44, no. 51. In (c), 𝔐 probably
stems from a marginal variant to נשיתי (on the latter compare 𝔊 λαμβανω,
Syr Vulg; and σ' λημματι for נשא). The crux lies in verses 36-38. Neither 𝔐 nor 𝔊 presents a text free of problems, and it is difficult to

decide how the divergence developed.  One cannot, in any case, suppose
that the ⌀ omissions are intentional.  Would the translator purposely
have omitted the clause ‏···חיים אלהים דברי את והפכתם‎, which does not
repeat previous material, but introduces a new idea?  And if he had
chosen to eliminate the parallel to verse 35, would he have left the
clause ‏יהוה דבר ומה‎ high and dry and out of context?[35]

9.  25.1  ‏בבל מלך לנבוכדראצר הראשנית השנה היא‎] om. ⌀.  Rudolph (p.
147):  "von ⌀ aus Animosität gegen Babel weggelassene Synchronismus."
Given the frequent and varied reference to Babylon and Nebuchadrezzar in
the book, the last place one would look for an expression of animosity
would be in deletion of something as innocuous as a synchronismus.  While
a similar synchronism in 52.12 is omitted in ⌀ (against 𝔐 and 2 Kgs.
25.8 𝔐 ⌀), a third synchronism in 32.1 is translated.  Here, as in 52.12,
the 𝔐 plus is a most likely sort of scribal gloss (so also, e.g., Giesebrecht, Duhm; cf. Bright, p. 160).

10.  25.3  ‏אלי יהוה דבר היה‎] om. ⌀.  Volz (p. 200):  "Om. ⌀ und die
meisten neueren Exegeten; aber die Wegnahme empfielt sich nicht, denn es
soll deutlich gesagt werden, dass die Worte Jeremias auf dem Wort Jahwes
beruhen.  ⌀ kürzt absichtlich, weil ihm der Stil Baruchs zu breit ist."
The presence or absence of the phrase is bound up with the identity of
the speaker in these verses (Jeremiah in 𝔐, Yahweh in ⌀), and it is
doubtful that the translator's objections to Baruch's prolix style would
have led him also to change the speaker of verses 3-5 from Jeremiah to
Yahweh.  Various attempts have been made to square verses 3-5 with the
Yahweh-speech in verses 6-7.[36]  But it is not necessary to go outside
verse 3; we hold it to be decisive that the cliché ‏העדתי\למד\א\השלח\ואדבר‎
‏העד\למד\שלח\ודבר אליכם···השכם‎ occurs elsewhere only with Yahweh as
speaker or subject.[37]  ‏אלי יהוה דבר היה‎ probably arose as part of a harmonizing process, after the mistaken gloss ‏הנביא ירמיהו‎ on the verb ‏דבר‎
in verse 2 (which arose perhaps from the latter's proximity to verse 1).

11.  26.22  Rudolph (p. 158):  "dl das überflüssige 'Männer nach
Ägypten'; ⌀ lässt statt dessen 22b weg, aber eine solche Nachricht ist
unerfindlich.  ⌀ wollte wohl nicht Word haben, dass ein Jude einen sol-
chen Auftrag ausführte...und ging dabei in den Bahnen von 𝔐 weiter, wo
der Zusatz in 22a ermöglicht, 22b bei der Verlesung in der Synagogue weg-
zulassen."  If readings 22a and 22b were indeed in ⌀-*Vorlage*, one could
explain the absence of the latter quite sufficiently by haplography,

without recourse to the strained explanation given by Rudolph.[38]   But,
as argued elsewhere, 22a and 22b are conflated variants.[39]

    12.  27.7  Om. ₵.  Some have taken 𝕸 as a *vaticinium ex eventu*,
while others retain 𝕸 as original and explain ₵ as intentional deletion.
The two positions may be summarized as follows:

    (a)  There is no difficulty in accepting the verse's genuineness,
as it accords with other forecasts of the limited duration of Babylonian
suzerainty.[40]  The phrase "him,...and his son, and his son's son" was
not meant literally, but signified merely descendants or successors.[41]
However, the Greek translator, reading the phrase literally, deleted the
verse either because of the non-fulfillment of the prophecy (Graf, Wambacq, Rudolph), or because of its opposition to chapter 29.10 (Wambacq,
Rudolph).

    (b)  The whole thrust of Jeremiah's oracle to the neighboring states
(27.5-11) is to urge submission to Nebuchadrezzar's yoke, and verse 7
represents a digression from, and a weakening of, this thrust (Cornill,
Nötscher).  The duration of the Babylonian empire elsewhere is expressed
in the phrase "seventy years" (25.11, 12, 29.10), and "him,...and his
son, and his son's son" accordingly is suspect (Cornill).  The omission
in ₵ therefore is decisive, and the verse is a *vaticinium ex eventu*.
From this point of view, the phrase "him,...and his son, and his son's
son" may be explained in one of two ways:  the glossator apparently knew
that the seventy-year prophecy had not come true, and therefore chose an
expression which would not collide directly with the facts.  The phrase
was used simply to mean "his successors" (Cornill).  Or the glossator,
who lived in much later times, and therefore was no longer familiar with
the actual details of neo-Babylonian royal succession, arrived at the
triple-reign through a combination of the Daniel traditions (Nebuchadrezzar and Belshazzar) and the reference in Jer. 52.31 = 2 Kgs. 25.27 to
Evil-Merodach (Duhm, Giesebrecht).

    A closer examination of the implications of the first view makes
it apparent that it labors under a burden of improbability.  Was it the
translator who excised the verse?  We question the degree of precise
historical knowledge of sixth century Babylon imputed to Jewish scribes
living in third or second century Alexandria.  If they knew anything
about Babylon, they would be more likely to know, and to be impressed by,
its (predicted) sudden *end* (cf. the Daniel traditions), than the number

and dynastic interrelationships of its kings.  Therefore, to excise the
whole verse because of "streng wörtlichen Verstandniss des Sohn und
Sohnes Sohn" (Graf), or "um die Nichterfüllung der Weissagung zu ver-
tuschen" (Rudolph), would have been to throw out the baby with the bath-
water.  The same objection applies to the possibility that verse 7 was
suppressed in $\mathcal{G}$-*Vorlage* by Alexandrian scribes.

Nor will it do to argue that the verse was suppressed while events
were still fresh (shortly after 539) and thus well known.  For one thing,
it is highly improbable that the divergence of the archetypes of $\mathfrak{M}$ and
$\mathcal{G}$-*Vorlage* can be placed early enough to allow for this explanation of
the absence of the verse in $\mathcal{G}$ and its presence in $\mathfrak{M}$.[42]  For another, it
is inconceivable that scribes would delete such a choice and explicit
forecast of their erstwhile captors' downfall.  It would be simpler (and
more likely) for them to harmonize the bothersome phrase to fit the
events.  But when it is noted that the likewise literally inaccurate
forecast of seventy years of exile (25.11, 12, 29.10) gave no trouble to
anyone, this whole line of reasoning falls apart.[43]

In view of these difficulties in the deletion theory, the following considerations ought to leave little doubt that the verse is secondary:  There was no apparent ground (e.g., haplography) for accidental
omission.  The verse digresses from, and weakens, the thrust of the
oracle.[44]  The verse is closely related in phraseology to 25.14--which
is also missing in $\mathcal{G}$, and certainly secondary--and probably is to be
attributed to the same hand.

Now, if verse 7 is a *vaticinium ex eventu*, how should we understand
the phrase "him,...and his son, and his son's son?  Cornill's suggestion
seems a bit too contrived.  One could take the phrase as meaning simply
"him and his successors"; but, occurring as a gloss after the event, the
words suggest a more specific reference.  The suggestion of Duhm and
Giesebrecht is possible, but likewise contrived; nevertheless, it points
in the right direction.  With the help of recent developments in the
study of the Daniel traditions, we may explain the glossator's mention
of three kings as a straightforward reference to the history as it was
popularly remembered in his day.

In 1948, H. L. Ginsberg argued strongly that the handwriting on
the wall in Daniel 5.24-28 originally represented three kings of the neo-
Babylonian empire.  He proposed that מנא, תקל, and פרס stood for

Nebuchadrezzar, Evil-Merodach, and Belshazzar.[45] Discovery of the Prayer of Nabonidus[46] has enabled D. N. Freedman to place Ginsberg's proposal beyond reasonable doubt, with the modification that the three kings of the tradition were Nebuchadrezzar, *Nabonidus*, and Belshazzar. Freedman writes:

> In the earlier Babylonian recension of the complex Daniel 3-5, there were stories about *three* different kings. It is clear that the missing king between Nebuchadnezzar (chap. 3) and Belshazzar (chap. 5) was...Nabonidus (chap. 4). These three then are respectively the mina, the shekel, and the half-mina of Dan. 5.26,28.[47]

We have here clear evidence that post-exilic Jewish historical memory about Babylon focused upon *three* kings,[48] after the last of which the divinely appointed end came. Jer. 27.7 now is seen to be a capsule statement of this theme, and it is highly probable that the gloss owes its inspiration to the historical-theological traditions reflected in Dan. 3-5, and especially in 5.24-28.[49]

13. 27.18-21, 22 Giesebrecht, Volz, and Rudolph see the abridging tendency of ₲ at work, though differing in details. For our discussion of these verses, see pp. 45-47, nos. 66-73.

14. 28.9 דבר הנביא] του λογου (= הדבר); Bo = verbum eius = Vulg. Volz (p. 215): "Der umständliche Satz des Baruch ist absichtlich wie eine juristiche Formel stilisiert, vgl. den Stil des Deut.; die Kürzungen der Verss. sind begreiflich." In view of the secondary addition of הנביא no less than eleven times elsewhere in this chapter,[50] it is better to attribute 𝕸 here to the same process than to argue for 𝕸 on grounds of juristic style.[51]

15. 29.6 ותלדנה בנים ובנות] om. ₲. Volz (p. 217): "Kürzungen der Verss. sind begreiflich; aber die eindringliche Ausführlichkeit war Absicht." It is not impossible that the verse has been glossed by a common phrase (cf., e.g., verse 6a, Deut. 28.41, Ezek. 23.4). On the other hand, if in the preceding phrase we were to read ₲ not as ανδρασι δοτε (Ziegler, adopting B-S-538) but as δοτε ανδρασι (rel.[-198 764]), the omission in ₲ might be due to haplography in Greek.

ΔΟΤΕ ΑΝΔΡΑΣΙ

ΚΑΙ ΤΕΚΝΟΠΟΙΗΣΑΤΩΣΑΝ ΚΑΙ ΘΥΓΑΤΕΡΑΣ

ΚΑΙ ΠΛΗΘΥΝΕΣΘΕ

Certainty is not possible. But in view of the ease with which elements drop out of serial statements, the ascription of intentional abbreviation

is not conclusive. By coincidence, the phrase is missing in Kennicott 82;
yet no one would attribute *Tendenz* to the medieval scribe!

16. 29.21 אל אחאב בן קוליה ואל צדקיהו בן מעשיה] επι αχιαβ και
επι σεδεκιαν. Rudolph (pp. 170-171): "₵ unterdrückt bei beiden Ver-
brechern die Bezeichnun 'Sohn des,...' um sie als 'Söhne eines Niemand'
verächtlich zu machen." It is at least as plausible--and in view of the
pronounced tendency of 𝕸 to fill out names, more likely--that אחאב and
צדקיהו were later provided with patronyms.[52] It is highly suggestive
that the only other occurrence of the name קוליה in the O.T. is in Neh.
11.7: ‏‎סלא...בן קוליה בן מעשיה‎!

17. 32.5 עד פקדי אתו נאם יהוה כי תלחמואת הכשדים לא תצליחו] om.
₵. Giesebrecht (p. 176): "Für den v., der fast ganz in LXX fehlt,
spricht der Umstand, dass er nicht in Erfüllung gegangen ist, LXX scheinen
deswegen gekürzt zu haben." Similarly Rudolph. It is not certain whether עד פקדי אתו is to be read as a promise or a threat, since both are
possible.[53] In favor of the first option is the close similarity of the
phrase to 27.22; but while this interpretation would seem to indicate the
early status of the promise (before events turned out otherwise), the
resemblance to the gloss in 27.22 suggests its origin from the same later
hand.

It is to be noted that in verse 5a ₵ reads και καθιεται (A-106' C'-
239-613 Arab και εκει αποθανειται!), which does not seem to translate
ושם יהיה.[54] It is not impossible that the summary statement in verses
3-5 originally ended on some such general note, and that this was later
made more pointed in A-(etc.) and 𝕸 on the basis of 34.4-5, 52.11.

In any case, it is doubtful that the translator deleted an unfulfilled promise, since this view leaves unexplained the ₵ omission of
verse 5b. The latter is anticlimactic as  an ending, after 5a, and probably is to be taken as a gloss.

18. 34.18 ונתתי את האנשים העברים את ברתי אשר לא הקימו את דברי
הברית אשר כרתו לפני העגל אשר כרתו לשנים ויעברו בין בתריו] και δωσω τους
ανδρας τους παρεληλυθοτας την διαθηκην μου τους μη στησαντας την διαθηκην
μου ην εποιησαν κατα προσωπον μου τον μοσχον ον εποιησαν εργαζεσθαι αυτω.
also, in verse 19, העברים בין בתרי העגל] om. ₵. Rudolph (p. 206): "₵
ändert 18b ab und streicht 19b, um die ihm anstössige Zeremonie der Selbst-
verfluchung nich berichten zu müssen." Volz (p. 255): "Kürzt ₵ und
weicht stark ab. Er verstand die hier beschriebene alte Zeremonie nicht

mehr, oder war sie ihm zu fremdartig; daher übersetzte er frei."

The textual problems of the passage are difficult, and in our view
any conclusions must be tentative. The most serious divergence is in
verse 18b, where τον μοσχον ον εποιησαν εργαζεσθαι αυτον stands in sharp-
est possible contrast to הָעֵגֶל אֲשֶׁר כָּרְתוּ לִשְׁנַיִם וַיַּעַבְרוּ בֵּין בְּתָרָיו. The latter
refers, of course, to the rite of covenant-making, while the former is a
pointed allusion to Aaron's calf and the rebellion at Mt. Sinai (cf. Ex.
32.4, 8, 35). It is often asserted that ₵ is a tendentious alteration of
M. But would such a drastic alteration move in the direction of greater
obscurity? While there is no mistaking the allusion in ₵, its syntactic
connection with the context is puzzling, to say the least. Moreover, if
the translator had concocted the reading as a substitute for M, would he
not have written τον μοσχον ον εποιησαν <u>οι πατεροι αυτων</u> εργαζεσθαι αυτω,
or the like? It is clear that the allusion could not have been intended
to refer to Zedekiah and company! But that ₵ is no free substitute for
M is suggested by the clear reflection of וַיַּעַבְרוּ in εργαζεσθαι αυτω
(לַעֲבֹד),[55] and the trace of לִשְׁנַיִם in εποιησαν (עָשָׂה). If verse 18b M is
original, ₵ may be an attempt to render as faithfully as possible a damaged context. In our view, such an interpretation is required by the
irrelevancy of verse 18b ₵ to its context.[56]

הָעֹבְרִים בֵּין בְּתָרֵי הָעֵגֶל] om. ₵. No doubt it is the combination of this
omission and the variant reading in verse 18b which has led to the view
that the ₵ omissions are tendentious. But however 18b is to be explained,
this zero variant in verse 19 is most easily explained as an M gloss,
based on verse 18b M, and similar to scores of other expansions in Jer.
M.[57]

On the question of ₵ abbreviations elsewhere in chapter 34,[58] see
pp. 50-51, nos. 101-113.

19. 35.18-19 Volz (p. 259): "₵ hat auch hier starke Kürzungen."
Similarly Bright, cf. Giesebrecht and Rudolph. Duhm and Cornill prefer
₵. The texts are as follows:

|  |  |
|---|---|
|  | וְלַבֵית הָרֵכָבִים אָמַר יִרְמְיָהוּ |
| δια τουτο ουτως ειπε κυριος | כֹּה אָמַר יְהוָה צְבָאוֹת אֱלֹהֵי יִשְׂרָאֵל |
| επειδη ηκουσαν υιοι Ιων. υιου ρηχαβ | יַעַן אֲשֶׁר שְׁמַעְתֶּם עַל מִצְוַת יְהוֹנָדָב אֲבִיכֶם |
| την εντολην του πατρος αυτων | וַתִּשְׁמְרוּ אֶת כָּל מִצְוֹתָיו |
| ποιειν καθοτι ενετειλατο αυτοις ο πατηρ αυτων | וַתַּעֲשׂוּ כְּכֹל אֲשֶׁר צִוָּה אֶתְכֶם |
|  | לָכֵן כֹּה אָמַר יְהוָה צְבָאוֹת אֱלֹהֵי יִשְׂרָאֵל |

ου μη εκλιπη ανηρ των υιων ιων. υιου ρ.          לא יכרת איש ליונדב בן רכב

παρεστηκως κατα προσωπον μου πασας τας ημερας της γης    עמד לפני כל הימים

That M is heavily expanded is shown by the characteristic readings in
verse 17a (divine name),[59] 17b (from 7.13), 18a (divine name), and 19a
(formula and divine name). The three clauses שמעתם···ותשמרו···ותעשו are
not likely original. Though ותשמרו את כל מצותיו may be missing in ₡ by
homoioarchon, more likely it is a conflated variant of the preceding
clause.[60] The protasis originally read[61] יען אשר שמעו את מצות אביהם
לעשות כאשר צום אביהם; compare the sequence in verses 8a, 10b.

Rudolph's argument, "₡ schliesst 18 ohne die Einleitung (also unter
Vermeidung des Namens Jer) mit 'darum' direkt an 13–17 an; die Sinnlosig-
keit dieses 'darum' zeigt, dass ₡ sekundar ist,"[62] is not compelling.
לכן in verse 18 is parallel to לכן in verse 17, and the two verdicts follow chiastically upon the indictments in verses 15b, 16.[63] We would maintain that the above-indicated expansions in verses 17–19 were accompanied
by a recasting of the Rechabite oracle into the second person, and the
addition of ולבית הרכבים אמר ירמיהו.

20.  36.6  [וקראת במגלה אשר כתבת מפי את דברי יהוה באזני העם καL
αναγνωση εν τω χαρτιω τουτω εις τα ωτα του λαου. Giesebrecht (p. 196):
"אשר bezieht sich auf במגלה zurück. את דברי יהוה is abhangig von וקראת
cf. v. 10, die Konstrukt. haben LXX nicht verstanden und daher den Relativ-
satz und א' ד' יהוה ausgelassen.... Dass LXX die Worte vorfanden, aber
wegliessen, ergibt sich daraus, dass sie תקראם mit Suff. allerdings nur
als αυτοις erhalten, aber da dies sinnlos, wohl = αυτους gelesen haben."
It must be admitted that the plain antecedent of the suffix ם(תקרא) is
את דברי יהוה, and Streane's attempt to make it refer to המגלה is weak.[64]
Giesebrecht's argument, that ₡ αυτους reflects the suffix and thereby
demonstrates that את דברי יהוה was in ₡-Vorlage, is not without merit.
Yet a number of problems remain: If the translator felt free to delete
five words because he did not understand their syntax, why would he reproduce a pronoun (if indeed αυτους does render ם[ותקרא]) for which he had
removed the antecedent? If the translator misunderstood the syntax, why
did he not simply translate it after the sense of verse 4 מפי (ברוך) ויכתב
ירמיהו את כל דברי יהוה? If the clause were original in verse 6, we suggest it would have to be read like the similar clause in verse 4.[65]  In
our view, the case for intentional omission is weak, and there is a good
possibility that M has been glossed from verse 4.

21.  36.9  קראו צום לפני יהוה כל העם בירושלם וכל העם הבאים מערי

יהודה בירושלם] εξεκαλησιασαν νηστειαν κατα προσωπου κυριου πας ο λαος εν
ιερουσαλημ και οικος ιουδα. Giesebrecht (p. 197): "Auch hier haben LXX
den Text zusammengezogen." Similarly Rudolph.[66] On the other hand,
Streane and Duhm prefer ₵, and take M as expanded from verse 6. Cornill
combines M and ₵, inserting ובית יהודה before וכל העם. As Duhm points
out, the contemporaneous juxtaposition of the two groups in verse 9
clashes with the sequential picture in verse 6,[67] so that M is suspect.
On the other hand, ₵ does not seem superior, since if בית יהודה refers to
the royal house it should precede כל העם בירושלם, and if it refers to the
people of Judah generally it is no less awkward.[68] We propose that 36.9
originally read קראו צום לפני יהוה כל העם בירושלם. ₵ and M reflect two
different glosses, the first from verse 3, the second from verse 6.[69]

22.  36.32  וירמיהו לקח מגלה אחרת ויתנה אל ברוך בן נריהו הספר ויכתב

עליה מפי ירמיהו] και ελαβε βαρουχ χαρτιον ετερον και εγραψεν επ αυτω απο
στοματος ιερεμιου. Volz (p. 264): "Der Text des ₵ beruht deutlich auf
Kürzung, nicht etwa auf einem bessern Urtext. Jeremiah muss als der
eigentliche Träger der Handlung vorausstehen." So also Giesebrecht and
Rudolph; in favor of ₵ are Streane, duhm and Cornill. For discussion,
see p. 72, no. 9.

23.  37.1  וימלך <צדקיהו> בן יאשיהו תחת כניהו בן יהויקים  .om  כניהו
בן ₵. Rudolph (p. 217): "[Baruch] aus der ganz kurzen Zeit Jojachins
nichts zu berichten hat, was das Schicksal Jer's entscheidend berührt (₵
lässt deshalb Jojachin ganz weg, kommt aber so in der Formulierung des
Satzes mit der Geschichte in Konflikt)." That a translator who took
pains to make such a sophisticated emendation should be oblivious to historical problems thereby created, is hardly likely. He was well aware
of Jehoiachin's reign and affiliation (22.24, 24.1, 29.2 etc.). The explanation of the ₵ omission is surely much simpler.[70] Jehoiakim is one
of the chief *dramatis personae* in chapter 36 (cf., e.g., 36.32). Coming
to 37.1, therefore, it would be easy for the copyist to overlook Coniah,
who had not figured in the narrative for several chapters, and to move
on to Jehoiakim as the name most familiar from context (thereby *inadvert-
ently* producing a historical error).

24.  43.10  עבדי] om. ₵. On the argument that the translator exer-
cised the offensive epithet, see pp. 54-57, no. 160.

25. Chapter 44. Volz (p. 287): "Das Kapitel ist stark aufgefüllt
und bildet ein Beispiel der späteren homilie-artigen Erweiterung ursprüng-
lich kürzerer Worte.... 𝔊 hat kürzeren Text; aber daraus folgt nicht not-
wendig der Schluss auf eine kürzere hebräische Vorlage des 𝔊; wahrscheinlich kürzte 𝔊 selbst aus Gründen des Sprachgefühls." The majority of 𝔊
shorter readings in this chapter have already been analyzed and shown to
be superior.[71] In addition, in verses 18, 29, 30, 𝔊 is shorter by haplography. Of the few remaining variants, most are minor glosses and
embellishments,[72] and provide little ground for the suggestion that 𝔊
abridged "aus Gründen des Sprachgefühls." On verse 19 להעצבה] om. 𝔊 Syr,
Volz comments, "𝔊 om. das Wort, wie manchmal, wenn der Grieche ein Wort
nicht verstand; ebenso S." This is less likely than that the word is a
gloss on the preceding phrase. Volz's proposal faces the following problems: If the translator did not know the word, why did he not transliterate it, as he had done with the previous rare word (χαυωνας for
כונים)? Or, conversely, why did he transliterate the previous word, and
not omit it as well? The evidence of α' σ' ϑ' and O suggests the secondary origin of the peculiar form להעצבה:

| α' | χαυωνας αυτη (αυτης cod.) ασιβα | 86 |
| α' | εις κακωσιν (s. εν κακωσει) | Syh |
| anon. | των γλυπτων αυτης | Q |
| σ' | χαβωνας  των γλυπτων αυτης | 86 |
| σ' | τω γλυπτω αυτης | Syh |
| σ' | και σοββα | Q |
| ϑ' | και σοββα | 86 |
| O | και σοβα (σοβνα 88) | |

Without sorting out which sigla are correct, we may note that: not one
of the revisions reflects an understanding of the form as a verb (except
α'-Syh, which however is so far off 𝔐 that it offers no clue to the Hebrew
form); α'-86 presupposes a form לָ֣ךְ עָצְבָּה, which suggests that at one time
the rare word כונים was glossed with עצבה, and that the two words were
conflated to produce לה כונים לה עצבה; σ'-Q ϑ'-86 O would seem to reflect
a Hebrew text in which the conflation took the form לה כונים ועצבה; anon.-
Q σ'-86 σ'-Syh likewise seem to reflect a Hebrew text with the conflation
in the form לה כונים עצבה.

26. 46.5 om. 𝔊. Volz (p. 295): "Om. 𝔊, aber willkürlich, weil
es ihm unbequem war." 𝔐 does appear to be the superior reading. Presumably

Volz refers to ₵'s "anti-anthropomorphic" reaction to רֵאִיתִי with God as
subject. But the translations of 7.11, 13.27, 23.13, 14, cast serious
doubt on his proposal. ₵ (or its *Vorlage*) is defective by simple scribal
lapse.

27. 48.26 הִשְׁכִּירֻהוּ כִּי עַל יְהוָה הִגְדִּיל וְסָפַק מוֹאָב בְּקִיאוֹ וְהָיָה לִשְׂחֹק גַּם

הוּא μεθυσατε αυτον οτι επι κυριον εμεγαλυνθη και επικρουσει μοαβ εν
χειρι αυτου και εσται εις γελωτα και αυτος (α' θ' εν τω εμετω αυτου).
Volz (310): "₵ ändert absichtlich anstössige Ausdrucke, während umge-
kehrt die Änderung des ₵-Textes in den M-Text schwer begreiflich wäre."
M probably is superior, as *lectio difficilior*. Volz's proposal seems on
the surface to be plausible. Yet a closer examination suggests that the
variant is to be explained otherwise:

(a) The meaning of סָפַק is not perfectly clear. Its usage elsewhere is literal, meaning to clap hands together (Num. 24.10, Jb. 27.23,
[34.37], Lam. 2.15) or on the thigh (Jer. 31.19, Ezek. 21.17), or to
slap/chastise someone (Job 34.26). If the same root is used in Jer.
48.26, its usage here is figurative[73] and obscure. All the versions have
trouble with the verb. If a different root is used (cf. Gesenius-Bühl:
סָפַק II = sich erbrechen), the problem remains the same, only now it is a
*hapax legomenon* which all the versions misunderstand.

(b) As סָפַק elsewhere is accompanied by כַּפַּיִם, either explicitly (3
times) or implicitly, a shift בקיאו > כפיו represents simply a change in
the direction of customary usage, a common type of unconscious harmonization. Whether such a shift occurred in ₵ or ₵-*Vorlage*, we cannot say,
though the graphic similarity between כפיו and בקיאו inclines us to the
latter.

28. 52.20 Rudolph (p. 296): "Umständlicher Text, den ₵ und 2 R
25.16 in verschiedener Weise kürzen." Since Rudolph in an earlier sentence states his preference for the shorter text of Kings, it is not
clear where in the latter text he finds deliberate deletions. It is
doubtful that ₵ omissions are intentional, as the following analysis
shows:

[1]B$] και την θαλασσαν μιαν N rell A.        [2]So also O 106 Arm.

## Jeremiah 52.20

| L | G | M |
|---|---|---|
| και τον χαλκον | και οι στυλοι | העמודים |
| των στυλων | δυο | מספר |
| των δυο | και η θαλασσα | הים |
| της θαλασσης | μια | אחד |
| της μιας | και οι μοσχοι | הבקר |
| και των μοσχων | δωδεκα | מספר שנים |
| των δωδεκα | χαλκοι | הנחשת |
| των χαλκων | υποκατω | אשר תחת |
| των υποκατω | της θαλασσης | המכנות |
| της θαλασσης | α εποιησεν | אשר עשה |
| ων εποιησεν | ο βασιλευς | המלך |
| ο βασιλευς | Σαλομων | שלמה |
| Σαλομων | εν οικω | לבית |
| εν οικω | κυριου | יהוה |
| κυριου | | |
| ουκ ην | ουκ ην | לא היה |
| σταθμος | σταθμος | משקל |
| του χαλκου αυτων | του χαλκου αυτων | לנחשתם |
| παντων | παντων | כל |
| των σκευων τουτων | των σκευων τουτων | הכלים האלה |

## 2 Kings 25.16

| L | καιγε | M |
|---|---|---|
| και των στυλων | στυλους | העמודים |
| των δυο | δυο | מספר |
| και των βασεων | η θαλασσα [1] | הים |
| | η μια | אחד |
| | | |
| και της θαλασσης | και τα μεχωθ | המכנות |
| ων εποιησεν | α εποιησεν | אשר עשה |
| ο βασιλευς | | |
| Σολομων | Σαλομων | שלמה |
| εν οικω | εν οικω | לבית |
| κυριου | κυριου | יהוה |
| ων ελαβε | | |
| ναβοβζαρδαν | | |
| ο αρχιμαγειρος | | |
| ουκ ην | ουκ ην | לא היה |
| σταθμος | σταθμος | משקל |
| του χαλκου | του χαλκου | לנחשת |
| παντων | παντων | כל |
| των σκευων | των σκευων | הכלים |

(a) ‏והבקר שנים עשר נחשת אשר תחת‎] om. Kgs. As many have pointed out, the bulls long since had been removed from the temple (2 Kgs. 16.17), so that Jer. 52.20 is anachronistic[74] and secondary, probably from 1 Kgs. 7.44 ‏אשר תחת המכנות‎. Now Jer. M ‏ואת הים האחד ואת הבקר שנים עשר עשר תחת הים‎. does not make sense, and we must suppose that the addition once included ‏הים‎ (= $\mathcal{G}$), which fell out of M by haplography, ‏הים והמכנות‎.

(b) Kgs L και των στυλων των δυο και των βασεων και της θαλασσης. In view of other evidence of harmonization with 1 Kgs. 7.38-51 (see above, (a), below, (c)), L may well be superior in omitting ‏(ה)אחד‎ (cf. Jer. 52.17//2 Kgs. 25.13, and fn. 74 above). ‏(ה)אחד‎ in Jer$^{M\mathcal{G}}$ Kgs$^{\mathcal{G}καιγε}$ probably is secondary from 1 Kgs. 7.44).

(c) ‏לנחשת‎ Kgs. M $\mathcal{G}$ Jer. O L] ‏לנחשתם‎ Jer. M $\mathcal{G}$. Also, ‏כל הכלים האה‎ Jer M] om. Jer. $\mathcal{G}$; om. ‏האלה‎ Kgs. L καιγε. The suffix ‏ם-‎ and ‏כל הכלים‎ ‏האלה‎ are alternate objects referring back to the items listed in the long *casus pendens*; M is conflate. (‏כל הכלים (האלה‎ appears to be secondary from 52.18//25.14; cf. also 1 Kgs. 7.45 (M-Qere $\mathcal{G}$ Vulg) and 7.47.

(d) ‏המכנות‎ Jer. M] om. Jer. $\mathcal{G}$. Perhaps haplography occurred: και (των βασεων)⌒και οι μοσχοι (but this would require in Jer. $\mathcal{G}$ an order which paralleled 2 Kgs. $\mathcal{G}^{L}$, or the like). Or, the secondary addition described in (a) above may have *replaced* ‏והמכנות‎, with M conflating these two variants.

(e) Cornill (p. 526) conjectures that "da hier offenbar die ein- zelnen ehernen Gegenstände aufgezählt werden sollen, so ist in allen Texten vor dem mittelbar folgenden ‏אשר‎ das Zahlwort ‏עשר‎ ausgefallen und zu schreiben ‏והמכנות עשר‎." But as we have seen, the reference to the twelve bulls is secondary, as is ‏אחד‎. The only enumerated item is ‏העמודים שנים‎, and this probably because of the following detailed refer- ence to ‏העמוד האחד‎ and ‏העמוד השני‎.

The original text of Jer. 52.20//2 Kgs. 25.16, as we would recon- struct it, is ‏העמודים שנים הים והמכנות אשר עשה המלך שלמה לבית יהוה לא היה‎ ‏משקל לנחשתם‎.

29. Finally, the following variants in introductory sentences have been attributed to *Tendenz* in $\mathcal{G}$:

(a) 2.1-2 ‏ויהי דבר יהוה אלי לאמר הלך וקראת באזני ירושלם לאמר‎] και ειπε $\mathcal{G}$.

(b) 7.1-2 ‏הדבר אשר היה אל ירמיהו מאת יהוה לאמר עמד בשער בית יהוה‎ ‏וקראת שם את הדבר הזה ואמרת שמעו דבר יהוה כל יהודה הבאים בשערים האלה להשתחות‎

‏ℭ. הבאים‴ליהוה‴הדבר and ‏הדבר‴ליהוה [om. ‏ואמרת‴ליהוה

(c)  16.1-2  ‏ויהי דבר יהוה אלי לאמר לא תקח לך אשה ולא יהיו לך בנים
‏ובנות] και συ μη λαβης γυναικα λεγει κυριος ο θεος ισραηλ και ου γενηθη-
σεται σοι υιος ουδε θυγατηρ = ‏מאתה לא תקח (לך) אשה נאם יהוה אלהי ישראל
‏ולא יהיו לך בנים ובנות.

(d)  46.1  ‏אשר היה דבר יהוה אל ירמיהו הנביא על הגוים [om. ‏ℭ.

(e)  47.1  ‏אשר היה דבר יהוה אל ירמיהו הנביא אל פלשתים בטרם יכה פרעה
‏את] עזה] επι τους αλλοφυλους ℭ.

(f)  50.1  ‏הדבר אשר דבר יהוה אל בבל אל ארץ כשדים ביד ירמיהו הנביא]
λογος κυριου ον ελαλησεν επι βαβυλωνα ℭ.

On (a) Rudolph says "ℭ hat die ganze Einleitung zu και ειπεν ver-
kürzt" (p. 12). On (b) he says "ℭ kürzt in 1 f. sehr stark wie in 2. 1
f,"[75] and on (e) "in ℭ fehlt 46.1, weil dort 25.13bβ die Überschrift
über die Fremdorakel bildet."[76]  On (f) Bright says "LXX is abbreviated"
(p. 339).  Gerstenberger attributes ℭ deletion to the translator's lack
of understanding of, or interest in, the redactoral organization of Jer.
2-25.[77]

Not all these variants can be explained with any sort of finality.
To some extent, one's conclusions will depend on his understanding of
the place of the introductory statements in the redactoral organization
of the book and on one's estimate of the character of the two text traditions.  Against arguments from form criticism of the redactoral process,
it is sufficient to note that the formula ‏הדבר אשר היה אל ירמיהו מאת יהוה
‏לאמר, which generally appears with C material as one of its criteria, is
not a *sine qua non* of this source, and does appear in other contexts as
well.[78]  It would appear already from this that there are primary and
secondary levels within the editorial catch lines.  To this evidence may
be added the theoretical consideration, that in a work which is composed
of disparate materials, woven together so that passages stand together
which originally had no relation to each other, the tendency to provide
captions or introductions would continue beyond the initial redaction,
especially at points where there is a sudden transition in the material.[79]
That is to say, given two text traditions, one *less* systematic in its
editorial structure and the other *more* systematic, we should identify
the first type as earlier, unless we have clear indication that the less
systematic tradition is corrupt.[80]

Against the view that $\mathcal{G}$ deleted or abbreviated in the above readings, it may be observed that in the great majority of instances $\mathcal{G}$ translates the introductory formulas exactly.  It is difficult to believe that
the translator vacillated so erratically between careful and arbitrary
translation method.

A few comments may be made on individual variants:

(a)  The transition in $\mathcal{G}$ from direct divine speech to prophetic
speech admittedly is abrupt.[81]  Perhaps chapter 2 originally opened
directly with כה אמר יהוה, and ויאמר and ויהי דבר יהוה אלי לאמר are variant secondary transitional glosses.  The opening clause in M is likely
an expansion from 1.4, 11, 13; for הלך···, see 3.12 and elsewhere.  If
the translator had had M text before him, we might have expected him to
abbreviate to και ειπεν ιερεμιας.

(b)  For detailed discussion of this variant, see p. 36, no. 9;
also, n. 78 on p. 112.

(c)  This is an odd variant.  Would the translator delete one prophetic formula, to introduce another of similar substance and length?
It is not impossible that $\mathcal{G}$ preserves a text which stood one stage closer
than M to a poetic form, in which Jeremiah was instructed not to marry.
The original poetic form later was elaborated to its present prose form.
In $\mathcal{G}$, it follows smoothly and continuously upon the second-person divine
address in chapter 15.  If Rudolph is correct in identifying 16.1-13 (18)
as C material, we have further cause to doubt that ויהי דבר יהוה אלי לאמר
is an integral part of the redactoral framework.

(d)  This reading is bound up with two other problems, neither of
which can be given full treatment here: the position and order of the
Oracles against Foreign Nations; the origin of the anomalous formula אשר
היה דבר יהוה אל ירמיהו.

It is true that in $\mathcal{G}$ the Oracles against Foreign Nations as a group
are headed by the statement which in M constitutes 25.13bβ (אשר נבא
ירמיהו על {כל} הגוים), and that therefore one would not expect to find
both general superscriptions.  But if, as most recent commentators agree,
the position of the Oracles at the end of the book is secondary, the
clear likelihood is that 46.1 M was inserted secondarily after the shift,
which left the original heading at 25.13.[82]

The secondary character of the sentence is further suggested by
the fact that not one of the אשר היה דבר יהוה formulas (14.1, 46.1, 47.1,

49.34) is textually stable. In 47.1, 𝔊 reads simply επι τους αλλοφυλους
(see p. 112, e). The shorter catch line has the appearance of originality, resembling the catch lines לאדום, לבני עמון, למואב, etc. For 49.34
אשר היה דבר יהוה אל ירמיהו הנביא אל עילם בראשית מלכות צדקיה מלך יהודה
לאמר, 𝔊 (26.1) reads εν αρχη βασιλευοντος σεδεκιου βασιλεως εγενετο ο
λογος ουτος περι αιλαμ. The term בראשית occurs in introductory prophetic
formulas only here and in Jer. 26.1, 27.1, 28.1 (compare Gen. 1.1).
Though 28.1 is conflate[83] and 27.1 is secondary from 26.1,[84] the latter
suggests the proper form for such an introduction, so that in 49.34 (=
26.1 𝔊) 𝔊 probably is original.

It may be, since two of the four אשר היה דבר יהוה formulas stand a
at the beginning of the 𝔐 and 𝔊 collections respectively,[85] that the
formula arose at the same time, and for the same purpose, as the עד הנה
formulas at 48.47 𝔐 and 51.64 𝔐 (see the Excursus at the end of this
chapter). The formula in 47.1 then would be expansion from these two
places, as would its occurrence in 14.1, where 𝔊 Syr read (surely correctly) אשר היה דבר יהוה אל ירמיהו. for 𝔐 ויהי דבר יהוה אל ירמיהו.

(f)   50.1b 𝔐 is expanded, partly from frequent occurrence in the
Oracle,[86] partly from 51.59 הדבר אשר צוה ירמיהו הנביא את שריה.

Finally, in all four of the above introductions to Oracles against
Foreign Nations (46.1, 47.1, 49.34, 50.1; cf. 46.13), the 𝔐 plus contains
the title ירמיהו הנביא, which suggests that these fuller introductions
arose after this title had become widespread in the text.[87]

## *Conclusion*

The common view, "das 𝔊 nach Kürzung strebt" (Rudolph), cannot be
sustained. Where it is invoked, insufficient attention is given to the
implications of such an explanation. For example, the view that 𝔊 omits
second occurrences of doublets is based upon a small percentage of the
doublets in Jeremiah, and fails to account for those doublets which are
rendered in both places. Again, the view that 𝔊 deliberately omitted
27.7 fails to reckon with the unlikely conditions which such an explanation presupposes. Further, a number of omissions are explained by such
far-fetched attributions of *Tendenz* that one cannot counter them with
argument, but only reject them out of hand.[88] In view of the clear character of 𝔐 as heavily expanded, of 𝔊 or its *Vorlage* as frequently

defective by haplography,[89] and of the lack of clear and cogent evidence
for abridgement by the translator, this latter hypothesis ought to be
abandoned once and for all.

*Excursus:*
*The Position and Order*
*of the Oracles against Foreign Nations*

The following is a brief sketch of our arguments for the priority
of the ¢ position and order of the Oracles against Foreign Nations:

*Position.*  Since the book of Jeremiah clearly is composed of a
number of sources, each of which had existed in an earlier form, it is
most probable that the Oracles against Foreign Nations also circulated
separately for a time.  We propose that their inclusion in the Jeremianic
corpus took place after the latter comprised substantially 1-25.13b (to
בספר הזה), 25.15-45.5.  The Oracles were inserted at 25.13 on the analogy
of the books of Isaiah and Ezekiel, where the Oracles against Foreign
Nations appear in the middle of the book,[90] and because of the existence
already in chapter 25 of oracular material relating to the foreign nations.
Now, this new form of the Jeremianic corpus would render a number of extant manuscripts obsolete.  We propose that, rather than destroy these
manuscripts (which had been produced with no small effort!), scribes
brought them up to date by the simple expedient of sewing an addition on
to the leather, and adding the new material as an appendix.  Subsequently,
in the final major stage of the book's growth, chapter 52 was added at
the end of the two forms of the corpus.

*Order.*  While there is general preference for the ¢ position of the
Oracles as a unit in chapter 25, most commentators prefer the M internal
order,[91] since the latter corresponds basically to the order of the
nations listed in 25.19-26 (e.g., Rudolph, p. 245), to roughly the chronological order of the history of the nations treated (Hyatt), or to the
geographical location of the nations (e.g., Pfeiffer, *Introduction*, p.
487); on the other hand, there is no discernible order to ¢.

It may be observed, however, that the collection of Oracles itself

gives evidence of being composed of one or more smaller groups. For
example, the Oracles לדמשק, לאדום, לבני עמון, למואב, may have constituted
one such group. But if the collection itself is a secondary compilation,
made before the addition of the whole to the book of Jeremiah, there is
no necessary reason for its order to have agreed with that of 25.15-26.
On the other hand, once the collection was joined to the Jeremianic
corpus, it would be natural subsequently to bring its order into conformity with the list in chapter 25. Thus, we can account for a secondary
development resulting in 𝔐 order, while no grounds can be given to account
for a secondary development producing 𝔊,[92] so that the latter form of the
text is to be preferred as *lectio difficilior*.

Other arguments for 𝔐, from geographical location or historical
sequence, do not carry separate weight, since such considerations could
have determined the order of the list in chapter 25, whence (secondarily)
the same order in the Oracles.

To these general considerations we may add one or two arguments of
detail. As proposed above, pp. 93-94, the location of the oracle of
hope in 46.27-28 is best explained as originating in a form of the text
in which the Oracle against Babylon followed the Oracle against Egypt.
The little Word to Jacob was intended as a gloss to the opening section
of the Oracle against Babylon, but was taken into the text (probably at
a paragraph break) between the Oracles against Egypt and Babylon. Later,
when the order was revised, the Word to Jacob was taken with the Oracle
against Egypt, and hence its present, seemingly inexplicable location
with the latter.

Also, the occurrence in 𝔐 of the related glosses עד הנה דברי ירמיהו
and עד הנה משפט מואב at the end of the 𝔐 order (51.64) and of the 𝔊 order
(48.47 𝔐) respectively, is very odd. Thackeray probably is correct in
associating this in some way with the secondary order of 𝔐.[93]

VI   Haplography

In a series of omissions, ₵ probably is defective by haplography.
In many instances it is impossible to say whether the omission occurred
in the transmission of ₵ or already in its *Vorlage*.  Certain or probable
instances of the latter are nos. 4, 5, 8, 10, 13, 16, 21, 22, 23, 26, 34,
36, 39, 41, 44, 45, 46, 48, 50, 53, 54, 55, 58, 59; of the former, no.
60.

*Data*

1.   2.13   בארות 1°⌢2°.
2.   5.15   גוי 2°⌢4°.  For another probably haplography in this
verse, see p. 97, no. 3.
3.   7.4   היכל 2°⌢3°.
4.   13.4   אשר 1°⌢2°.
5.   14.16   המה 2°⌢3°.
6.   15.12   ברזל 1°⌢2°.
7.   15.21   ולהצילך⌢והצלתיך.
8.   16.17   לא 1°⌢2°.
9.   17.1-4   יהוה 1°(17.5)⌢יהוה (16.21).
10.   17.12   מרום [מראשון מקום] מקדשנו.
11.   20.5   ואת 2°⌢3°.
12.   20.15   שמח⌢שמחה.
13.   21.4   אשר 1°⌢2°.
14.   22.29   ארץ 2°⌢3°.
15.   23.2   הרעים 1°⌢2°.
16.   23.22   מדדכם⌢(ו)מרע.
17.   24.3   תאנים 1°⌢2°.
18.   25.20   ואת כל 2°⌢3°.

19.   27.5   הארץ 1°^2°.

20.   27.8   אשרלא 1°^2°.

21.   27.12-14   תעבדו^ (v. 14)   ועבדו^ (v.12).

22.   27.20-21   מירושלם בבלה^וירושלם בבלה.   For another explanation
of this reading, see p. 46, no. 72.

23.   29.11   אנכי 1°^2°.

24.   29.16-20   בבלה [כי כה אמר יהוה''' בבלה] כה אמר יהוה.   Note that
verses 16-20 intrude upon the sequence of verses 15, 21-23. The order
once may have been verses 14, 16-20, 15, 21-23; the letter's reference to
the exiles (4-14) and to the Jerusalem remnant (16-20) would then parallel the similar reference in chapter 24 (4-7, 8-10). The disturbed order
of 𝕸 would have arisen from homoioteleuton, בבלה verse 20^verse 15, and
subsequent incorrect insertion of the dropped line before verse 16 (which
opens with the same phrase as verse 21).

25.   31.5   נטעו^נטעים.

26.   32.17   יהוה^הנה.

27.   36.26   עזריאל^עבדאל.

28.   37.15   בית 1°^2° (but see p. 22, no. 54).

29.   37.19   עליכם^ועל.

30.   38.4   הזאת^ראה.

31.   39.4-13   שרי מלך בבל^רבי מלך בבל 2°.   While it is most likely
that 𝕲 is defective by haplography, it is also possible that 𝕲 attests an
earlier stage of the text; for verses 4-10 surely are secondary (//52.7-
11, 13-16), and verse 13 may have originated as a correction to corruption
of the names in verse 3.

32.   42.19   כי העיוחתי^כי החעתים.

33.   44.10   ולא 1°^2°   But see p. 25, no. 58.

34.   44.18   והסך^חסרנו.

35.   44.29   עליכם 1°^2°.

36.   44.30   פרעה^הפרע.

37.   46.25   ועל פרעה 1°^2°.

38.   48.8   עיר^ועיר.

39.   49.12   יהוה^הנה.

40.   49.12   כי 1° (v. 13)^כי 2°.

41.   50.21   והחרם^אחריהם.

42.   50.36   חרב 1°^2°.

43.   51.22   ונפצתי 1°^2°.

44.   51.44   .בבל ב[בל].

45.   51.44-49   גמ′′° 2°° גם.   While it is most likely that ⅁ is defective by haplography, it is odd that verses 49b-53 contain much of the
same, or similar, phraseology, in somewhat different order. It may be
that 44b-49a and 49b-53 are old variants, conflated in M.

46.   52.15   השאיר [העם< ומדלות >העם (16)′′′.העם 1והנשארים.   For reconstruction of the conditions for haplography, see pp. 20-21, no. 44.

The following may also be due to haplography:

47.   1.18   .ולעמוד~ולחמות.

48.   9.16   .ותבואנה ותמהרנה.

49.   11.7-8   ולא עשו [כי העד העדתי אשר צויתי לעשות] ועשיתם אותם.
For discussion of this reading, with alternate explanations, see pp. 39-
40, no. 22.

50.   15.5   .לשאל~לשלום.

51.   20.6   .תבוא ושם~תמות ושם.

52.   22.27   לא ישובו [לשוב שם ושמה] נפשם.

53.   22.28   .נבזה~הזה כניהו   (Giesebrecht, p. xxxvi.)

54.   24.1   .יהוה~הנה.

55.   25.16   .והתגעשו~והתהללו.

56.   26.20   .על העיר הזאת~ועל הארץ הזאת.

57.   26.21   1°° 2°   .וכל.

58.   26.21   .וירא~ויבא.   For alternate explanation of the last three
readings, see pp. 21-22, no. 49-51.

59.   27.6   נתתי [ועתה אנכי].בעיני.   The likelihood of haplography
would be increased if we could suppose that, in place of אנכי, ⅁-*Vorlage*
read אני.

60.   29.6   Inner-Greek haplography ΑΝΔΡΑΣΙ ΚΑΙ...ΘΥΓΑΤΕΡΑΣ ΚΑΙ.
See p. 103, no. 15.

61.   30.19   והיו [והכבדתים ולא יצערו] ולא ימעטו.

62.   36.6   .וקראת [ובאת אתה].

63.   38.1   .שלמיהו מלכיה.

As noted earlier, instances of a shorter text in M are few and
relatively minor. Among them, only two are probably due to haplography:

4.3   ירושלם [ול]ישבי  ולמ יהודה  לאיש.   The full cliché probably is
original; cf. 4.4, and seven times elsewhere.

23.32   נבאי חלמות שקר [הנבאים] הנני על.   Cf. verses 30, 31.

*Conclusion*

In 𝔐, the very low incidence of haplography and the high incidence of conflation (see chapter II) point strongly to the conclusion that this is a recensional text. Recension, together with the broad transmission implied in the developed character of the text, resulted in the correction of such haplography as did occur in individual manuscripts, so that such omissions were unable to gain permanent footing in this text tradition.

On the other hand, 𝔊 is marked by a high incidence of haplography, which in many instances can be shown to have occurred in the Hebrew *Vorlage*. This, together with the general absence of correction toward 𝔐 plusses (especially the larger ones), suggests two conclusions: First, the *Vorlage* was the product of quite narrow transmission, so that, when haplography occurred, there was little pressure to correct from sister manuscripts, and the defective readings endured. Second, the *Vorlage* probably represented a pre-recensional text. This is supported by the rarity of doublets which can be attributed with any confidence to the *Vorlage* (see chapter II).

## VII  Miscellaneous Variants

In addition to those discussed in chapters I-VI, there are a number of zero variants which fall into no single easily defined category. Though in these instances a judgment may be made with greater or less probability, their evaluation is more difficult. Some of the readings no doubt have arisen through scribal lapse, as in the instances of haplography (chapter VI); other readings probably are to be taken as glosses, though the source or reason for these glosses may not be apparent. In an exhaustive analysis of the text, these readings require weighing and interpreting no less than the others. But for our purpose, which is to establish the character of the Septuagint and Masoretic text types of Jeremiah, their treatment is not necessary. The evidence already presented is sufficient to establish the text types, and these remaining readings would do little to modify the conclusions already drawn. Moreover, their interpretation is sufficiently ambiguous to render them unsuitable as evidence for our problem. A few readings are exceptions, and these will receive some comment. The rest I will merely list.

2.28 fin.] + και κατ'αριθμον διοδων της ιερουσαλημ εθυον τη βααλ = ומספר חצות ירושלם קטרו לבעל. $\mathcal{G}$ may be expanded from 11.13. But, as Cornill points out (following Ewald), the couplet in 11.13 is almost certainly secondary, deriving from 2.28, and therefore is an indirect witness to the superiority of $\mathcal{G}$ in the latter place.

10.6-8, 10. Om. $\mathcal{G}$. Also, in $\mathcal{G}$ verse 9 is located between 5a and 5b (after ידברו). Final evaluation of the variants would involve a close analysis of 10.1-16, which will not be attempted here. What is of importance for our purposes is the striking evidence from Qumrân that in these variants $\mathcal{G}$ is based on a Hebrew *Vorlage*. Part of a fragment of the Qumrân manuscript 4QJer[b] reads as follows:[1]

| | |
|---|---|
| רבז]הב ייפהו במקבות | 1. 5 |
| תכלת וארגמן[ | 1. 6 |
| יאבדן מן ארעא[ | 1. 7 |

Clearly there is no room for verses 6-8, or for verse 10; and the fragment is most satisfactorily reconstructed according to the ₵ position of
verse 9. As Cross has noted, "4Q transposes MT *bmsmrwt wbmqbwt* to read
*bmqbwt* [*w* <*b*> *msmrwt*] with LXX, εν σφυραις και ηλοις." This minor detail should give pause to the tendency to attribute other such transpositions[2] to the exigencies of Greek style.

25.14    כי עבדו בם גם המה גוים רבים ומלכים גדלים ושלחתי להם כפעלם
[וכמעשה ידיהם om. ₵. The verse is a secondary addition, *ex eventu*, similar to the addition in 27.7 (see pp. 101-103, no. 12), and in 25.26 (see
next reading below).

25.26    [ומלך ששך ישתה אחריהם om. ₵. The clause is no part of the
original list in verse 17-26, but was added, after the Oracles against
Foreign Nations were joined to the book, to correspond to the Oracle
against Babylon in chapters 50-51.[3]

52.28-30    𝕸] om. ₵ 2 Kgs. 25. There can be no doubt that these
verses are a later addition to Jer. 52 𝕸. They are absent from both Jer.
₵ and 2 Kgs., and for Nebuchadrezzar's regnal figures they follow (correctly) a different system of reckoning from the one contained in Kings
and elsewhere in Jeremiah.[4] Yet, that the verses are literarily secondary in chapter 52 does not necessarily reflect on their authenticity.
The combination of correct regnal dates and precise totals suggests that
the verses are an excerpt from some sort of official record.[5] This is,
then, a good example of a substantial piece of material added to proto-𝕸
after the divergence of the archetypes of 𝕸 and ₵.

33.14-26    Om. ₵. This is the largest single block of 𝕸 material
absent from ₵. Two issues are involved: Is the passage Jeremianic, or
non-Jeremianic? Was it absent from ₵-*Vorlage* or did the translator
delete it intentionally? The two issues obviously have some bearing on
one another. Yet, the solution of the first issue does not settle the
second, since the presence of, for example, 10.1-16 (which a consensus
holds to be non-Jeremianic) in both 𝕸 and ₵ shows that material common to
both text traditions may be Jeremianic or otherwise. We may, therefore,
bypass the first question and concentrate upon the second.

If the passage was intentionally deleted, what was the motive?
Omission of the second occurrence of material? So Graf argues, and Lindblom; and Volz does not rule out the possibility.[6] It is noted that
verses 15-16 are a doublet of 23.5-6, and that the following verses have

a close parallel in 31.35–37. But if this was the motive, why not delete
just verses (14) 15–16? The parallels to 31.35–37 are not at al verbally
precise. If these be called doublets, then we can cite numerous such
"doublets" in the book which are translated both times. Moreover, why
would the translator omit material (verses 17–18, 21–22) which has no
parallel, either in wording or in substance, elsewhere in the book? Graf
proposes that the latter material was omitted because of non-fulfilment
of the promise to David and the Levitical priests. But the translator
seems to have felt no compunction in translating other types of hope
oracles, at the time still unfulfilled (e.g., 16.14–15, 46.27–28). Moreover, one may ask, what is the time limit on a non-specific oracle of
hope, after which it is presumed to be incapable of fulfilment? The
intensity of post-exilic eschatological hope stood in no necessary relation to external signs of its fulfilment. Swete allows that "possibly
the Messianic hope which [the passage] emphasizes had less interest for
a subject of the Ptolemies than for the Jews of Palestine."[7] In the
absence of independent evidence of a disinterest in Messianic hope among
Alexandrian Jews of the period, this conjecture is weak. Certainly the
translator thought it worthwhile to render the parallel in 23.5–6.

In short, there are no clear gounds for supposing that the passage
was tendentiously omitted in translation. It is, of course, possible
that it dropped out by scribal lapse. But in view of the pronounced expansionist character of M, extending to substantial blocks of material
(e.g., 52.28–30), and, we may note, what appear to be post-Jeremianic
elements in the eschatological expectation, it is likely that the pericope was added to the proto-M tradition after the divergence of the two
text traditions.[8]

1.3 תם, 4 לאמר, 11 and 13 אני ראה, 17 אליהם, 18 ואני and עַל ()הארץ.

2.25 לוא (cf. 18.12).

3.1 לאמר.

4.22 המה, 23 תהו ר', 24 המה, 27 כי, 30 שדוד.

5.1 שמנו עשתו 28 ישור משך, 26 לאמר, 20 לוא, 10 ואם, 2 איש אם יש,
ויצליחו, דברי רע.

6.9 ידך, 20 הטוב, 28 סרי.

7.28 ונפרתה.

8.3 הרעה, 4 ואמרת אליהם, 8 אבן הנה, 13 ואתן להם יעברום, 14 שם, 22
כי.

9.6   אֵיךְ, בם 8, ונהי 9, 16 ו', התבוננו 23, אותי.

10.3   כי 2°, 9 כלם חכמה מעשה, 13 תתו לקול (cf. 51.16), 18 בפעם.

11.16   פרי, 19 כי.

12.3   תראני ו', לטבחה כצאן התקם, כי 5, 14 בית.

13.1   אלי, 3 שנית, ואלך 5, העם 10, 17 תדמע ודמע.

14.5   כי 1°, 6 כתנים, כן 10, להם 13, 22 אלהינו יהוה.

15.5   כי 6, עליך 7, לוא שבו 8, להם 10, איש 11, 2° לא אם 13, לא 15, ופקדתיך 21, תקחני, אתה ידעת.

16.5   כי 1°, 6 להם 2°, 18 ראשונה.

17.17   אליי, 19 אתה.

18.17   1° כי 22, אל 18, ערף ולא פנים.

19.11   אליהם.

20.3   בלבי 9, ויהי ממחרת.

22.14   28 אחרת 26, כי 21, והיו הזה, והיו אחות 18, אז טוב 16, האמר, לא יצלח בימיו 30, העצב.

23.15   לאמר 33, בינה 20, (cf. 30.23), 17 אמר, 19 ראש, על הנבאים.

24.8   כי.

25.15   2° אליהם 30, הנה 29, אתו, אלי, כי.

26.1   לאמי, נבא 18, 1° לאמר 11, לאמר 17, אליהם 4, ערי 2, לאמר.

27.2   אלי, היה 8, אליכם לאמר 9, 12 בבל מלך בעל.

28.8   ולרעה ולדבר.

29.6   שם 10, הטוב 12, והלכתם ותי וקראתם 24, לאמר 25, אל ספרים, ירושב 32, הזה 29, ואל כל הכהנים, כל העם אשר בירושלם.

30.5   כי, והיה 8, אשר 9, אותך 14, אהלי 18, 23 ראש (cf. 23.19).

31.7   רבו 13, ונחמתים 14, דשן 17, לגלולם 20, ושבו בנים, עוד 27 בית, וכל העמק הפגרים והדשן 40, עוד 39, כל האדם 30, עוד 29, 1° and 2°.

32.8   כדבר יהוה 19, פקחות 23, לעשות 24, והנך ראה 27, הנה 36, לכן.

33.5   באים.

34.4   עליך לא תמות בחרב,, הראשנים אשר היו 5, להם 8, 16 אתם ותכבשו, להיות.

35.2   ודברת אותם 14, אלי 15, אלי.

36.1   ויהי 18 להם, בדיו 25, אליהם שמע ולא 28, הראשנים הראשנה, 31 את ענם.

37.1   מלך (M dittography), רשמו 13, בביתו 17, ויאמר, 20 שמע-נא.

38.6   השליכו אל הבור 27, ממנו 28, בלכדה ירושלם כאשר, ויקחו את ירמיהו 9, האנשים האלה את כל אשר, ירמיהו הנביא את אשר.

39.14   אל הבית 15, עצור בהיותו 16, לאמר 16, ביום ההוא 16 לפניך והיו.

40.1 ‏אסור והוא‎, 4-5 ‏שמה ללכת‏''‏בעיניך רע ואם‎ 5 ‏ישוב לא ועודנו‎,
‏או ,ארחה‎ 15 ‏לאמר.‎

41.2 ‏פגרי‎ 9 ‏אליהם,‏ ‏ויהי כפגש אתם,‏ ‏מן המצפה הלך‎ 6 ‏בחרב וימת אתו‎
‏האנשים,‎ 10 ‏וישבים ישמע אל בן נתניה.‎

42.2 ‏שם‎ 16 1° and 2°. ‏ועתה‎ 15 ‏לאמר,‏ ‏לא‎ 14 ‏ממנו,‎ 11 ‏אתכם,‎ 4 ‏אתנו.‎

43.2 ‏אליהם,‎ 10 ‏אתה מדבר.‎

44.14 ‏כי,‎ 15 ‏העמדות,‎ 21 ‏אתם,‎ 25 ‏לאמר,‎ 26 ‏נקרא,‎ 28 ‏מן ארץ מצרים‎,
‏ממנו ומהם.‎

45.1 ‏כה,‎ 4 ‏לאמר.‎

46.8 ‏אתה,‎ 28 ‏וכנהרות יתגעשו מים.‎

47.6 ‏הוי.‎

48.2 ‏הרחקות,‎ 24 ‏עלה,‎ 15 ‏וארור,‎ 10 ‏צרי‎ 2°, 5 ‏כי,‎ 4 ‏זעקה,‏ ‏לכו ‏רי‎
‏והקרבות,‎ 27 ‏מדי דבריך,‎ 31 ‏ולמואב,‎ 38 ‏כלה מספד,‏ ‏את מאוב.‎

49.3 ‏ואחרי כן אשיב את שבות בני עמון‎ 6 ‏לנדד,‎ 5 ‏והתשוטטנה בגררות‎,
‏אחזתה כיולדה,‎ 30 ‏עליה‎ 2°. ‏צדה וחבלים‎ 24 ‏קולה,‎ 21 ‏ומי‎ 19 ‏כי הנה‎ 15 ‏הוא,‏ ‏שתו,‎ 12 ‏לך,‎ 9 ‏נאם יהוה‎

50.7 ‏והמשך‎ 19 ‏כי ליהוה חטאה‎ 14 ‏ציה וערבה,‏ ‏הנה,‎ 12 ‏יהוה,‎ 22
‏בארץ,‎ 25 ‏היא,‎ 38 ‏חרב,‎ 44 ‏נוה.‎

51.2 ‏כי,‎ 3 ‏ידרך אל ידרך)‎ M dittography), ‏ואל,‎ 7 ‏גוים,‎ 38 ‏ישאגו‎,
‏כי‎ 51 ,57 ‏וישבו שנת עולם ולא יקיצו.‎

52.6 ‏לקחו‎ 18 ‏מהעיר,‏ ‏ויברחו,‎ 7 (so also 2 Kgs. 25.3), ‏בחדש הרביעי‎
25 ‏מן העיר לקח‎ ‏שר,‎ 27 ‏וימתם,‏ ‏ויגל יהודה מעל אדמתו.‎

1.17 οτι μετα σου εγω ειμι του εξαιρεισθαι σε λεγει κυριος.

3.12 προς με.

4.2 τω θεω εν ιερουσαλημ, 10 ιδου, 15 ηξει, 16 ηκασιν, 26 ηφανισ-
θησαν.

5.24 υμιν.

6.1 γινεται, 9 οτι, 12 ταυτην, 16 κυριου, και ιδετε.

11.19 πονηρον λεγοντες δευτε και.

12.14 οτι.

13.7 ποταμον, 20 ειρουσαλημ.

22.18 ουαι επι τον ανδρα τουτον.

26.10 οικου (₵ clearly original).

29.1 επιστολην εις βαβυλωνα τη αποικια (probably inner-Greek).

31.27 δια τουτο.

37.9 οτι.

38.3  οτι.

40.10  εναντιον υμων, 14 προς σε.

42.19  και νυν.

43.2  λεγοντες.

48.3  οτι.

49.21  οτι.

50.46  οτι.

51.14  οτι.

VIII    The Character and Provenience of 𝕸 and 𝕲

The limitation of this study to the zero variants makes possible
only a *partial* assessment of the character of the texts of 𝕸 and 𝕲. Full
assessment will involve detailed examination of the content variants, and
of the transpositions (especially those concerning the Oracles against
Foreign Nations). Therefore, in this chapter we must not attempt to say
too much. Still, it is believed that the study has yielded enough evidence for us to make a number of significant statements about the character of each text, and, in a more speculative vein, about their provenience.

*Character*

*The Masoretic text*

The text of 𝕸 has undergone much secondary expansion. Names are
filled out frequently to their full form, and titles and epithets are
added to them, while pronoun objects and subjects of verbs are made explicit. The text is heavily interpolated from parallel, related, or
nearby passages. Many of these interpolations are innocuous, but many
others are of such size and character as to reflect conscious scribal
notation and harmonization. Particularly striking are the large doublets,
and the interpolations from O.T. passages outside Jeremiah.

The high incidence of conflation, together with the rarity of haplography, indicates that 𝕸 is a revised[1] text. Though a number of doublets no doubt reflect conflation of what we may call inner-familial variants, it is possible that 𝕸 does not represent a pure text type, but a
mixed text, to some degree infected by Egyptian readings. The presence
of the Egyptian Hebrew text type of Jeremiah in Palestine in the Hasmonaean period,[2] and the occasional trace of late retouching in 𝕸,[3] indicate

at least that circumstances would have allowed such mixing.

*The Alexandrian text*

The text of 𝔊 contains only a very small amount of secondary expansion. In the great majority of its zero variants, it preserves a text
superior to that of 𝔐. The evidence does not support the commonly held
theory that the translator abridged his *Vorlage*, so that, except where
scribal lapse is patent or must be assumed, 𝔊 may be taken as a substantially faithful witness to the Hebrew text at home in Alexandria. This
conclusion, if correct, closes one long-standing debate about the text
of Jeremiah.

The paucity of double readings which can be ascribed with any confidence to 𝔊-*Vorlage* (most are inner-Greek), together with the frequency
of haplography, suggests that behind 𝔊 stood a text which had not passed
through large-scale recensional activity and which had had only a short
transmission history.

*Provenience*

The following discussion proceeds within the framework of the theory
of local texts recently formulated by F. M. Cross. His theory may be
summarized as follows:[4]

Sometime in the Persian period, and probably in the fifth century,
local texts began to diverge and to develop in Palestine and Babylon.
This divergence originated in the introduction of the Babylonian text
into Palestine. After the beginning of the separate history of the
Palestinian text, it in turn was introduced into Egypt, where a local
text began to develop. (The Egyptian and Palestinian texts are more
closely affiliated than either is with the Babylonian.) This second
divergence may be dated roughly as follows: in the Pentateuch, no later
than the fourth century; in Samuel, perhaps no earlier than the fourth
century; in Isaiah the two texts are virtually identical, and the separation was quite late, if indeed the Greek *Vorlage* can be spoken of as a
distinct text type at all.

The Egyptian local text became the basis for the old Greek translation. In the late second or early first century B.C., this old Greek

text was revised in Palestine to the current Palestinian text, and is
extant, in part, in the proto-Lucianic stratum of the Greek Bible.  The
Babylonian text, which meanwhile had been transmitted in isolation from
the other two, was re-introduced into Palestine perhaps as early as the
Maccabean era, perhaps later in the second or first century B.C.  This
text became the basis of a second revision of the Greek text, no later
than the beginning of the first century A.D., known as proto-Theodotion
or καιγε.  The third and final recensional stage of the Greek Bible is
represented by Aquila's revision of ca. 130 A.D., by which time the
Hebrew Text had achieved fixed form as we know it in the Masoretic text.

Though at this stage of research generalizations must not be considered final, these local texts may be characterized as follows:  The
*Palestinian* text is characterized by conflations, glosses, expansions
from parallel passages, synoptic additions, and like editorial activity.
The *Egyptian* text is often, but not always, a full text (for example, in
the Pentateuch it is without the synoptic additions of the Palestinian
text, but not so conservative as the Masoretic text).  The *Babylonian*
text, where extant, is short and conservative.

How may the two texts of Jer. be fitted into this general theory?
In terms of the theory, the Hebrew text behind 𝔊 should represent the
Egyptian family.[5]  The primary question concerns the provenience of 𝔐:
is it Babylonian or Palestinian?

In developing his general theory, Cross is able to establish the
identity of the Palestinian text by a series of interlocking textual
affinities.  Thus, in Samuel the text of Chronicles, 4QSam[a b c], proto-
Lucian, and Josephus, and in the Pentateuch the Pentateuchal citations
in Chronicles, 4QEx[m] and 4QNum[b], the Samaritan Pentateuch, the old Greek,
and proto-Lucian, respectively converge in a manner which clearly establishes the Palestinian text.  The designation of 𝔐 as Babylonian is
largely by process of elimination combined with circumstantial evidence.

The problem in Jeremiah is that we have only *two* text types, so
that 𝔐 could have been at home in either Palestine or Babylon.  Further,
we have little external evidence by which to locate 𝔐 (but see below on
4QJer[a]).  Our argument will have to be based largely on analogy, and our
conclusions admittedly will be tentative.

1.  Since in the Pentateuch and the Former Prophets 𝔐 contains a
Babylonian text, it would be natural to assume the same for the Latter

Prophets, and therefore for Jeremiah Ṃ. However, if this were the case, Jeremiah Ṃ would be anomalous, since its expansionist and heavily revised text contrasts radically with the short, conservative text found in the first two parts of the Old Testament.

2. The text of Jeremiah Ṃ has a suggestive resemblance to other *Palestinian* texts. We may augment the above description of the latter text from the summary of the character of the Samaritan text given in the unpublished Harvard dissertation of Bruce K. Waltke. According to him, the text of the Samaritan Pentateuch has been supplemented and clarified by the insertion of additions and the interpolation of glosses from parallel passages. Small additions, such as the subject of the verb, appositives, and various nouns, have been added for clarity. The text has been harmonized and supplemented by parallel passages. As Gesenius said, "the Samaritan critics seem to have put forth a special effort to achieve complete consistency in the sacred text and to make sure that nothing would be omitted which seemed to be required for a complete statement."[6] That these features are not all sectarian, but are basically a common feature of the Palestinian text, is demonstrated by the textual support which the Samaritan text frequently receives from Chronicles,[7] ₵,[8] and the Palestinian exemplars 4QEx$^m$ and 4QNum$^b$. This description of the Palestinian text type agrees closely with our own description of the text of Jeremiah Ṃ.

3. Among the Qumrân manuscripts we have an early exemplar of a proto-Masoretic text of Jer. dating to ca. B.C. 200-175.[9] While it is possible that this manuscript derives from the Babylonian text tradition, the indications are against the presence of a Babylonian exemplar in Palestine at such an early date. According to Cross, the Babylonian text of the Latter Prophets is not found at all at Qumrân,[10] and appears in Palestine first in the Greek καιγε recension. In the Pentateuch, he is now inclined to think, genuine exemplars of the Babylonian text at Qumrân are exceedingly rare and late in date.[11] It is probable that--like the only two manuscripts to antedate it, 4QEx$^f$ and 4QSam$^b$[12]--4QJer$^a$ is a Palestinian exemplar, and affords external evidence for our proposal that the provenience of Jer Ṃ is Palestinian.

4. If Jer. Ṃ represents a Palestinian text type, this would account for the nonexistence of a distinctive proto-Lucianic text in Jer., different from ₵ on the one hand and Ṃ on the other. For, if Ṃ were Babylonian

and $\mathcal{G}$ Egyptian, we would have expected to find some evidence of a Greek
revision to the Palestinian text, similar to proto-Lucian in the Pentateuch and the Former Prophets.  But in Jer. the Lucianic text is basically the old Greek text corrected to the Hexaplaric recension.  Such
non-$\mathcal{G}$, non-Origenic readings as we have can best be described as proto-
$\mathfrak{M}$[13] and probably are to be associated with the καιγε recension, of which
there are traces in Jer.[14]

This last point is pertinent to the Greek text of Isa. and Ezek.,
where evidence for a Greek recension differing from $\mathcal{G}$ and $\mathfrak{M}$ in the manner above described is likewise lacking.  Taken together with indications
that $\mathfrak{M}$ in Isa. and Ezek. exhibits the expansionist features of Jer. and
the Palestinian text generally,[15] this points most naturally to a Palestinian provenience for $\mathfrak{M}$ in *all* the Latter Prophets.  The contrast between
the great divergence of Jer. $\mathfrak{M}/\mathcal{G}$ and the narrow divergence of $\mathfrak{M}/\mathcal{G}$ in Isa.
and Ezek. would be due simply to a different date for the divergence of
the respective Greek *Vorlagen* from the Palestinian text.  While Isa. and
Ezek. diverged quite late, the evidence points strongly to a very early
divergence of the text of Jer.

### Date of Divergence of the Archetypes of $\mathfrak{M}$ and $\mathcal{G}$

Controls on the problem are not tight, and any proposal must be in
broad terms.  It will be best to establish the extreme chronological
horizons, and then to attempt to narrow the range of time within which
the divergence is most likely to have occurred.

The *terminus ad quem* is ca. 200 B.C., the date of 4QJer[a] with its
fully developed text.  But we must allow a substantial length of time
for this text to have developed so fully.  It is difficult to see the
text common to $\mathfrak{M}$ and $\mathcal{G}$ coming down later than the late fifth or early
fourth century.  This estimate is based on the projection of Cross for
the divergence of the Egyptian and Palestinian texts of the Pentateuch
(no later than the fourth century) and Sam. (no earlier than the fourth
century).  The more pronounced difference between Jer. $\mathfrak{M}$ and $\mathcal{G}$ seems to
require a date prior to either of these.

The *terminus a quo* is provided by the date of the latest commonly
transmitted material.  This date we may deduce by proceeding in stages,
moving downward in time.

The two texts contain material which takes us at least into the middle-Exilic period; but (if Bright and Freedman are right), no substantial blocks of material require a post-Exilic date.[16]

М and Ꞡ represent one and the same basic redaction of the book. With the exception of the position of the Oracles against Foreign Nations, and the material in 33.14-26 and 52.28-30, the differences between М and Ꞡ are those which characterize the textual, rather than the redactoral, phase of development of a Biblical book.[17] We cannot go back into the Exilic period for our divergence, and the common redaction attested in М and Ꞡ probably brings us down at least to the end of the sixth century or slightly later.[18]

Internal evidence makes it unlikely that the divergence occurred soon after the redaction of the book. The text common to М and Ꞡ contains corruptions and expansions which indicate that it was transmitted for some time before it branched into two streams of transmission. The following examples have been gleaned from textual notes in the commentaries of Rudolph and Bright; detailed examination of the common text doubtless would produce more:

*Corruptions.* 10.1-16 The passage is almost universally considered to be non-Jeremianic. Affinities with Exilic[19] and post-Exilic[20] passages suggest its inclusion in the book in the post-Exilic period (similarly, perhaps, 10.25, which is from the Exilic Psalm 79.7). Aside from the zero variants in verses 6-8, 10, the passage has undergone disturbance and development at a common stage of transmission. The position of verse 9 is original in neither М nor Ꞡ (between 5a and 5b), and it may have belonged originally after 4a.[21] Also, the Aramaic verse 11 is an obvious gloss on the preceding verses. The corruption and development of the common text thus indicates that some time elapsed between the inclusion of this passage in the book and the divergence of М and Ꞡ archetypes.[22]

11.18-12.6 The passage has suffered dislocation: "Dass der jetzige Textzusammenhang nicht befriedigt, hat man längst empfunden" (Rudolph). For example, 12.4 "are doubtless words of Jeremiah, but apparently from another context" (Bright). For detailed discussion, see Rudolph, pp. 75-76, and Bright, pp. 84-90.

23.7-8 On our proposal that the transposition of these verses in both text traditions resulted from haplography in the common archetype, see pp. 92-93.

31.40 הַשְׁרֵמוֹת [הַשְׁרֵמוֹת] ασαρημωθ. Corruption of (ה)מוֹת(הַשַׁדְ (cf. Rudolph, p. 188, Bright, p. 283).

31.40 עַד [עַד] εως. Corruption of עַל from following עַד.

44.19 The sentence should be preceded by וְהַנָּשִׁים אָמְרוּ (so L' 88 Syh^mg; cf. Syr) or the like.

*Expansions.* (a) Clarifying glosses. 17.13 אֶת יְהוָה, 23.13 אֶת יִשְׂרָאֵל, 32.8 אֲשֶׁר בְּאֶרֶץ בִּנְיָמִין (in M after בַּעֲנָתוֹת, אֲשֶׁר, in Ø before), 42.17 και παν- τες οι αλλογενεις] 43.2 הַזֵּדִים,^23 43.13 אֲשֶׁר בְּאֶרֶץ מִצְרַיִם, 44.14 כִּי אִם פְּלֵטִים.

(b) From parallel or related passages. 3.13 תַּחַת כָּל עֵץ רַעֲנָן (from verse 6), 3.17 וְנִקְווּ אֵלֶיהָ כָל הַגּוֹיִם (Isa. 2.1-3, 18.7, 60.9),^24 5.1 וּבֵית יְהוּדָה (3.7-10), 6.27 מִבְצָר and verse 28 נְחֹשֶׁת וּבַרְזֶל (1.18), 7.6 וְדָם נָקִי אַל (7.18-19), 8.19 מַדּוּעַ הִכְעִסוּנִי בִּפְסִלֵיהֶם בְּהַבְלֵי נֵכָר (22.3), תֻּשְׁפְּכוּ בַמָּקוֹם הַזֶּה 11.2 הוּא וְעָבְדוּ וְעָמוֹ (verse 6), 22.4 שִׁמְעוּ אֶת דִּבְרֵי הַבְּרִית הַזֹּאת (verse 2), 26.8 וְכָל הָעָם (verse 7), 44.24 ר' (כֹּל)הָעָם (verses 15, 20), 52.20 וְהַבָּקָר אֶל (כֹּל)הָעָם (1 Kgs. 7.44) שְׁנַיִם עָשָׂר נְחֹשֶׁת אֲשֶׁר תַּחַת (הַיָּם) (see pp. 109-111).

(c) Other. 2.31 הַדּוֹר אַתֶּם רְאוּ דְבַר יְהוָה "seems to be a marginal comment by a later reader" (Bright, p. 13, following Duhm and Rudolph). Ø has a corrupt version of the gloss = וְלֹא יְרֵאתֶם שִׁמְעוּ דְבַר יְהוָה.

12.15-17 For discussion, cf. Rudolph, p. 83, and Bright, p. 88.

15.12-14 The verses clearly are intrusive, and in origin related to 17.1-4 (Rudolph, Bright). This doublet may have arisen like many other doublets in Jer. as a scholarly marginal cross-reference. But what would attract these verses as a gloss to 15.11ff?^25 It is to be noted that 15.11ff and 17.1-4 would have stood in adjacent columns of an ancient manuscript. 15.12-14 may have originated as a marginal variant to 17.1-4 (note the numerous variants between the two basically similar passages), *or* as a correction (since corrupted) of haplography in the common archetype of 17.1-4 (still reflected in Ø), wrongly restored.^26 In either case, 15.12-14 and 17.1-4 would represent conflation in M of two manuscript traditions.^27

17.25 וְשָׂרִים; dittography of the following יֹשְׁבִים (Rudolph and Bright); or, more likely, conflation of an early corruption וְשָׂרִים > יֹשְׁבִים.

25.31 נְאֻם יְהוָה; "Vorher nicht Jahwe redet" (Rudolph).

25.33 Prose intrusion (cf. Rudolph, p. 153, Bright, p. 162).

30.13 אֵין דָּן דִּינֵךְ לְמָזוֹר רְפֻאוֹת//תְּעָלָה אֵין לָךְ. Verse 13a is metri- cally too long (compare 46.11), and דָּן דִּינֵךְ probably is intrusive (cf. Bright, Rudolph).

38.9  מפני הרעב כי אין הלחם עוד בעיר  (cf. Volz, Rudolph, Bright).

45.4  ותאמר אליו.

46.17  מלך מצרים.  Expansion of the title פרעה.

48.33  הידד לא הידד.[28]

49.25  לא  (cf. Rudolph and Bright).

51.34  נבוכדראצר.  Addition before מלך בבל, as frequently in Jer.
M.

In at least seven instances, a jointly attested כה אמר יהוה (צבאות)
(אלהי ישראל) clearly is intrusive: 8.4, 9.16, 17.5,[29] 30.5, 31.2, 31.15,
32.14. These secondary insertions of this formula are to be compared
with nine instances of insertion in M alone (see pp. 84-86).

*Doublets*. The book of Jeremiah contains a considerable number of
doublets common to M and ₵, for example: 2.28//11.13, 5.9//5.29//9.8,
6.22-24//50.41-43, 7.16//11.14//14.11, 7.31-32//19.5-7//32.35, 7.33//
16.4//19.7//34.20.[30] It would be hazardous to suggest that all such
instances are secondary, and arose in the transmission of the text.[31]
Nevertheless, on the basis of the evidence of ₵ that some doublets are
secondary in M (see pp. 91-96), and of at least one instance where a
commonly attested doublet is secondary,[32] it is probable that the common
doublets at least to some degree witness to textual development in the
archetype common to M and ₵.

As the above examples indicate, we must suppose an appreciable lapse
of time between the redaction of the book and the divergence of the two
text traditions. If the redaction was carried out at the end of the sixth
century, the common text development would carry us at least to the mid-
fifth century. We propose that the most likely period was mid-fifth or
early fourth century.

But why would the Egyptian text of Jeremiah diverge from the Palestinian so much earlier than the text of Isaiah and Ezekiel? Factors not
know to us may account for this. Perhaps the explanation is in some way
related to the fact that Jeremiah and Baruch were taken to Egypt, and--we
may be morally certain--consequently from the beginning of the exile the
Egyptian Jewish community was never without some form of the text.[33] This
is not to suggest that the present Greek text represents such a tradition, for, as we have seen, it must have passed through the hands of the
Exilic community in Babylon. But, for some reason or another, the traditions concerning Jeremiah's last years in Egypt may have been operative

in the acquisition of a Palestinian text of the book during the period I
have projected.  A sole copy of the text in Egypt, deriving from the
prophet himself,[34] may have become lost or worn out, so that a replacement was necessary; or, awareness of the defective character of a pre-
Exilic text may have led to the acquisition of a Palestinian exemplar.

These suggestions are no more than speculations in the dark.  What
we may hold to be established are the following conclusions:  the integrity and superiority of the ₵ text of Jeremiah in those zero variants
which are not demonstrably due to scribal lapse; the late, developed
character of the Masoretic text; and, somewhat more tentatively, the
Palestinian provenience of the Masoretic text type; and the divergence
of the Egyptian archetype from the Palestinian text sometime in the
period 450-350.

APPENDICES

## Appendix A

### *Human Names in Jeremiah*

| | | M | ₵ |
|---|---|---|---|
| A | | נבוכדראצר מלך בבל | |
| 1 | 20.4 | מלך בבל | מלך בבל |
| 2 | 21.2 | נבוכדראצר מלך בבל | מלך בבל ---------[1] |
| 3 | .4 | מלך בבל | --- --- |
| 4 | .7 | נבוכדראצר מלך בבל | --- --- --------- |
| 5 | .10 | מלך בבל | מלך בבל |
| 6 | 22.25 | נבוכדראצר מלך בבל | --- --- --------- |
| 7 | 24.1 | נבוכדראצר מלך בבל | ובוכדנאצר מלך בבל[2] |
| 8 | 25.1 | נבוכדראצר מלך בבל | * |
| 9 | .9 | נבוכדראצר מלך בבל | * |
| 10 | .11 | מלך בבל | * |
| 11 | .12 | מלך בבל | --- --- |
| 12 | .26 | מלך ששך | * |
| 13 | 27.6 | נבוכדנאצר מלך בבל | מלך בבל ---------[3] |
| 14 | .8 | נבוכדנאצר מלך בבל | ** |
| 15 | .8 | מלך בבל | מלך בבל |
| 16 | .9 | מלך בבל | מלך בבל |
| 17 | .11 | מלך בבל | מלך בבל |
| 18 | .12 | מלך בבל | * |
| 19 | .13 | מלך בבל | ** |
| 20 | .14 | מלך בבל | מלך בבל |
| 21 | .17 | מלך בבל | * |
| 22 | .20 | נבוכדנאצר מלך בבל | מלך בבל --------- |
| 23 | 28.2 | מלך בבל | מלך בבל |
| 24 | .3 | נבוכדנאצר מלך בבל | * |
| 25 | .4 | מלך בבל | מלך בבל |
| 26 | .11 | נבוכדנאצר מלך בבל | מלך בבל --------- |
| 27 | .14 | נבכדנאצר מלך בבל | מלך בבל --------- |
| 28 | 29.1 | נבוכדנאצר | * |
| 29 | .3 | נבוכדנאצר מלך בבל | מלך בבל --------- |

| # | Ref | | |
|---|---|---|---|
| 30 | .21 | נבוכדראצר מלך בבל | מלך בבל --------- |
| 31 | .22 | מלך בבל | מלך בבל |
| 32 | 32.1 | $=$ Syr$^4$ I --- --- נבוכדראצר | נבוכדנאצר מלך בבל |
| 33 | .2 | מלך בבר | מלך בבל |
| 34 | .3 | מלך בבל | מלך בבל |
| 35 | .4 | מלך בבל | מלך בבל |
| 36 | .28 | נבוכדראצר מלך בבל | מלך בבל --------- |
| 37 | .36 | מלך בבל | מלך בבל |
| 38 | 34.1 | נבוכדראצר מלך בבל | נבוכדנאצר מלך בבל |
| 39 | .2 | מלך בבל | מלך בבל |
| 40 | .3 | מלך בבל (עיני) | עיניו ... ... |
| 41 | .7 | מלך בבל | מלך בבל |
| 42 | .21 | מלך בבל | מלך בבל |
| 43 | 35.11 | נבוכדראצר מלך בבל | נבוכדנאצר --- --- |
| 44 | 36.29 | מלך בבל | מלך בבל |
| 45 | 37.1 | נבוכדראצר מלך בבל | נבוכדנאצר --- --- |
| 46 | .17 | מלך בבל | מלך בבל |
| 47 | .19 | מלך בבל | מלך בבל |
| 48 | 38.3 | מלך בבל | מלך בבל |
| 49 | .17 | מלך בבל | מלך בבל |
| 50 | .18 | מלך בבל | * |
| 51 | .22 | מלך בבל | מלך בבל |
| 52 | .23 | מלך בבל | מלך בבל |
| 53 | 39.1 | נבוכדראצר מלך בבל | נבוכדנאצר מלך בבל |
| 54 | .3 | מלך בבל | מלך בבל |
| 55 | .3 | מלך בבל | מלך בבל |
| 56 | .5 | נב'$^5$ (52.9,2 Kgs. 25.6) מלך בבל | * or ** (--מלך בבל |
| 57 | .6 | מלך בבל | * or ** |
| 58 | .6 | מלך בבל | * or ** |
| 59 | .11 | נבוכדראצר מלך בבל | * or ** |
| 60 | .13 | מלך בבל | * or ** |
| 61 | 40.5 | מלך בבל | מלך בבל |
| 62 | .7 | מלך בבל | מלך בבל |
| 63 | .9 | מלך בבל | מלך בבל |
| 64 | .11 | מלך בבל | מלך בבל |
| 65 | 41.2 | מלך בבל | מלך בבל |
| 66 | .18 | מלך בבל | מלך בבל |

| | | | |
|---|---|---|---|
| 67 | 42.11 | מלך בבל | מלך בבל |
| 68 | 43.10 | נבוכדראצר מלך בבל | נבוכדנאצר מלך בבל |
| 69 | 44.30 | נבוכדראצר מלך בבל | נבוכדנאצר מלך בבל |
| 70 | 46.2 | נבוכדראצר מלך בבל | נבוכדנאצר מלך בבל |
| 71 | .13 | נבוכדראצר מלך בבל | --------- מלך בבל |
| 72 | .26 | נבוכדראצר מלך בבל | ✳ |
| 73 | 49.28 | נבוכדראצר מלך בבל | נבוכדנאצר מלך בבל |
| 74 | .30 | נבוכדראצר מלך בבל | --------- מלך בבל |
| 75 | 50.17 | נבוכדראצר מלך בבל | --------- מלך בבל |
| 76 | .18 | מלך בבל | מלך בבל |
| 77 | .43 | מלך בבל | מלך בבל |
| 78 | 51.31 | מלך בבל | מלך בבל |
| 79 | .33 | (-תח) בבל | (-תחי) מלך בבל |
| 80 | .34 | נבוכדראצר מלך בבל | נבוכדנאצר מלך בבל |
| 81 | 52.3 | מלך בבל = 2 Kgs. 24.20 ⏐ | ✳ or ✲✳ |
| 82 | .4 | = 2 Kgs. 25.1 = נבוכדראצר מלך בבל | נבוכדנאצר מלך בבל |
| 83 | .9 | = 2 Kgs. 25.6 = מלך בבל | מלך בבל |
| 84 | .10 | (2 Kgs. 25.7 vid. --- ---) מלך בבל | מלך בבל |
| 85 | .11 | (2 Kgs. 25.7 --- ---) מלך בבל | מלך בבל |
| 86 | .12 | = 2 Kgs. 25.8 M ⏐[6] נבוכדראצר מלך בבל | ✳ |
| 87 | .12 | = 2 Kgs. 25.8 = מלך בבל | מלך בבל |
| 88 | .15 | = 2 Kgs. 25.11 ⏐ מלך בבל | ✲✳ |
| 89 | .26 | = 2 Kgs. 25.20 = מלך בבל | מלך בבל |
| 90 | .27 | = 2 Kgs. 25.21 = מלך בבל | מלך בבל |
| 91 | .28 | נבוכדראצר ✳ | ✳ |
| 92 | .29 | נבוכדראצר ✳ (Syr + מלכא דבבל) | ✳ |
| 93 | .30 | נבוכדראצר ✳ | ✳ |

B  צדקיהו בן יאשיהו מלך יהודה

| | | | |
|---|---|---|---|
| 1 | 1.3 | צדקיהו בן יאשיהו מלך יהודה | צדקיהו בן יאשיהו מלך יהודה |
| 2 | 21.1 | המלך צדקיהו | המלך צדקיהו |
| 3 | .3 | ---- ---- צדקיהו | צדקיהו מלך יהודה |
| 4 | .7 | צדקיהו מלך יהודה | צדקיהו מלך יהודה |
| 5 | 24.8 | צדקיהו מלך יהודה | צדקיהו מלך יהודה |
| 6 | 27.3 | צדקיהו מלך יהודה | צדקיהו מלך יהודה |
| 7 | .12 | צדקיהו מלך יהודה | צדקיהו מלך יהודה |
| 8 | 28.1 | צדקיהו מלך יהודה | צדקיהו מלך יהודה |

| | | | |
|---|---|---|---|
| 9 | 29.3 | צדקיהו מלך יהודה | צדקיהו מלך יהודה |
| 10 | 32.1 | צדקיהו מלך יהודה | המלך צדקיהו |
| 11. | .2 | (בית-) מלך יהודה | ---- המלך (בית-) |
| 12 | .3 | צדקיהו מלך יהודה | המלך צדקיהו |
| 13 | .4 | צדקיהו מלך יהודה | ---- --- צדקיהו |
| 14 | .5 | צדקיהו | צדקיהו |
| 15 | 34.2 | צדקיהו מלך יהודה | צדקיהו מלך יהודה |
| 16 | .4 | צדקיהו מלך יהודה | צדקיהו מלך יהודה |
| 17 | .6 | צדקיהו מלך יהודה | המלך צדקיהו |
| 18 | .8 | המלך צדקיהו | המלך צדקיהו |
| 19 | .21 | צדקיהו מלך יהודה | צדקיהו מלך יהודה |
| 20 | 37.1 | מלך צדקיהו בן יאשיהו[7] | ----- צדקיהו בן יאשיהו |
| 21 | .3 | המלך צדקיהו | המלך צדקיהו |
| 22 | .17 | המלך צדקיהו | ---- צדקיהו |
| 23 | .18 | המלך צדקיהו | ------ המלך |
| 24 | .20 | אדני המלך | אדני המלך |
| 25 | .21 | המלך צדקיהו | ------ המלך |
| 26 | 38.4 | המלך | המלך |
| 27 | .5 | המלך צדקיהו | ------ המלך |
| 28 | .5 | המלך | המלך |
| 29 | .7 | המלך | המלך |
| 30 | .8 | המלך | המלך |
| 31 | .9 | אדני המלך | ------ ---- |
| 32 | .10 | המלך | המלך |
| 33 | .14 | המלך צדקיהו | ------ המלך |
| 34 | .15 | צדקיהו | המלך |
| 35 | .16 | המלך צדקיהו | ------ המלך |
| 36 | .17 | (אל-) צדקיהו | אליו |
| 37 | .19 | המלך צדקיהו | ------ המלך |
| 38 | .24 | צדקיהו | המלך |
| 39 | .25 | המלך | המלך |
| 40 | .25 | המלך | המלך |
| 41 | .26 | המלך | המלך |
| 42 | .27 | המלך | המלך |
| 43 | 39.1 | לצדקיהו מלך יהודה (52.4 למלכו = 2 Kgs. 25.1) I | לצדקיהו מ' י' = |
| 44 | .2 | לצדקיהו (Syr צדקיא מלכא = 52.5 2 Kgs. 25.2) I | לצדקיהו |

| 45 | .4 | צדקיהו מלך יהודה | | * or ** |
| 46 | .5 | צדקיהו (= 52.8 M; 52.8 𝔊 אזו = | | * or ** |
| | | 2 Kgs. 25.5) | | |
| 47 | .6 | צדקיהו = 52.18 2 Kgs. 25.7 | | * or ** |
| 48 | .7 | צדקיהו = 52.11 2 Kgs. 25.8 | | * or ** |
| 49 | 44.30 | צדקיהו מלך יהודה | צדקיהו מלך יהודה | |
| 50 | 49.34 | צדקיהו מלך יהודה | צדקיהו המלך | |
| 51 | 51.59 | צדקיהו מלך יהודה | צדקיהו מלך יהודה | |
| 52 | 52.1 | צדקיהו = 2 Kgs. 24.18 = 2 Chr. | צדקיהו | |
| | | 36.11 = | | |
| 53 | .3 | (Syr מלכא צדקיא) צדקיהו | | * or ** |
| 54 | .5 | המלך צדקיהו = 2 Kgs. 25.2 = | המלך צדקיהו | |
| 55 | .8 | המלך = 2 Kgs. 25.5 = | המלך | |
| 56 | .8 | (את-) צדקיהו    2 Kgs. 25.5 = | את | |
| 57 | .9 | המלך = 2 Kgs. 25.6 = | המלך | |
| 58 | .10 | צדקיהו = 2 Kgs. 25.7 = | צדקיהו | |
| 59 | .11 | צדקיהו = 2 Kgs. 25.7 = | צדקיהו | |

| C | | יהויקים בן יאשיהו מלך יהודה | | |
| 1 | 1.3 | יהויקים בן יאשיהו מלך יהודה | יהויקים בן יאשיהו מלך יהודה | |
| 2 | 22.18 | יהויקים בן יאשיהו מלך יהודה | יהויקים בן יאשיהו מלך יהודה | |
| 3 | 25.1 | יהויקים בן יאשיהו מלך יהודה | יהויקים בן יאשיהו מלך יהודה | |
| 4 | 26.1 | יהויקים בן יאשיהו מלך יהודה | ----- --- יהויקים בן יאשיהו | |
| 5 | .21 | המלך יהויקים | המלך יהויקים | |
| 6 | .21 | המלך | ---- | |
| 7 | .22 | המלך יהויקים | ------- המלך | |
| 8 | .23 | המלך יהויקים | ------- המלך | |
| 9 | 27.1 | יהויקים בן יאשיהו מלך יהודה | * | |
| 10 | 35.1 | יהויקים בן יאשיהו מלך יהודה | יהויקים ------ מלך יהודה | |
| 11 | 36.1 | יהויקים בן יאשיהו מלך יהודה | יהויקים בן יאשיהו מלך יהודה | |
| 12 | .9 | יהויקים בן יאשיהו מלך יהודה | המלך יהויקים | |
| 13 | .16 | המלך | המלך | |
| 14 | .20 | המלך | המלך | |
| 15 | .20 | המלך | המלך | |
| 16 | .21 | המלך | המלך | |
| 17 | .21 | המלך | המלך | |
| 18 | .21 | המלך | המלך | |

| | | | |
|---|---|---|---|
| 19 | .22 | המלך | המלך |
| 20 | .24 | המלך | המלך |
| 21 | .26 | המלך | המלך |
| 22 | .27 | המלך | המלך |
| 23 | .28 | יהויקים מלך יהודה | המלך יהויקים |
| 24 | .29 | יהויקים מלך יהודה | ----- --- ------- |
| 25 | .30 | יהויקים מלך יהודה | יהויקים מלך יהודה |
| 26 | .32 | יהויקים מלך יהודה | ----- --- יהויקים |
| 27 | 45.1 | יהויקים בן יאשיהו מלך יהודה | יהויקים בן יאשיהו מלך יהודה |
| 28 | 46.2 | יהויקים בן יאשיהו מלך יהודה | יהויקים -- ------- מלך יהודה |
| 29 | 52.2 | יהויקים = 2 Kgs. 24.19 ‖ | * or ** |

**D**   (יכניהו /כניהו/) יהויכין בן יהויקים מלך יהודה

| | | | |
|---|---|---|---|
| 1 | 22.24 | כניהו בן יהויקים מלך יהודה | יכניהו בן יהויקים מלך יהודה |
| 2 | .28 | כניהו | יכניהו |
| 3 | 24.1 | יכניהו בן יהויקים מלך יהודה | יכניהו בן יהויקים מלך יהודה |
| 4 | 27.20 | יכניה בן יהויקים מלך יהודה | ----- --- ------- -- יכניה |
| 5 | 28.4 | יכניה בן יהויקים מלך יהודה | ----- --- ------- -- יכניה |
| 6 | 29.2 | יכניה המלך | יכניה המלך |
| 7 | 37.1 | כניהו בן יהויקים | ------ -- יהויקים |
| 8 | 52.31 | יהויכין מלך יהודה | ιωακιμ מלך יהודה |
| 9 | .31 | יהויכין מלך יהודה | ιωακιμ מלך יהודה |

**E**   יאשיהו בן אמון מלך יהודה

| | | | |
|---|---|---|---|
| 1 | 1.2 | יאשיהו בן אמון מלך יהודה | יאשיהו בן אמון מלך יהודה |
| 2 | 3.6 | יאשיהו המלך | יאשיהו המלך[8] |
| 3 | 22.11 | יאשיהו | יאשיהו |
| 4 | 25.3 | יאשיהו בן אמון מלך יהודה | יאשיהו בן אמון מלך יהודה |
| 5 | 36.2 | יאשיהו -- ---- | יאשיהו מלך יהודה |

**F**   חזקיהו מלך יהודה

| | | | |
|---|---|---|---|
| 1 | 26.18 | חזקיהו מלך יהודה | חזקיהו מלך יהודה |
| 2 | .19 | חזקיהו מלך יהודה | ----- --- חזקיהו |

**G**   שלם בן יאשיהו מלך יהודה

| | | | |
|---|---|---|---|
| 1 | 22.11 | שלם בן יאשיהו מלך יהודה | שלם בן יאשיהו --- ----- = Syr ‖ |

| H | | ירמיהו הנביא | | |
|---|---|---|---|---|
| 1 | 1.1 | ירמיהו בן חלקיהו | | ירמיהו בן חלקיהו |
| 2 | .11 | ירמיהו | | ------ |
| 3 | 7.1 | ירמיהו | | * |
| 4 | 11.1 | ירמיהו | | ירמיהו |
| 5 | 14.1 | ירמיהו | | ירמיהו |
| 6 | 18.1 | ירמיהו | | ירמיהו |
| 7 | .18 | ירמיהו | | ירמיהו |
| 8 | 19.14 | ירמיהו | | ירמיהו |
| 9 | 20.1 | ירמיהו (Syr + נביא) | | ירמיהו |
| 10 | .2 | (את) ירמיהו הנביא | | אתו |
| 11 | .3 | ירמיהו | | ירמיהו |
| 12 | .3 | ירמיהו | | ירמיהו |
| 13 | 21.1 | ירמיהו | | ירמיהו |
| 14 | .3 | ירמיהו | | ירמיהו |
| 15 | 24.3 | ירמיהו | | ירמיהו |
| 16 | 25.1 | ירמיהו | | ירמיהו |
| 17 | .2 | ירמיהו הנביא | | ----- ------ |
| 18 | 26.7 | ירמיהו (Syr + נביא) | | ירמיהו |
| 19 | .8 | ירמיהו | | ירמיהו |
| 20 | .9 | ירמיהו | | ירמיהו |
| 21 | .12 | ירמיהו | | ירמיהו |
| 22 | .20 | ירמיהו | | ירמיהו |
| 23 | .24 | ירמיהו | | ירמיהו |
| 24 | 27.1 | ירמיהו | | * |
| 25 | 28.5 | ירמיה הנביא | | ----- ירמיהו |
| 26 | .6 | ירמיה הנביא Syr = | | ----- ירמיהו |
| 27 | .10 | ירמיה הנביא | | ----- ירמיהו |
| 28 | .11 | ירמיה הנביא | | ----- ירמיהו |
| 29 | .12 | ירמיה (Syr + נביא) | | ירמיהו |
| 30 | .12 | (צואר) ירמיה הנביא | | צוארו |
| 31 | .15 | ירמיה הנביא | | ----- ירמיהו |
| 32 | 29.1 | ירמיה הנביא | | ----- ירמיהו |
| 33 | .27 | ירמיה הענתתי | | ירמיהו הענתתי |
| 34 | .29 | ירמיה הנביא | | ----- ירמיהו |
| 35 | .30 | ירמיהו | | ירמיהו |
| 36 | 30.1 | ירמיהו | | ירמיהו |

| | | | |
|---|---|---|---|
| 37 | 32.1 | ירמיהו | ירמיהו |
| 38 | .2 | ירמיהו הנביא | ירמיהו ----- |
| 39 | .6 | ירמיהו | ירמיהו (.vid) |
| 40 | .26 | (אל) ירמיהו | אלי |
| 41 | 33.1 | ירמיהו (Syr + נביא) | ירמיהו |
| 42 | .19 | ירמיהו | * |
| 43 | .23 | ירמיהו | * |
| 44 | 34.1 | ירמיהו | ירמיהו |
| 45 | .6 | ירמיהו הנביא | ירמיהו ----- |
| 46 | .8 | ירמיהו | ירמיהו |
| 47 | .12 | ירמיהו | ירמיהו |
| 48 | 35.1 | ירמיהו | ירמיהו |
| 49 | .12 | (אל) ירמיהו | אלי |
| 50 | .18 | ירמיהו | * |
| 51 | 36.1 | (אל) ירמיהו | אלי |
| 52 | .4 | ירמיהו | ירמיהו |
| 53 | .4 | ירמיהו | ירמיהו |
| 54 | .5 | ירמיהו | ירמיהו |
| 55 | .8 | ירמיהו הנביא | ירמיהו ----- |
| 56 | .10 | ירמיהו | ירמיהו |
| 57 | .18 | ----- | I Syr = ירמיהו |
| 58 | .19 | ירמיהו | ירמיהו |
| 59 | .26 | ירמיהו הנביא | ירמיהו ----- |
| 60 | .27 | ירמיהו (Syr + נביא) | ירמיהו |
| 61 | .27 | ירמיהו | ירמיהו |
| 62 | .32 | ירמיהו | ברוך |
| 63 | .32 | ירמיהו | ירמיהו |
| 64 | 37.2 | ירמיהו הנביא | ירמיהו ----- |
| 65 | .3 | ירמיהו הנביא | ירמיהו ----- |
| 66 | .4 | ירמיהו | ירמיהו |
| 67 | .6 | ירמיהו הנביא | ירמיהו ----- |
| 68 | .12 | ירמיהו | ירמיהו |
| 69 | .13 | ירמיהו הנביא | ירמיהו ----- |
| 70 | .14 | ירמיהו | ------ |
| 71 | .14 | ירמיהו | ירמיהו |
| 72 | .15 | ירמיהו | ירמיהו |
| 73 | .16 | ירמיהו | ירמיהו |

| 74 | .16 | ירמיהו | —————— |
| 75 | .17 | ירמיהו | —————— |
| 76 | .18 | ירמיהו | ירמיהו |
| 77 | .21 | את ירמיהו | את |
| 78 | .21 | ירמיהו | ירמיהו |
| 79 | 38.1 | ירמיהו | ירמיהו |
| 80 | .6 | ירמיהו | * |
| 81 | .6 | את ירמיהו | את |
| 82 | .6 | ירמיהו | —————— |
| 83 | .7 | ירמיהו | ירמיהו |
| 84 | .9 | ירמיהו הנביא | האיש הזה |
| 85 | .10 | (Syr לארמיא) את ירמיהו הנביא | את |
| 86 | .11 | ירמיהו | ירמיהו |
| 87 | .12 | ירמיהו | * |
| 88 | .12 | ירמיהו | ירמיהו |
| 89 | .13 | את ירמיהו | את |
| 90 | .13 | ירמיהו | ירמיהו |
| 91 | .14 | את ירמיהו הנביא | את |
| 92 | .14 | אל ירמיהו | אליו |
| 93 | .15 | ירמיהו | ירמיהו |
| 94 | .16 | אל ירמיהו    = 86-'0 I | אליו |
| 95 | .17 | ירמיהו | ירמיהו |
| 96 | .19 | ירמיהו | ירמיהו |
| 97 | .20 | ירמיהו | ירמיהו |
| 98 | .24 | אל ירמיהו | אליו |
| 99 | .27 | ירמיהו | ירמיהו |
| 100 | .28 | ירמיהו | ירמיהו |
| 101 | 39.11 | ירמיהו | * or ** |
| 102 | .14 | ירמיהו | ירמיהו |
| 103 | .15 | ירמיהו | ירמיהו |
| 104 | 40.1 | ירמיהו | ירמיהו |
| 105 | .2 | לירמיהו (sic!) | את |
| 106 | .6 | ירמיהו | —————— |
| 107 | 42.2 | ירמיהו הנביא (Syr om. נביא) | ירמיהו הנביא |
| 108 | .4 | ירמיהו הנביא | ————— ירמיהו |
| 109 | .5 | ירמיהו | ירמיהו |
| 110 | .7 | ירמיהו | ירמיהו |

| # | Ref | | |
|---|---|---|---|
| 111 | 43.1 | ירמיהו | ירמיהו |
| 112 | .2 | ירמיהו | ירמיהו |
| 113 | .6 | (Syr om. נביא) ירמיהו הנביא | ירמיהו הנביא |
| 114 | .8 | ירמיהו | ירמיהו |
| 115 | 44.1 | ירמיהו | ירמיהו |
| 116 | .15 | ירמיהו | ירמיהו |
| 117 | .20 | ירמיהו | ירמיהו |
| 118 | .24 | ירמיהו | ירמיהו |
| 119 | 45.1 | (Syr om. נביא) ירמיהו הנביא | ירמיהו הנביא |
| 120 | .1 | ירמיהו | * |
| 121 | 46.1 | ירמיהו הנביא | ירמיהו ----- |
| 122 | .13 | ירמיהו הנביא | * |
| 123 | 47.1 | ירמיהו הנביא | * |
| 124 | 49.34 | ירמיהו הנביא | ----- ------ |
| 125 | 50.1 | ירמיהו הנביא | * |
| 126 | 51.59 | (Syr om. נביא) ירמיהו הנביא | ירמיהו הנביא |
| 127 | .60 | ירמיהו | ירמיהו |
| 128 | .61 | ירמיהו | ירמיהו |
| 129 | .64 | ירמיהו | * |

### I  חנניה בן עזור הנביא

| # | Ref | | חנניה בן עזור הנביא |
|---|---|---|---|
| 1 | 28.1 | חנניה בן עזור הנביא | חנניה ----- |
| 2 | .5 | חנניה הנביא | חנניה ----- |
| 3 | .10 | חנניה הנביא | חנניה ----- |
| 4 | .11 | חנניה | חנניה |
| 5 | .12 | חנניה הנביא | חנניה ----- |
| 6 | .13 | (Syr + נביא) חנניה | חנניה |
| 7 | .15 | חנניה הנביא | חנניה ----- |
| 8 | .15 | חנניה | * |
| 9 | .17 | חנניה הנביא | * |

### J  ברוך בן נריה בן מחסיה

| # | Ref | | ברוך בן נריה בן מחסיה |
|---|---|---|---|
| 1 | 32.12 | ברוך בן נריה בן מחסיה | ברוך |
| 2 | .13 | ברוך | ברוך בן נריה |
| 3 | .16 | ברוך בן נריה | ברוך בן נריה |
| 4 | 36.4 | ברוך בן נריה | ---- |
| 5 | .4 | ברוך | |

| | | | |
|---|---|---|---|
| 6 | .5 | ברוך (Syr + ברכריא) | ברוך |
| 7 | .8 | ברוך בן נריה | ברוך -- ---- |
| 8 | .10 | ברוך | ברוך |
| 9 | .13 | ברוך | ברוך |
| 10 | .14 | ברוך | ברוך בן נריה |
| 11 | .14 | ברוך בן נריה | ברוך -- ---- |
| 12 | .15 | ברוך | ברוך |
| 13 | .16 | ברוך | ---- |
| 14 | .17 | ברוך | ברוך |
| 15 | .18 | ברוך | ברוך |
| 16 | .19 | ברוך | ברוך |
| 17 | .26 | ברוך הספר | ברהך ---- |
| 18 | .27 | ברוך | ברוך |
| 19 | .32 | ברוך בן נריהו הספר | * |
| 20 | 43.3 | ברוך בן נריה | ברוך בן נריה |
| 21 | .6 | ברוך בן נריה | ברוך בן נריה |
| 22 | 45.1 | ברוך בן נריה | ברוך בן נריה |
| 23 | .2 | ברוך | ברוך |

K  גדליהו בן אחיקם בן שפן

| | | | |
|---|---|---|---|
| 1 | 39.14 | גדליהו בן אחיקם בן שפן | גדליהו בן אחיקם בן שפן |
| 2 | 40.5 | גדליה בן אחיקם בן שפן = 2 Kgs.25.22 = גדליה בן אחיקם בן שפן |
| 3 | .6 | גדליה בן אחיקם | גדליה -- ----- |
| 4 | .7 | גדליהו בן אחיקם = 2 Kgs. 25.23 ‖ גדליהו -- ----- |
| 5 | .8 | גדליה = 2 Kgs. 25.23 = גדליה |
| 6 | .9 | גדליהו בן אחיקם בן שפן = 2 Kgs. 25.24 ‖ גדליהו -- ----- |
| 7 | .11 | גדליהו בן אחיקם בן שפן | גדליהו בן אחיקם -- --- |
| 8 | .12 | גדליהו | גדליהו |
| 9 | .13 | גדליהו | גדליהו |
| 10 | .14 | גדליהו בן אחיקם | גדליהו -- ----- |
| 11 | .15 | גדליהו | גדליהו |
| 12 | .16 | גדליהו בן אחיקם | גדליהו -- ----- |
| 13 | 41.1 | גדליהו בן אחיקם | גדליהו -- ----- |
| 14 | .2 | גדליהו בן אחיקם בן שפן ---- -- -- = 2Kgs.25.25 ‖ גדליהו |
| 15 | .3 | גדליהו = 2 Kgs. 25.25 ‖ ------ |
| 16 | .4 | גדליהו | גדליהו |
| 17 | .6 | גדליהו בן אחיקם | גדליהו -- ----- |

| | | | |
|---|---|---|---|
| 18 | .9 | ביד גדליהו | בור גדול |
| 19 | .10 | גדליהו בן אחיקם | גדליהו בן אחיקם |
| 20 | .16 | גדליהו בן אחיקם | \* |
| 21 | .18 | גדליהו בן אחיקם | גדליהו -- ----- |
| 22 | 43.6 | גדליהו בן אחיקם בן שפן | גדליהו בן אחיקם -- --- |

### L    יונדב בן רכב

| | | | |
|---|---|---|---|
| 1 | 35.6 | יונדב בן רכב | יונדב בן רכב |
| 2 | .8 | יהונדב בן רכב | יונדב -- --- |
| 3 | .10 | יונדב | הונדב |
| 4 | .14 | יהונדב בן רכב | יהונדב בן רכב |
| 5 | .16 | יהונדב בן רכב | יהונדב בן רכב |
| 6 | .18 | שמעותם | (בני) יונדב בן רכב) |
| 7 | .18 | יהונדב    vv.18-19 ₵ aliter { | ------ |
| 8 | .19 | יונדב בן רכב | יונדב בן רכב |

### M    יוחנן בן קרח

| | | | |
|---|---|---|---|
| 1 | 40.8 | יוחנן ויונתן בני קרח   ‖ 2 Kgs. 25.23 = | יוחנן ------ בן קרח ----- |
| 2 | .13 | יוחנן בן קרח | יוחנן בן קרח |
| 3 | .15 | יוחנן בן קרח | יוחנן -- --- |
| 4 | .16 | יוחנן בן קרח | יוחנן -- --- |
| 5 | 41.11 | יוחנן בן קרח | יוחנן בן קרח |
| 6 | .13 | יוחנן בן קרח | יוחנן -- --- |
| 7 | .14 | יוחנן בן קרח | יוחנן -- --- |
| 8 | .15 | יוחנן | ----- |
| 9 | .16 | יוחנן בן קרח | יוחנן -- --- |
| 10 | 42.1 | יוחנן בן קרח | יוחנן -- --- |
| 11 | .8 | יוחנן בן קרח | יוחנן -- --- |
| 12 | 43.2 | יוחנן בן קרח | יוחנן בן קרח |
| 13 | .4 | יוחנן בן קרח | יוחנן -- --- |
| 14 | .5 | יוחנן בן קרח | יוחנן -- --- |

### N    נבוזראדן רב טבחים

| | | | |
|---|---|---|---|
| 1 | 39.9 | נבוזראדן רב טבחים = 52.15, 2 Kgs. 25.11 ‖ | \* or \*\* |
| 2 | .10 | נבוזראדן רב טבחים = 52.16 M; 52.16 ₵, 2 Kgs. 25.12 om. נב' ‖ | \* or \*\* |
| 3 | .11 | נבוזראדן רב טבחים | \* or \*\* |

| | | | | |
|---|---|---|---|---|
| 4 | .13 | נבוזראדן רב טבחים | | ** or * |
| 5 | 40.1 | נבוזראדן רב טבחים | | נבוזראדן רב טבחים |
| 6 | .2 | רב טבחים | | רב טבחים |
| 7 | .5 | רב טבחים (Syr. pr. נבוזרדן) | | רב טבחים |
| 8 | 41.10 | נבוזראדן רב טבחים | | רב טבחים -------- |
| 9 | 43.6 | נבוזראדן רב טבחים | | נבוזראדן ----- -- |
| 10 | 52.12 | נבוזראדן רב טבחים = 2 Kgs. 25.8 = | | נבוזראדן רב טבחים |
| 11 | .14 | רב טבחים = 2 Kgs. 25.10 = | | רב טבחים |
| 12 | .15 | נבוזראדן רב טבחים = 2 Kgs. 25.11 (Syr om. ר'ט') | | ** |
| 13 | .16 | נבוזראדן רב טבחים I 2 Kgs. 25.12 = | | רב טבחים -------- |
| 14 | .19 | רב טבחים = 2 Kgs. 25.15 = | | רב טבחים |
| 15 | .24 | רב טבחים = 2 Kgs. 25.18 = | | רב טבחים |
| 16 | .26 | נבוזראדן רב טבחים = 2 Kgs. 25.20 = | | נבוזראדן רב טבחים |
| 17 | .30 | נבוזראדן רב טבחים | * | * |

| | | | | |
|---|---|---|---|---|
| 0 | | ישמעאל בן נתניה בן אלישמע | | |
| 1 | 40.8 | ישמעאל בן נתניהו | | ישמעאל בן נתניהו |
| 2 | .14 | ישמעאל בן נתניה | | ישמעאל -- ----- |
| 3 | .15 | ישמעאל בן נתניה | | ישמעאל -- ----- |
| 4 | .16 | ישמעאל | | ישמעאל |
| 5 | 41.1 | ישמעאל בן נתניה בן אלישמע = 2Kgs.25.25= ישמעאל בן נתניה בן אלישמע | | ישמעאל בן נתניה בן אלישמע |
| 6 | .2 | ישמעאל בן נתניה | | ישמעאל -- ----- |
| 7 | .3 | ישמעאל | | * |
| 8 | .6 | ישמעאל בן נתניה | | ישמלאל -- ----- |
| 9 | .7 | ישמעאל בן נתניה | | ישמעאל -- ----- |
| 10 | .8 | ישמעאל | | ישמעאל |
| 11 | .9 | ישמעאל | | ישמעאל |
| 12 | .9 | ישמעאל בן נתניהו | | ישמעאל -- ----- |
| 13 | .10 | ישמעאל | | ישמעאל |
| 14 | .10 | ישמעאל בן נתניה | | * |
| 15 | .11 | ישמעאל בן נתניה | | ישמעאל -- ----- |
| 16 | .12 | עם ישמעאל בן נתניה | | עמו |
| 17 | .13 | ישמעאל | | ישמעאל |
| 18 | .14 | ישמעאל | | * |
| 19 | .15 | ישמעאל בן נתניה | | ישמעאל -- ----- |
| 20 | .16 | ישמעאל בן נתניה | | ישמעאל -- ----- |
| 21 | .18 | ישמעאל בן נתניה | | ישמעאל -- ----- |

**P** <u>עבד מלך הכושי</u>

| | | | |
|---|---|---|---|
| 1 | 38.7 | עבד מלך הכושי איש סריס | עבד מלך הכושי --- ---- |
| 2 | .8 | עבד מלך | --- --- |
| 3 | .10 | עבד מלך הכושי | עבד מלך ----- |
| 4 | .11 | עבד מלך | עבד מלך |
| 5 | .12 | עבד מלך הכושי | ----- --- --- |
| 6 | 39.16 | עבד מלך הכושי | עבד מלך הכושי |

**Q** <u>אלישמע הספר</u>

| | | | |
|---|---|---|---|
| 1 | 36.12 | אלישמע הספר | אלישמע הספר |
| 2 | .20 | אלישמע הספר | אלישמע ----- |
| 3 | .21 | אלישמע הספר | אלישמע ----- |

**R** <u>פשחור בן אמר הכהן</u>

| | | | |
|---|---|---|---|
| 1 | 20.1 | פשחור בן אמר הכהן | פשחור בן אמר הכהן |
| 2 | .2 | פשחור | ----- |
| 3 | .3 | פשחור | פשחור |
| 4 | .3 | פשחור | פשחור |
| 5 | .6 | פשחור | ----- |
| 5 | .3 | מגור מסביב | מגור ----- |

**S** <u>צפניה בן מעשיה הכהן</u>

| | | | |
|---|---|---|---|
| 1 | 21.1 | צפניה בן מעשיה הכהן | צפניה בן מעשיה הכהן |
| 2 | 29.25 | צפניה בן מעשיה הכהן | צפניה בן מעשיה הכהן |
| 3 | .29 | צפניה הכהן | צפניה ---- |
| 4 | 37.3 | צפניה בן מעשיה הכהן | צפניה בן מעשיה הכהן |
| 5 | 52.24 | צפניה כהן המשנה = 2 Kgs. 25.18 I | ----- כהן המשנה |

**T** <u>שמעיה הנחלמי</u>

| | | | |
|---|---|---|---|
| 1 | 29.24 | שמעיהו הנחלמי | שמעיהו הנחלמי |
| 2 | .31 | שמעיה הנחלמי | שמעיה הנחלמי |
| 3 | .31 | שמעיה | שמעיה |
| 4 | .32 | שמעיה הנחלמי | שמעיה ------ |

**U** <u>חנמאל בן שלם דד\-</u>

| | | | |
|---|---|---|---|
| 1 | 32.7 | חנמאל בן שלם דדך | חנמאל בן שלם דדך |
| 2 | .8 | חנמאל בן --- דדי = Syr I | חנמאל בן שלם דדי |

| | | | |
|---|---|---|---|
| 3 | .9 | חנמאל בן דדי | חנמאל בן דדי |
| 4 | .12 | Syr = ‖ חנמאל -- דדי | חנמאל בן דדי |

**V** אוריה בן שמעיהו

| | | | |
|---|---|---|---|
| 1 | 26.20 | אוריהו בן שמעיהו | אוריהו בן שמעיהו |
| 2 | .21 | אוריהו | אוריהו |
| 3 | .23 | את אוריהו | אתו |

**W** אלנתן בן עכבור

| | | | |
|---|---|---|---|
| 1 | 26.22 | אלנתן בן עכבור | * |
| 2 | 36.12 | אלנתן בן עכבור | [9]יונתן בן עכבור |
| 3 | .25 | אלנתן | אלנתן |

**X** נרגל שר אצר

| | | | |
|---|---|---|---|
| 1 | 39.3 | נרגל שר אצר | נרגל שר אצר |
| 2 | .3 | נרגל שר אצר רב מג | נרגל שר אצר רב מג |
| 3 | .13 | נרגל שר אצר רב מג | * or ** |

**Y** אחאב בן קוליה

| | | | |
|---|---|---|---|
| 1 | 29.21 | אחאב בן קוליה | אחאב -- ----- |
| 2 | .22 | אחאב | אחאב |

**Z** צדקיהו בן מעשיה

| | | | |
|---|---|---|---|
| 1 | 29.21 | צדקיהו בן מעשיה | צדקיהו -- ----- |
| 2 | .22 | צדקיהו | צדקיהו |

**AA** פשחור בן מלכיה

| | | | |
|---|---|---|---|
| 1 | 21.1 | פשחור בן מלכיה | פשחור בן מלכיה |
| 2 | 38.1 | פשחור בן מלכיה | ----- -- ----- |

**BB** *Names of one occurrence with variant*[10]

| | | | |
|---|---|---|---|
| 1 | 36.26 | שלמיהו בן עבדאל | ----- -- ------ |
| 2 | 52.24 | שריה כהן הראש = 2 Kgs. 25.18 ‖ | ---- כהן הראש |

**CC** *Names of more than one occurrence with no variants*

| | | | | | | |
|---|---|---|---|---|---|---|
| 1 | 36.14 | יהודי בן נתניהו בן שלמיהו בן כושי | 3 | .21 | יהודי |
| 2 | .21 | יהודי | 4 | .23 | יהודי |

| | | | | | |
|---|---|---|---|---|---|
| 5 | 36.10 | גמריהו בן שפן הספר | | 7 | .25 | גמריהו |
| 6 | .12 | גמריהו בן שפן | | | | |
| | | | | | | |
| 8 | 37.15 | יהונתן הספר | | 11 | 51.59 | שריה בן נריה בן מחסיה |
| 9 | .20 | יהונתן הספר | | 12 | .59 | שריה |
| 10 | 38.26 | יהונתן | | 13 | .61 | שריה |
| | | | | | | |
| 14 | 36.11 | מיכיהו בן גמריהו בן שפן | | 16 | 36.12 | דליהו בן שמעיהו |
| 15 | .13 | מיכיהו | | 17 | .25 | דליהו |
| | | | | | | |
| 18 | 37.3 | יהוכל בן שלמיה | 20 | 37.13 | יראייה בן שלמיה בן חנניה[11] |
| 19 | 38.1 | יוכל בן שלמיהו | 21 | .14 | יראייה[11] |

## NOTES TO APPENDIX A

1. The long dash indicates omission of all or part of a name. Thus,
גדליהו -- ----- -- --- :גדליהו בן אחיקם בן שפן indicates that בן אחיקם
בן שפן are omitted in ₵. An asterisk indicates that the larger context
in which the name occurs is absent in ₵ and secondary in M. A double
asterisk indicates that the context of the name is secondarily absent in
₵.

2. The spelling with נ is given only to indicate Greek Ναβουχοδονοσορ, not to suggest that ₵-*Vorlage* read this spelling (though it probably
did). Otherwise, the spelling in the ₵ column corresponds to M spelling
in each specific reference.

3. On my interpretation of the divided Greek evidence, see pp. 54-57.

4. Where Syr is not specifically cited, it agrees with M.

5. BH[2]: נבוכדנאצר.

6. Om. המלך Syr (Jer. Kgs.) ₵ (Kgs.) BA+mss. Cf. 32.1 τω βασιλει
ναβουχοδονοσορ βασιλει Βαβυλωνος B-S A(om. βασιλει 2°)-106' Aeth Arab(om.
βασ. βαβ.).

7. מלך is dittography from immediately preceding וימלך.

8. B-family is split: B-S-106-538 La Sa Aeth = M; 410-130-239 Bo
join the majority of witnesses of Q-V-family, two cursives of L, and C'
in reading המלך יאשיהו. It may be that the uncertainty is an indication
that both traditions represent corrections from an earlier יאשיהו = A
Arab.

9. The Greek witness is split on this first name, primarily between
B-S and congeners (Ιωναθαν) and A Q and congeners (ναθαν), with weak
attestation of ελναθαν.

10. The name שלם בן יאשיהו מדך יהודה occurs only once (22.11). But
since it is a king's name, and involves only the zero variant מלך יהודה,
it is treated as behaving textually like the other royal names, in B-G
above.

11. ₵: Σαρουιαμ.

## APPENDIX B

*Divine Names in Prophetic Clichés*

### Table B.1

כה אמר יהוה Outside of Jeremiah[a]

| Book | Total occurrences | כה אמר יהוה | כה אמר אדני י׳ | כה אמר י׳ צבאות | כה אמר א׳ י׳ צב׳ | כה אמר י׳ אל׳ ישראל | Other |
|---|---|---|---|---|---|---|---|
| Exodus | 10 | 5 | -- | -- | -- | 2 | 3 — כה אמר י׳ אל׳ העברים |
| Joshua | 2 | -- | -- | -- | -- | 2 | -- |
| Judges | 1 | -- | -- | -- | -- | 1 | -- |
| Samuel | 8 | 4 | -- | 2 | -- | 2 | -- |
| Kings | 33 | 24 | -- | -- | -- | 8 | 1 — כ׳א׳י׳ אלהי דוד אביך |
| Chronicles | 4 | 3[b] | -- | -- | -- | -- | 1 — כ׳א׳י׳ אלהי דוד אביך |
| Amos | 14 | 11 | 2 | -- | 1[c] | -- | -- |
| Micah | 2 | 2 | -- | -- | -- | -- | -- |
| 1 Isaiah | 12 | 6[d] | 2 | -- | 2 | -- | 2 — כה אמר קדש ישראל / כה א׳ אדני קדש ישראל |
| Nahum | 1 | 1 | -- | -- | -- | -- | -- |
| Ezekiel | 126 | 3 | 123 | -- | -- | -- | -- |
| 2 Isaiah | 27 | 20 | 3 | -- | -- | -- | 4 — כה אמר האל יהוה / כה אמר רם ונשא / כה אמר מלך ישראל / כה א׳ אדניך י׳ אלהיך |
| Haggai | 5 | -- | -- | 5 | -- | -- | -- |
| 1 Zechariah | 19 | 2 | -- | 17 | -- | -- | -- |
| 2 Zechariah | 1 | -- | -- | -- | -- | -- | 1 — כה אמר יהוה[e] אלהי |
| Malachi | 1 | -- | -- | 1 | -- | -- | -- |
| Obadiah | 1 | -- | 1 | -- | -- | -- | --- |
| Total | 267 | 81 | 131 | 25 | 3 | 15 | 12 |
| Less Ez. | 141 | 78 | 8 | 25 | 3 | 15 | 12 |
| Less HZM[f] | 242 | 79 | 131 | 2 | 3 | 15 | 12 |
| Less Ez.+HZM | 116 | 76 | 8 | 2 | 3 | 15 | 12 |

## Table B.2

### כה אמר יהוה in Jeremiah

| | The forms in M and 𝒢, by types of variant (𝒢 zero variants in parentheses) | |
|---|---|---|
| 76 | M = 𝒢 | כה אמר יהוה | a |
| 5 | M = 𝒢 | כה אמר יהוה אלהי ישראל | b |
| | | | |
| 8 | | כה אמר יהוה (אלהי ישראל) | c |
| 16 | | כה אמר יהוה (צבאות) | d |
| 2 | | כה אמר יהוה צבאות (אלהי ישראל) | e |
| 9 | | כה אמר יהוה (צבאות) אלהי ישראל | f |
| 17 | | כה אמר יהוה (צבאות אלהי ישראל) | g |
| 2 | | כה אמר יהוה (אלהי צבאות אלהי ישראל) | h |
| 1 | | כה אמר יהוה (אלהי) צבאות (אלהי ישראל) | i |
| 1 | | כה אמר יהוה (אלהי) צבאות | j |
| 1 | | כה אמר (אדני) יהוה | k |
| 1 | | כה אמר יהוה\יהוה ταδε λεγει κυριος ο θεος | l |
| | | | |
| 8 | | (כה אמר יהוה) | m |
| 1 | | (כה אמר יהוה אלהי ישראל) | n |
| 3 | | (כה אמר יהוה צבאות) | o |
| 3 | | (כה אמר יהוה צבאות אלהי ישראל) | p |

| | The forms in M and 𝒢, by totals | | |
|---|---|---|---|
| M | 𝒢 | | |
| 85 | 120 | כה אמר יהוה | q |
| 14 | 14 | כה אמר יהוה אלהי ישראל | r |
| 19 | 4 | כה אמר יהוה צבאות | s |
| 31 | -- | כה אמר יהוה צבאות אלהי ישראל | t |
| 1 | -- | כה אמר יהוה אלהי צבאות | u |
| 3 | -- | כה אמר יהוה אלהי צבאות אלהי ישראל | v |
| 1 | -- | כה אמר אדני יהוה | w |
| -- | 1 | ταδε λεγει κυριος ο θεος | x |
| 154 | 139[a] | | |

Table B.3

נאם יהוה and אמר יהוה Outside Jeremiah[a]

| Book | Total occur-rences | נאם יהוה | נאם אדני י' | נאם י' צבאות | נאם י' אלהי צבאות | האדון י' צבאות | נאם י' אלהי ישראל |
|---|---|---|---|---|---|---|---|
| Genesis | 1 | 1 | -- | -- | -- | -- | -- |
| Numbers | 1 | 1 | -- | -- | -- | -- | -- |
| Samuel | 2 | 1 | -- | -- | -- | -- | 1 |
| Kings | 4 | 4 | -- | -- | -- | -- | -- |
| Amos | 21 | 14 | 4 | -- | 3[b] | -- | -- |
| Hosea | 4 | 4 | -- | -- | -- | -- | -- |
| 1 Isaiah | 11 | 3 | -- | 4[c] | -- | 3[c] | 1 |
| Micah | 2 | 2 | -- | -- | -- | -- | -- |
| Zephaniah | 5 | 4 | -- | 1[d] | -- | -- | -- |
| Nahum | 2 | -- | -- | 2 | -- | -- | -- |
| Ezekiel | 85 | 4 | 81 | -- | -- | -- | -- |
| 2 Isaiah | 13 | 12 | 1 | -- | -- | -- | -- |
| Haggai | 12 | 6 | -- | 6 | -- | -- | -- |
| 1 Zechariah | 13 | 6 | -- | 7[e] | -- | -- | -- |
| 2 Zechariah | 7 | 5 | -- | 2[f] | -- | -- | -- |
| Malachi | 1[g] | 1 | -- | -- | -- | -- | -- |
| Obadiah | 2 | 2 | -- | -- | -- | -- | -- |
| Joel | 1 | 1 | -- | -- | -- | -- | -- |
| Psalms | 1 | 1 | -- | -- | -- | -- | -- |
| | | | | | | | |
| Total | 188 | 72 | 86 | 22 | 3 | 3 | 2 |
| Less Ez. | 103 | 68 | 5 | 22 | 3 | 3 | 2 |
| Less HZM | 162 | 59 | 86 | 9 | 3 | 3 | 2 |
| Less Ez. and HZM | 77 | 55 | 5 | 9 | 3 | 3 | 2 |

| | Total | אמר יהוה | אמר אדני י' | אמר י' אלהי\- | אמר י' אלהיך | אמר י' צבאות | אמר י' אלהי צבאות שמר | Other |
|---|---|---|---|---|---|---|---|---|
| Amos | 9 | 5 | 2 | -- | 1 | -- | 1 | -- |
| 1 Isaiah | 2 | 1 | -- | -- | -- | 1[h] | -- | -- |
| Zephaniah | 1 | 1 | -- | -- | -- | -- | -- | -- |
| 2 Isaiah | 16 | 10 | -- | 3 | -- | 1 | -- | 2 | אמר גאלך יהוה אמר רחמך יהוה |
| Haggai | 3 | 1 | -- | -- | -- | 2 | -- | -- |
| 1 Zechariah | 4 | -- | -- | -- | -- | 4 | -- | -- |
| Malachi | 24 | 3 | -- | -- | -- | 20 | -- | 1 | אמר יהוה אלהי ישראל |
| Total | 59 | 21 | 2 | 3 | 1 | 28 | 1 | 3 |
| Less HZM | 28 | 17 | 2 | 3 | 1 | 2 | 1 | 2 |

| | Total | נאם יהוה | נאם אדני יהוה | נאם יהוה צבאות | נאם אדני יהוה צבאות | נאם המלך י ׳ צבאות שמו | נאם יהוה אלהי ישראל | Other | |
|---|---|---|---|---|---|---|---|---|---|
| M | 175 | 164 | 1 | 4 | 3 | 3 | -- | --- | |
| ¢ | 110 | 102 | -- | -- | -- | 1 | 1 | 6 | ταδε λεγει κυρ. ο θεος |

| | Total | אמר יהוה | אמר יהוה צבאות | אמר י ׳ צבאות אלהי ישראל |
|---|---|---|---|---|
| M | 9 | 8 | -- | 1 |
| ¢ | 6 | 5 | 1 | -- |

## NOTES TO APPENDIX B

### *Table B.1*

[a]This table does not include occurrences in synoptic passages to Kings, in Isaiah and Chronicles, because in these books the passages are literarily secondary. They would be of interest only if they possessed variant readings, but in each instance the synoptic text is identical to that of Kings.

[b]2 Chr. 21.12 האלהים אמר כה] ταδε λεγει κυριος. On האלהים as a later replacement for יהוה in Chronicles, see Ralph W. Klein, "Studies in the Greek Texts of the Chronicler" (Ph.D. dissertation, Harvard University, 1966).

[c]Am. 5.16 אדני צבאות אלהי יהוה אמר כה   ταδε λεγει κυριος ο θεος ο παντοκρατωρ (> ο θεος 62 Aeth).

[d]Isa. 21.6, 21.16 אדני אמר כה, surely for יהוה אמר כה (in 21.16, 1QIsa[a] reads יהוה).

[e]Zech. 11.4 אלהי יהוה אמר כה] ταδε λαγει κυριος παντοκρατωρ; ...deus Ach (cf. 𝔐). 𝔊 (or 𝔊-*Vorlage*) probably has moved to the dominant pattern in Zech. (cf. also 𝔊 apparatus to 1.16, 8.3).

[f]In this appendix, the abbreviation HZM = Haggai, 1 Zechariah, Malachi.

### *Table B.2*

[a]Eight times, 𝔊 is superior in omitting the whole formula (see discussion in chapter IV); seven times the formula occurs in a larger context absent in 𝔊.

### *Table B.3*

[a]This table does not include the cliché in 2 Chr. 34.27, a synoptic parallel to 2 Kings 22.19.

[b]3.13 צבאות יהוה אדני נאם] λεγει κυριος ο θεος ο παντοκρατωρ. In 6.8 and 6.14, צבאות אלהי יהוה נאם is absent in 𝔊, and probably secondary in 𝔐.

[c]In 3.15, 𝔊 omits צבאות יהוה אדני נאם. Two occurrences of יהוה נאם

צבאות in 14.22.23 are textually sound. But this passage is a late addition to 1 Isaiah, so that the formulas here probably reflect the later usage of HZM.

[d]2.9 צבאות .om [נאם יהוה צבאות אלהי ישראל ¢.

[e]1.3 נאם יהוה צבאות] om. ¢. The verse is congested with prophetic clichés.

[f]13.2 נאם יהוה צבאות] om. צבאות ¢; cf. 12.4 נאם יהוה] + παντοκρα-τωρ. In both instances the plus is secondary from 1 Zech.

[g]In view of the normal usage of אמר יהוה, usually with צבאות (see below in this table), this single occurrence probably is secondary.

[h]22.4 אמר אדני יהוה צבאות] om. ¢.

APPENDIX C

*The Occurrences of* צבאות *in the Old Testament*

In a recent article,[1] Friedrich Baumgärtel has presented a thesis
concerning the occurrence of צבאות which differs radically from my own
conclusion and which on first reading seems quite plausible. But deeper
study of his argument reveals several major flaws which vitiate his conclusions. In what follows, sections A and C outline his general argument
and his discussion of textual problems, respectively; sections B and D
contain my critique.

A

In the two contemporary prophets Jeremiah and Ezekiel, there is a
striking difference in the designation of the deity, all the more so as
this difference is demonstrated within the same speech forms, as set
forth in Tables C.1 and C.2. These tables show that צבאות and אדני occur
predominantly within the prophetic formulas listed in the tables. In
fact, a closer examination of the data leads to the conclusion that all
free occurrences of these two epithets in the prophets are to be viewed
as secondary, being either redactoral glosses or metrically superfluous.
The only exceptions to this are the free occurrences of צבאות in Zech.
7-8, 14.16-21, and in 1 Isaiah. It is not impossible that in 1 Isaiah
the epithet, which occurs 43 times in free contexts (26 genuine, 8 ungen-
uine, 9 unclear), constitutes a special theologumenon.

Table C.1:  The usage of יהוה צבאות

| | Totals | כה אמר | נאם | אמר | שמר | Address | free י׳צ׳ |
|---|---|---|---|---|---|---|---|
| Samuel | 11 | 2 | – | – | – | 2 | 7 |
| Kings | 5 | – | – | – | – | – | 5 |
| I Isaiah[a] | 56 | 2 | 7 | 1 | – | – | 46 |
| II Isaiah | 6 | 1 | – | 1 | 4 | – | – |
| Jeremiah | 82 | 55 | 7 | – | 8 | 4 | 8 |
| Hosea | 1 | – | – | – | 1 | – | – |
| Amos | 9 | 1 | 3 | – | 2 | – | 3 |
| Micah | 1 | – | – | – | – | – | 1 |
| Nahum | 2 | – | 2 | – | – | – | – |
| Habakkuk | 1 | – | – | – | – | – | 1 |
| Zephaniah | 2 | – | 1 | – | – | – | 1 |
| Haggai | 14 | 5 | 6 | 2 | – | – | 1 |
| Zechariah | 53 | 17 | 9 | 4 | – | 1 | 22 |
| Malachi | 24 | 1 | – | 20 | – | – | 3 |
| Psalms[b] | 15 | – | – | – | – | 11 | 4 |
| Chronicles | 3 | 1 | – | – | – | – | 2 |
| With Isa.I | 285 | 85 | 35 | 28 | 15 | 18 | 104 |
| Minus Isa. I | 229 | 83 | 28 | 27 | 15 | 18 | 58 |

[a]Including chapters 36-39.

[b]Including the elohistic redaction.

Except in the prophets, צבאות stands predominantly outside these formulas. But here, the free occurrences stand virtually entirely in contexts having to do with the ark, or with Zion as the home of the ark. So much is certain: יהוה צבאות is the old cult name of Yahweh connected with the ark.

From Table C.1, it is seen that יהוה צבאות adheres above all to the formula כה אמר, and also to the formula נאם י׳ (צבאות appears in 85 of 479 occurrences of כה אמר יהוה, in 35 of 368 occurrences of נאם יהוה). So, it may be said that the name יהוה צבאות is connected to the ark, and to the old formula כה אמר. Is there any connection between the ark and כה אמר?[2]

Table C.2:  The usage of אדני יהוה[a]

| | Totals | כה אמר | נאם | אמר | אזה | נשבע | כה הראני | Address | Free אד״י |
|---|---|---|---|---|---|---|---|---|---|
| Genesis | 2 | – | – | – | – | – | – | 2 | – |
| Deuteronomy | 2 | – | – | – | – | – | – | 2 | – |
| Joshua | 1 | – | – | – | 1 | – | – | – | – |
| Judges | 2 | – | – | – | 1 | – | – | 1 | – |
| Samuel | 6 | – | – | – | – | – | – | 6 | – |
| Kings | 2 | – | – | – | – | – | – | 1 | 1 |
| I Isaiah | 4 | 3 | – | – | – | – | – | – | 1 |
| II Isaiah | 13 | 3 | 1 | – | – | – | – | – | 9 |
| Jeremiah | 8 | 1 | 1 | – | 4 | – | – | 1 | 1 |
| Ezekiel | 217 | 122 | 81 | – | 4 | – | – | 1 | 9 |
| Amos | 19 | 2 | 4 | 2 | – | 2 | 3 | 2 | 4 |
| Obadiah | 1 | 1 | – | – | – | – | – | – | – |
| Micah | 1 | – | – | – | – | – | – | – | 1 |
| Zephaniah | 1 | – | – | – | – | – | – | – | 1 |
| Zechariah | 1 | – | – | – | – | – | – | – | 1 |
| Psalms | 3 | – | – | – | – | – | – | 1 | 2 |
| | 283 | 132 | 87 | 2 | 10 | 2 | 3 | 17 | 30 |

[a]The phrases 'dny yhwh ṣb'wt and the like are classified with yhwh ṣb'wt;
'dny in these forms is probably a later inserted Qere.

The connection of a "liturgical" formula כה אמר to the ark can con-
sist only in this, that the communication of the divine דבר comes from
יהוה צבאות, the God of the ark.  If the ark originally had something to
do with oracles, then כה אמר would be the old oracle formula.  To be
sure, it is the ephod which is the oracle locus proper, while the ark is
the throne of Yahweh.  Yet (following von Rad) each--ephod and ark--be-
longs to the other, and cannot exist for itself.  If the ark was not the
oracle locus proper, yet one sought in its presence the oracle, because
it was a fulsome contemporizing of God.  Now, the oracle was not always
answered yes or no; sometimes a full answer (e.g., Jud. 20.27-28) was
given, which often came in the form ויאמר יהוה.  But, translated into a
ritual context, this could be none other than כה אמר יהוה.  The prophets,

therefore, later made use of the old formula speech of the priestly oracle ritual which stood in relation to the ark, opening their communication of the divine will with כה אמר יהוה צבאות.

Thus the name יהוה צבאות, which early was a living term, in the time of the great prophets became a mere residium as a style form of prophetic speech. The one exception is 1 Isaiah, who (probably owing to his unique relation to Zion, the temple and its cult) uses the term in free contexts as a special theologumenon.[3]

Finally, the question arises: why did Ezekiel not use צבאות, espepecially since he too was intimately associated with the ark? And why did he substitute אדני יהוה for it in the prophetic formulas?[4] Ezekiel was far from Zion in Babylon. After 587, the God of Zion could no more be called יהוה צבאות ישב הכרובים, for the temple was destroyed and the ark was taken. When in post-Exilic times the old festal formula with יהוה צבאות again rang out, this indicates only that this phrase no longer possessed strong inner connections with the God of the covenant ark.

B

Baumgärtel's argument for an original formula כה אמר יהוה צבאות as introductory to the priestly oracle associated with the ark breaks down in at least two places: First, an original connection of צבאות primarily to כה אמר cannot be sustained. It is predicated upon the higher proportion of occurrences of צבאות in כה אמר יהוה, as compared to נאם יהוה: 82:421 :: 38:363 (or 1 in 5.1 to 1 in 9.5).[5] However, when we consider the data apart from Jeremiah, Ezekiel, and Haggai-Zechariah-Malachi, the ratio is reversed: 5:116 :: 15:77 (or 1 in 23.2 to 1 in 5.1)! Thus, the statistics on which Baumgärtel's argument rests are fattened from Jeremiah (textually problematical) and Haggai-Zechariah-Malachi (post-Exilic); otherwise, occurrences of צבאות with כה אמר יהוה are rare. If anything, this indicates that the formula כה אמר יהוה צבאות is not early, but late, and--from the point of view of literary or tradition history-- secondary.[6] Further, 1 Isaiah's penchant for צבאות as a theologumenon makes problematical his failure to use צבאות in כה אמר יהוה to any degree. If to him alone among the prophets the epithet was anything more than a residium frozen in a cliché, if he was unique among the

prophets in his closeness to Zion, temple, and ark, we should expect him
above all to use the old form connected with the ark as locus for the
oracle.

Second, the attempt to trace the original *Sitz im Leben* of כה אמר
יהוה to ritual giving of the priestly oracle in association with the ark
is unconvincing. It is methodologically bad to try to derive the form
through reconstruction (from ויאמר יהוה), when another usage of this same
formula, well attested in the Old Testament, gives a perfectly adequate
explanation of the origin of the prophetic usage. There is abundant evidence that כה אמר יהוה is standard Hebrew epistolary style for introducing the words of the sender to the recipient. It is clear that the prophet, as messenger of Yahweh, uses the standard introductory form to sig-
nal the beginning of the message of his lord to the recipients.[7] Thus,
the prophetic usage is simply a specialization of epistolary form, and
the attempt to tie the origin of כה אמר יהוה to priestly oracles in connection with צבאות fails. But one might still wish to argue, from some
other point of origin, an "enge, sicher uralte Verbindung zwischen כה אמר
und יהוה צבאות."[8] This leads to our second major criticism.

Baumgärtel fails in his attempt to establish צבאות as an integral
element of the prophetic formulas. As we have demonstrated in Appendix
B, Tables B.2 and B.3, the formulas occur predominantly *without* epithets
after the divine name; apart from Jeremiah, Ezekiel, and Haggai-Zechariah-
Malachi, צבאות is present only rarely (20 of 193 occurrences),[9] while it
is only in the late books and Jeremiah that Baumgärtel's pattern emerges.
To argue from this to original usage is incomprehensible.

Even if Baumgärtel's dismissal of most free occurrences of צבאות is
legitimate, the remaining evidence establishes the epithet as not bound
exclusively to the formulas. To label the genuine occurrences in 1
Isaiah and Zechariah as a special theologumenon does not relieve his argument of the embarrassment their existence constitutes. The occurrences
in the phrase יהוה···שמו tell us nothing. For one thing, this phrase
occurs in two forms, one with צבאות and one without (see p. 79). In any
case, it is a hymnic element, and stands in no integral relation to the
prophetic formulas, and therefore in no way supports the argument. Similarly, the category "address" is in no way a valid type of prophetic
formula; that צבאות occurs in address contexts only shows that the speaker
(or writer) was familiar with a "free" usage of the epithet.[10]

Baumgärtel's tables (C.1 and C.2) seem, at first glance, to present strikingly similar patterns. But any inner connection, such as he wishes to find, is dissolved by my criticism of his argument. The dissimilarity between Tables C.1 and C.2 is further indicated by the fact that, whereas in the rest of the Old Testament (except for Haggai-Zechariah-Malachi) the formulas occur predominantly without צבאות, in Ezekiel the formulas are virtually solid with אדני. It can be argued that in the latter case we have a late usage leveled through in one book, and later infecting formulaic contexts in a few instances elsewhere, analogous to the manner in which the special usage with צבאות in Haggai-Zechariah-Malachi secondarily infected the text of Jeremiah. But this brings us to a consideration of Baumgärtel's text-critical method.

C

Baumgärtel's study, as he acknowledges, has proceeded on the tacit assumption that יהוה צבאות and אדני יהוה represent the original divine names. But, he asks, can conclusions be drawn on such assumptions, when 𝕲 shows far different readings of the divine names? He proceeds to investigate the textual situation, as follows:

יהוה צבאות. In Jeremiah the double name is represented almost throughout with κυριος, in both translators.[11] The dozen or so exceptions, where 𝕲 reads κυριος παντοκρατωρ, etc., have no significance. The integrity of the Masoretic text is shown in that secondary leveling of צבאות into just the formulas would be inconceivable—what would be the basis for such exclusive leveling? The presence of the exceptions in both halves of Jeremiah 𝕲 shows that παντοκρατωρ is secondary correction to 𝔐, after Jeremiah α and β have been joined.

But why does Jeremiah 𝕲 render the double name only with κυριος? As the variety of renderings in the Greek Old Testament shows, there was difficulty in translating the name. What would a Greek-speaking community understand by κυριος σαβαωθ? κυριος των δυναμεων was ambiguous in a world haunted by "powers." κυριος παντοκρατωρ had to appear as a way out, a way which the scholars, who were concerned with literal translation, took besides the other two attempts. It was simplest and clearest to translate with only κυριος.

In Isaiah, κυριος σαβαωθ appears in both Isaiah α and β (α and β indicate two translators). It is inconceivable that two translators, who otherwise were so different, should agree on such a translation. Rather, as with παντοκρατωρ in Jeremiah, σαβαωθ is secondary correction to M after the union of Isaiah α and β.

The Book of the Twelve: By analogy with what has been found in Jeremiah and Isaiah, it may be surmised that, because of the above-mentioned practical difficulties, the translators here also rendered the double name with κυριος, and παντοκρατωρ is correction to M.

אֲדֹנָי יהוה. The Greek translation would reflect synagogue practice. But in the synagogue, one no doubt read aloud just אֲדֹנָי, and not אֲדֹנָי אֲדֹנָי. So, the translators rendered only κυριος. This can be seen at work, for example, with the cliché אֹהָה אֲדֹנָי יהוה, which is rendered in Codex B two times with δεσποτη κυριε, two times with κυριε κυριε, and six times simply with κυριε. Unless we are to suppose that אֲדֹנָי was secondarily leveled through the cliché, it seems clear that 𝔊 was striving strongly to reduce אֲדֹנָי יהוה to simple κυριος. This *Bestreben zur Reduzierung* can be seen at work throughout the Greek Old Testament. Instances where 𝔊 presents a double name are later corrections to M.

Baumgärtel concludes: "Als *Ergebnis* der textkritischen Untersuchung ist festzustellen: die 'צ'י und die 'י'דא des M sind, von Einzelfällen abgesehen, den andersartigen LXX-Lesarten unbedingt vorzuziehen. *Von der textkritischen Seite her lassen sich also die oben entwickelten Thesen nicht anfechten.*"[12]

D

The above summary does not indicate many small details of Baumgärtel's textual analysis; but it does present the turning points of his discussion, and will suffice to allow us to make an evaluation. At the outset, it may be stated categorically that both his methods and his conclusions are totally unacceptable. His exclusive reliance upon the uncial codices of the Greek text tradition (to the neglect of the cursive and other witnesses), and the resultant lack of any attempt to reconstruct critically the old Greek text, let alone his failure to make any use of the Göttingen critical edition of the Septuagint in the Prophets, already gives some notion of both the vintage and the caliber of his textual methods. His analysis also breaks down in the following details:

His argument concerning the translation of יהוה אדני is not implausible. As I have indicated above, no less a textual critic than Joseph
Ziegler has also acknowledged the difficulty of interpreting the Septuagint evidence on this name.[13] Nevertheless, as Ziegler's study of similar readings in Isaiah shows, and as I maintain is indicated at least
partially in Jeremiah, the evidence of 𝔊 cannot be dismissed out of hand,
nor can 𝔐 readings of אדני יהוה be taken for granted as superior.

The variety of Greek renderings of צבאות does not of itself indicate that translation was problematical; many terms in the Old Testament
are rendered by a variety of Greek words, and their primary status in 𝔊
is not thereby called into question. Further, the problems with κυριος
σαβαωθ and κυριος των δυναμεων, which Baumgärtel attributes to the Alexandrian Jewish community, are non-existent. As Barthélemy has shown,[14]
the various renderings do not represent different old Greek renderings
but, in the main, recensional stages of the Greek text, wherein παντοκρατωρ is old Greek and κυριος των δυναμεων belongs to the late pre-Hexaplaric
recension which he designates as καιγε (the usage in Isaiah of σαβαωθ is
anomalous, and not explained as yet). But apart from Barthélemy's work,
it ought to have been clear from the full witness to the Greek text of
Jeremiah that παντοκρατωρ was not a later literalizing rendering, but the
earliest 𝔊 witness to the epithet, and certainly earlier than των δυναμεων. The latter rendering enters the cursive witness (and, rarely, the
uncials) only when παντοκρατωρ was absent in the old Greek, and then it
is taken from the pre-Hexaplaric recension identified in the Hexaplaric
apparatus as θ'.

Baumgärtel's dismissal of instances where 𝔊 (in Jeremiah and the
Twelve) reads παντοκρατωρ as secondary corrections to 𝔐 is nothing else
than getting rid of contrary evidence.

The argument that the presence of παντοκρατωρ in Jeremiah α and β,
and of σαβαωθ in Isaiah α and β, shows their secondary character does not
hold up. Whether the respective parts are the product of different translators or of recensional activity, there is nothing to forbid the appearance in both sections of some common renderings. As Ziegler points out,
concerning the character of Jeremiah α and β, "es kann...beobachtet werden,
dass sich in der ganzen Ier.-LXX einheitliche Züge finden, die sie von
anderen Büchern abheben."[15]

Baumgärtel doubts the basis for a supposed leveling of צבאות predominantly[16] in the prophetic clichés.  In view of the several weaknesses
in Baumgartel's argument, I maintain that it is easier to suppose that
the Masoretic text has been heavily infected by the special usage of the
late prophets Haggai, 1 Zechariah, and Malachi, according to the pattern
presented above, in chapter IV, section B.

Summing up, we may say that Baumgärtel's thesis is erected upon
shaky textual foundations, proceeds against the clear implications even
of the data in M, and fails completely in nearly every one of its major
arguments.

## NOTES TO APPENDIX C

1. F. Baumgärtel, "Zu den Gottesnamen in den Büchern Jeremia und Ezechiel," *Verbannung und Heimkehr* (Festschr. Wm. Rudolph), ed. Arnulf Kuschke (Tübingen, 1961), pp. 1-29.

2. In passing, it is noted that נאם and כה אמר have separate origins. נאם has its own independent meaning, in the sense of divinatory presentiment, of inspiration. Again and again it occurs in eschatological clichés, and its thrust is general and abstract. On the other hand, כה אמר is used in the context of mediation of the divine will in the form of דבר, and the thrust is entirely concrete and specific. Also, כה אמר never ends, while נאם never begins, an oracle. So, one can pursue the close connection between יהוה צבאות and כה אמר without regard for נאם, to whose sphere יהוה צבאות originally probably had no connection.

3. At the same time, 1 Isa. uses the prophetic forumlas only seldom. Compare:

| | | | | | | |
|---|---|---|---|---|---|---|
| כה אמר יהוה | 1 Isa. | 19 | Jer. | 202 | Ezek. | 125 |
| נאם יהוה | 1 Isa. | 13 | Jer. | 169 | Ezek. | 85 |

4. The latter name in the O.T. is generally (in genuine contexts) related to cultic prayer, and as such it may possibly be related to an old cultic name of God.

5. Baumgärtel's figures (85:479 and 35:368) are simply wrong. For example, he lists 202 occurrences of כה אמר יהוה for Jeremiah ("Zu den Gottesnamen...," p. 21); a thorough doublecheck in both Mandelkern and Lizowsky reveals no more than 154 occurrences.

6. Using Baumgärtel's argumentation, one could maintain with equal plausibility that the original formula was כה אמר יהוה אלהי ישראל! After all, this form occurs much more often outside the prophets (see Appendix B, Table B.1) than does כה אמר יהוה צבאות; and the designation יהוה אלהי ישראל certainly is an early one.

7. Examples of epistolary style may be found in Gen. 32.5, Num. 20.14, Jud. 11.14-15, 2 Kgs. 18.19, 28-29. The formal similarity between Gen. 32.5 and the prophetic form in 2 Sam. 7.8 is especially noteworthy. A similar adoption of epistolary usage to introduce the message of the divine messenger is seen in the Ugaritic myths. For example, *PRU* II 14.1ff (also *UM* 18.1-3) may be compared with *UT* 51.VIII 29-35. On this general point, see further Claus Westermann, *Basic Forms of Prophetic*

*Speech* (Westminster, 1967), pp. 100–128, against whose results Baumgärtel's objections are without weight.

    8.  Baumgärtel, p. 23.

    9.  In Baumgärtel's table (C.1), his listing of כה אמר יהוה צבאות
in 2 Isaiah and Chronicles is misleading; the latter occurrence is in a
synoptic parallel to 2 Sam. 7.8, and is therefore not an independent
datum, while the occurrence in 2 Isaiah (45.14) is only in LXX, not in MT.
Unfortunately, these are not the only instances of imprecision in Baumgartel's presentation of the data (see, e.g., n. 5 above).

    10.  One suspects that this category was set up to correspond to
the same category in Baumgartel's table (C.2), implying thereby an even
closer correspondence between his two tables.  But, for that matter, the
category in Table C.2 really tells us nothing.  For the very form אֲדֹנָי
indicates that (like אֲדֹנָי) originally it must have stood predominantly
in address contexts!

    11.  Accepting the identification in Jeremiah 𝔊 of two translators,
α (chaps. 1–29) and β (chaps. 30–51), by H. St.–John Thackeray, in "The
Greek Translators of Jeremiah," *JTS* (1903), pp. 245–266.

    12.  Baumgärtel, p. 20 (italics Baumgärtel's).

    13.  See pp. 81–82 and Ziegler's work there cited.

    14.  *Les Devanciers d'Aquila* (Leiden, 1963), pp. 82–83.

    15.  *Ieremias*, p. 128, n. 1.

    16.  Not exclusively; there are some 𝔐 plusses with צבאות which are
in free contexts.

## APPENDIX D

*Hebrew Texts of Jeremiah from Qumrân*

This appendix presents, in a preliminary form, transcriptions of most of the extant fragments of the Qumrân Jeremiah fragments 4QJer[a] and 4QJer[b]. These fragmentary manuscripts, both from Cave IV, will be published with photographs in the official series by Frank M. Cross. Meanwhile, Professor Cross has enabled me to study the photographs and to discuss with him the decipherment of broken letters. The present transcription has been checked, in part, with him; but final responsibility of course rests with me.

No attempt is made here to reconstruct the original columns; and, except where considerations of space clearly suggest reconstruction of lacunae in accordance with 𝔐 or 𝔊, textual notes will discuss only readings on the leather. Again, merely orthographic variants will be ignored. The interest for this study is chiefly in the textual position of the two Qumrân manuscripts in relation to 𝔐 on the one hand and 𝔊 on the other. Since, as will be quickly seen, the text type of the two manuscripts is quite unambiguous, there is no need for extended discussion beyond the textual notes. One general comment may be made here: When the reader considers how the readings of 4QJer[b] agree with 𝔊 in ways which quintessentially characterize the divergence of 𝔊 from 𝔐, and if the reader will extrapolate from the extant fragments of 4QJer[b] to a consideration of what the manuscript as a whole must have been like, then he should be left in little doubt that 𝔊 is emphatically, even if not perfectly, a witness to a short Hebrew text of the Book of Jeremiah.

# APPENDIX D

*4QJer^a*

1.  *7.29-9.2*

[כי מאס vacat
[יהוה שמר שקציהם]
[במות התפת אשר בגיא]
[יהם באש אשר לא צויתי]

[בה העם הזה
[הקשבתי ואשמע
[במראתם כסוס
[עגור ישמרו את

[חנני במדבר]
[גדים וידרכו]
רעה יצאו ואת]
[ מואבה כדאלה]

The long omission seems to be a scribal error on the part of the copyist.  The restoration begins between paragraphs, continues down the left margin, and concludes (with a line upside down!) along the lower margin.

7.31 במות ‪M‬Q] τον βωμον 𝔊.

8.3 נאם יהוה צבאות ‪M‬] om. 𝔊.  The restoration of the long scribal omission ends with ‪[הוה צבאות‬, thus agreeing with ‪M‬.

8.5 שובבה ‪M‬Q.  The participle does not agree in gender with its subject, עם, and the ה is taken as dittography.  This agreement in error helps to show the close family connection of ‪M‬ and 4QJer^a.

8.5 העם הזה ‪M‬Q] ο λαος μου 𝔊.

8.6 ‏הק שבתי ואשמע‎ [MQ ενωτισασθε δε και ακουσατε ₡.

2. *9.7-14*

‏[חטו ] נם מרמה דבר בפיו]‎

‏[לה לא אפקד בם נאם יהוה אם בגוי אשר כזה]‎

‏על הרים אשא בכי ונהי ועל נאות מדבר]‎

‏שמעו קול מקנה מעוף השמים ועד בהמה]‎

‏מעון תנים ואת ערי יהודה אתן שממה מב]‎

‏[ה‎                                                  ‏מֵ˚‎¹           ‏[חכם ויבן את זאת ואשר דבר]‎

‏[תי‎       ‏[ה על עׂזׄבׄם את]‎      ‏[וׄה על עׂזׄבׄם את]‎   ‏[נצתה כמדבר מבלי עבר]‎

‏[בה וילכו אחרי ש]‎      ‏[לי ולא]‎      ‏לפניהם ולא]‎

‏[                      vacat                      [‎      ‏אשר למדו˚]‎

‏[ל הנני מאׄכׄלם א]‎      ‏לכן כה אמר]‎

9.7 ‏דבׄר בפיו‎ [MQ τα ρηματα του στοματος αυτων ₡.

9.8 ‏בם‎ MQ] om. ₡.

9.9 ‏ההרים‎ [M₡ ‏הרים‎ Q, by haplography.

9.9 ‏אשא‎ MQ] λαβετε ₡.

9.9 ‏ונהי‎ MQ] om. ₡.

9.12 ‏יהוה‎ MQ] + προς με ₡.

9.12 ‏ולא הלכו בה‎ MQ] om. ₡.

9.14 ‏את העם הזה‎ M] om. ₡.   The phrase is ungrammatical after
‏מאכילם‎, and arose by conflation (see p. 11, no. 7).   Q] ‏מאׄכׄלם‎, in agreement with M, attests the earliness of the conflation.

3. *10.9-14*

‏[ארׄגׄמׄן]‎

‏[מֵלך עולם מקצ]‎

‏[ה תאמרו¹ להם]‎

‏אלה              vacat

vacat

‏עשה]‎

‏[וׄׄצא רוחׄ]‎

‏[רוח בׄ]‎

10.9 ‏ארגמן‎ MQ] this word indicates that, contra ₡ which displays
verse 9 in the middle of verse 5 (as does 4QJer[b]), Q contains the M order
of the text.

10.10  M̶Q] om. verse 10 𝒢.

10.9  כלם חכמים מעשה [M̶ 𝒢 has a text somewhat like this, in the colon before תכלת וארגמן לבושם, but not *after* the latter. If reconstructed with M̶ text in the lacuna, Q displays a line of 55 letters, or what one expects in this scroll.

10.12  עשה M̶Q] ᴋυριος ο ποιησας 𝒢.

10.13  רוח M̶ Q] φως 𝒢.

4.  *11.3-6*

דברי הברית[

תם מארץ מצרים מכור הברזֹ֗ל [ם֗ל]

ס֗ ככל אשר אצוה אתכם והייתם לי לעֹ֗ם

להים למען הקים את השבועה אשר נשבעתי        mg.

ם֗ ארץ]        ]ל[        הזה ראֹ֗ע]

הוה אֹ֗ל]

11.5  השבועה M̶Q] του ορᴋου μου 𝒢.

5.  *12.3-6*

תֹ֗קֹם בֹ֗]

רֹ֗ץ וֹ֗עֹ֗שֹ֗ב כל הֹ֗שֹ֗]

כֹ֗י אמרו לוא יראֹ֗ה יהֹ]

תֹ֗חרה את הסוסים בֹ֗א[]ץ֗]

וֹ֗דֹ ובית אביך גם הֹ֗]

ם֗ כי ידברו אליֹ֗]

הֹ֗ נפֹ֗]

12.3  לטבחהו כצאֹן הֹתקם [M̶ om. 𝒢. Q בֹ֗ל תֹ֗קם[ indicates agreement with M̶.

12.4  כל השדה ועֹשב [M̶Q] ᴋαι πας ο χορτος του αγρου 𝒢.

12.4  יראה [M̶ יראֹה Q. ֹ is unclear; it most resembles כ, and may represent an erased letter. In any case, the problem is internal to Q.

12.4  יראה [M̶ + ο θεος 𝒢/ + יהֹ] Q. Q and 𝒢 may represent different glosses of the previous verb; or they may variously reflect an original subject lost in M̶. In either case, the agreement between Q and 𝒢 is indirect at best, and by itself does not bespeak close familial relation.

12.5  ובארץ [M̶𝒢] ו om. Q, restored above the line.

6.  *12.13-16*

בשׁר מתב]

[שׁכב]                         [אמר]

[נתושׁם]          עמי את ישׁ]   mg.

אן תשׁי]               מ]

[אם למד י]

[מי להשׁבל]

12.13   מתבואתיכם [MQ απο καυχησεως υμων ₵ = (or read) מתפארתכם or
the like.

12.14   כה אמר יהוה [M οτι ταδε λεγει κυριος ₵.  Q lacuna leaves no
room for כי at the beginning of the line.  Letter count suggests that the
previous line was less than column-long and that verse 14 was begun fresh
on the present line.  In a personal communication, Patrick W. Skehan
observes further that "4QJer[a] regularly has a *P*-type interval where MT
calls for *P*, but does *not* observe *s*'s at all, except for a narrow interval after 17.10, so that after 12.13 one must presume a *P*-type interval
and no *ky* at the end of *that* line."  This increases the likelihood that
in this reading Q joins M against ₵.

12.14   נתשׁם [M נתושׁם Q.  Probably error for plene נותשׁם.

7.  *12.17-13.7*

                          vacat

רבשׁתי את] [י ההוא נתוש ואבד נאם יהוה]

כה אמר יהוה א] [הלוך וקנית לך אזור פשתים ו]

תבאהו ואקנה את האזור כדבר יהוה ואשׂם על מתני ו]הה]

שׁנית לאמר קח את האזור אשׁר קנית אשׁר לך מתניך ו]   [פרתה]

שׁם בנקיק הסלע ואלך ואטמנהו בפרתה]   [צוה יהוה]   [הי מקץ ימים

[רבים]   [הוה אלי קום לך]   [שׁר צויתך לטמנו

[שׁמה]

12.17   נאם יהוה [MQ om. ₵.

13.1   אלי [MQ om. ₵.

13.3   שׁנית [MQ om. ₵.

13.3   אשׁר קנית [MQ om. ₵.

13.5   ואלך [MQ om. ₵.

8.   *14.4-7*

באר̇ץ̇ בש̇ר̇ אכ̇ל̇[ו̇]ם̇]

דשא ורפאים עמדו על שפא̇ים שפאו רוח כתנים כלו עיניהם]

[בנו יהוה עשה למען שמך כי רבו מש̇]                    [ל̇ל̇]

14.4   בארץ [M̥Q] om. ₵.

14.6   שפ̇א̇ים [M] שפים Q.   The dots are in the manuscript, to delete erroneous aleph.

14.6   שאפו [M] שפאר Q.   By dittography from the previous error!

14.6   כתנים [M̥Q] om. ₵.

14.7   עשה [M̥Q] + υμιν ₵.

14.7   למען שמך [M̥Q] ενεκεν σου ₵.


9.   *15.1-2*

[מעל פני וה]

[ר למות]

15.1   מעל פני [M̥Q] om. ₵.


10.   *17.8-26*

[ות פרי]       [ב̇ ה]       [

[ש כדרכו כפרי מעליו       קרא ד] [לא ילד]

[עו̇זב̇א̇ו̇ ובאחריתו יהיה נבל       כ̇]       [שרן מן ס̇ם̇]

[       ]       [ח̇יים את יהוה       כל עזביך ימשר יסורי בארץ]

[תהלתי הנה המה אמרים אלי איה]       רפני יהו̇ה̇ וארפה התשעני ו̇]

[נא ואני אצתי מרעה אחריך]       [נרש לא ה̇]  [יתי̇ו]       [ת מרצא̇]

[מ̇חסי אתה ביום]       [כ̇ל̇]       נכח פ̇ד̇ך היה אל תהיה לי [

[ומשנה שבר̇ו̇ן̇]       [יא עליהם יום ש̇]       יחתו המה] [ל אחתה א̇ן̇

כה אמר יהוה [ ] [י ה̇פ̇ל̇ך̇ ו̇]  [שער בני עם אשר יבוא̇ מלך̇ייהודה   ואשר] [בו ובכל]

ירושלם ואמר] [ליהם שמעו] [ה מלכי יהודה וכל יהודה וכל ישבי יר]       [ס̇]

האלה  כה א̇]  [וה השא̇י̇]  [נפ̇ש̇כ̇ם̇ ואל תשא̇ משא ביום השבת והבא]

[צ̇יארו]       [מ̇ב̇ת̇יכם ביום ה]  [בת  וכל מלאכה לא תעשר וקדשתם את]

צ̇] [יתי את אבותיכם ולא שמעו] [לא הטו את אזנם ויקשר את ערפם ל]

רהיה אם שמוע תשמעו̇] אלי בא]       [לבלתי הביא משא בש̇ע̇]

את יום השבת לבלתי עשות בו̇]       [כה ו̇ב̇א̇ו̇ בש̇ע̇]

[א דויד רכבים       ברכב̇]  [בסוסים]

[מ̇ערי יה] [       ה̇]

17.10 כדרכו M[K]Q] κατα τας οδους αυτου ¢M[Q] = 32.19 כדרכיו (¢ κατα την οδον αυτου).

17.10 כפרי MQ] και κατα τους καρπους ¢ = 32.19 וכפרי.

17.10 מעליו Q for מעלליו M is simple haplography.

17.12 שוך מ[קו]ם Q = מראשון מקום M] om. ¢.

17.18 ומשנה MQ] δισσον (om. ו) ¢.

17.19 אלי MQ] om. ¢.

17.19 בשער···בו···בו MQ] εν πυλαις···εν αυταις···εν αυταις ¢.

17.19 עם M[K]Q] λαου σου ¢, העם M[Q].

17.19 יבוא···מלכי Q] יבאו···מלכי M = ¢. Q originally read singular, but is partly corrected (note final kaph) to the prevailing plural tradition. Q's plural reading, with MQ, in verse 20 (מלכי יהודה) suggests that the reading יבוא מלך in verse 19 is internal to Q.

17.20 ישבי MQ] om. ¢.

17.21 בנפשותיכם M] בנפשׁ‎ תיכם Q. ¢ translates both types of phrase in the plural, elsewhere (cf., e.g., Jer. 6.16, 19.7, 48.6), so its reading τας ψυχας υμων cannot be controlled. Since the singular noun with plural suffix occurs about 3 times as often as the plural noun with plural suffix, in M generally, the copyist may simply have rendered according to the more frequent form, and then corrected his own text, and may not reflect a non-M text tradition here.

17.23 ערפם MQ] + υπερ τους πατερας αυτων ¢.

17.24 תשמעון M] תשמעו ן Q. Again, while Q may reflect a non-M tradition, corrected to an M text type, the hand seems to be that of the copyist, perhaps simply correcting his own inadvertent normalizing tendency.

17.24 בה MQ] om. ¢ (see p. 40, no. 33, and n. 15).

11. *18.15-19.1*

top margin

]לם ללכת נתיבות דרך לא סלולה לשום[

]ר עליה ישום ויניד בראשו כרׄ[ ]חׄ קדׄוׄם[

]אם ביום֯ אידם ]

]מרו לכו ונחשבה על ירמיהו מחש[

ודבר מנביא לכו ונכנהו בלשון ואל[

margin ]אל[ ]שׄמע לקול ////ע[ ]ר֯יבי הישלם[

]֯ [ ]֯ לפ֯[ ]לדבר ע֯ל֯[ ]ו֯בה להשיב[

]ו֯ [ ]י֯ חרב ותהינה נש֯[

[כי חרב במלחמ֯ה תשמ֯]
[שיחה ל֯] ל֯ [ופחים]
[תכפ֯ר֯] מ֯ [ ///אא// ]
[הם ]
ו֯ תמ[ז֯קני]

18.16 כל עובר עליה ישם ויניד בראש MQ] παντες οι διαπορευομενοι δι᾽αυτης εκστησονται και κινησουσι την κεφαλην αυτων 𝕲.

18.17 ועדף ולא פנים MQ] om. 𝕲.

18.18 ונחשבה MQ] om. ו 𝕲 (cf. 18.18b, where 𝕲 = MQ ולכו ונכהו).

18.18 ונכנהו Q] ונכהו M = και παταξωμεν αυτον 𝕲. Q is corrupt.

18.18 אל MQ] om. 𝕲.

18.18 כי כרו שוחה לנפשי M] οτι συνελαλησαν ρηματα κατα της ψυχης μου και την κολασιν αυτων εκρυψαν μοι 𝕲. Q is broken here; but M fills the lacuna perfectly, to a line of about 54 characters (in a column of 51–54 letters generally), whereas there is no room for a reading as full as 𝕲. On 𝕲, see pp. 27–28.

18.21 תהיינה. This form of this verb, it may be noted, is spelled תהיינה over 40 times in M generally (including 3 times in Jeremiah), according to Mandelkern. Only twice, in Jer. 48.6 and here, does M read תהינה. Q at this place indicates the earliness of this atypical spelling.

18.22 תשמע MQ] γενηθητω 𝕲.

18.22 שיחה M^KQ] שוחה M^Q = 18.20 M (18.20 is in a Q lacuna).

12. *22.4–16*

[עשר תעשו] א֯ת֯ הד֯]
[ו֯ רכבים ברכב בסוסי]
[נאם יהוה כי לחרבה יהיה]
[גלעד אתה לי ראש הלבנון אם ל֯]
[ש֯חתים איש וכליו וכרתו מבחור]
[אמרו איש֯ על רעהו על מה]
[א֯מ֯ר] [הוה אלהיהם וישא֯ח]

vacat

[ל תגידו לו ב] ל[הולך כי לא ישוב עוד וראה א֯ת]
[ל֯ שלם ב֯] י[אשי] [מלך יהודה֯] [ך תחת יאשיהו אב]
[ל֯ א֯תו] [֯א ל֯ ]
[א[ משפ]

נֹהֹ[]י בית מדות ועליות מ[ ] חֶ֯ים וקרע֯
[תה מ] [חֹ]רה בארז אביך הלוא א֯ל
[ ] ‏ ≥ ‏ ראביין אז טוב הלוא הוא]
end of column

22.4   רכבים [MQ καὶ επιβεβηκοτες ₡.

22.4   ובסוסים [M] בסוסים [Q/ καὶ ιππων ₡.

22.7   מבחור ארזיך [M] מבחר ארזיך Q.   Cf. מבחור בראשיו in 2 Kgs.
19.23 (= מבחר ··· Isa. 37.24), and עיר מבחור 2 Kgs. 3.19.  The same imagery
marks all the passages.  Occurring in three different places, מבחור may
not be "scribal error...for מבחר" (BDB, p. 104b), but a genuine variant
form obscured in M of Isa. 37.24 and Jer. 22.7.

22.8   על רעהו [M] אל רעהו Q.  Copyist's error, in anticipation of
the following על-מה.

22.11   מלך יהודה [MQ] om. ₡.

22.14   ועליות [MQ] om. ו ₡.

22.14   וקרע [MQ] διεσταλμενα ₡.

22.15   בארז [MQ] εν Αχας ₡.

22.15-16 M and ₡ diverge at several points.  A number of them occur
in Q lacunae.  The M text fills the Q lacunae nicely, to give lines of
about 54 letters, the average for this column.  As for readings on the
leather:

    (a) verse 16 עני ואביון M is reflected by Q: ////ראביין , in con-
        trast to ουδε κρισιν πενητος ₡.

    (b) verse 16 אז טוב [MQ] om. ₡.

22.16   היא [M] הוא Q (cf. BH[3]: K[Or] (הוא)/τουτο ₡.

*4QJer[b]*

1.   *9.22-10.18*

[מהו ואל יתה]

[ ] וצדקה בארץ כי

[ ]ק//////ה הישב[]ט

[א]ל-דרך הגוים

[ ] ב‏ ייפהו במקבות

[ ]תכלת וארגמן

[ ]יאבדו מן ארעה

[צה ]  וץ ברקים

[ בעת  פקדתים

[ל[ו]את ישבו]

This fragment appears to be from a column of some 95-105 letters in width, judging from lines where $\mathfrak{G}$ and $\mathfrak{M}$ are in basic quantitative agreement, and from lines in which $\mathfrak{M}$ text vastly overflows the lacunae and $\mathfrak{G}$ text fills them nicely. Given the extraordinary line length, it is impossible to judge Q's allegiance in questions of minor quantitative divergence between $\mathfrak{M}$ and $\mathfrak{G}$. But this broken text does witness dramatically to its family connections, in that, as Cross observes (*ALQ*[2], p. 187, n. 38), "with LXX, 4QJer[b] transposes v. 5 after v. 9, and omits vv. 6-8 and 10. It will be noted also that 4Q transposes MT *bmsmrwt wbmqbwt* to read *bmqbwt [w(b)msmrwt]* with LXX, εν σφυραις και ηλοις." Three other readings on the leather may also be noted.

10.2 ‫דרך‬ $\mathfrak{M}$Q] οδους $\mathfrak{G}$. Just the opposite variants appear in the similar verse, Jer. 12.16: ‫דרכי‬ $\mathfrak{M}$] ‫דרך‬ $\mathfrak{G}$. Such variants occur easily, even within text families, given the common occurrence of both ‫דרך‬ and ‫דרכי‬.

10.11 ‫מארעא‬ $\mathfrak{M}$] ‫מן ארעא‬ 4QJer[b]. The $\mathfrak{M}$ form represents Hebraicization of the properly uncontracted Aramaic form, an incidental hint that $\mathfrak{M}$ stems from a "busier" textual transmission history than Q and $\mathfrak{G}$-*Vorlage* generally.

10.15 ‫פקדתם‬ $\mathfrak{M}\mathfrak{G}$] ‫פקדתים‬ Q. See the discussion below, p. 218, n. 24. Q here is secondary.

## 2.  43.3-9

[חנו ב[ב]ל ]ו[לא]שמע י]וחנן[וכל]שרי הח[י]ליס͏̊ וכל

העם בקול יהוה לשבת בארץ יהודה ו]י[קח יו]חנן [וכל ש[רי]החֿ]ילם את כל שארית

יהודה אשר שבו לגור בארֿ[צ]מצרי[ם את הגברים ואת הנשים ואת הטף ואת בנות

המלך ואת ]כל{ הנפש אשר הני]חֿ נבוזרדן את גדליהו בן אחיקם ואת ירמיהו הנביא

ואת ברוך בן נריהו ויבאו א[רץ מצרים כי לא שמעו בקול יהוה]ויבֿאֿוֿ]תחפנחס

ויהי דבר יהוה אל ירמיהו]בתחפנחס לאמר קח בידך אבנים גדלות וטמנתם

[אשר בפתח בתחפנחס לעיני אנֿשים יהודים

Characters per line:  53, 53, 54/56, 53, 52.

43.4 ‫בן קרח‬ $\mathfrak{M}$] om. Q$\mathfrak{G}$.

## APPENDIX D

43.5   בן קרח [M] om. Q₡.

43.5   החילים [M₡] [החה]ילם Q; copyist's error.

43.5   מכל הגוים אשר נדחו שם [M] om. ₡. Q has a lacuna here, which cannot contain the M plus, but which fills out nicely with ₡ text. For fuller comment on this reading, see p. 53, no. 141.

43.5   בארץ יהודה [M] εν τη γη ₡/ בארץ[י][מצרי]ם Q. The tail of the ץ of ארץ is barely visible; but the final ם of מצרים is totally visible. The preceding verb לגור suggests that מצרים is original (cf. 42.15, 17.22, 43.2); a reference to resettlement in the homeland by the verb גור would be odd indeed (cf. the use of ישב in 42.10,13). M יהודה arose probably in connection with the inclusion of the long gloss in verse 5. Whether Q מצרים is a gloss, or ₡ om. is by error, is hard to say.

43.6   כל [M] om. ₡. Q has a lacuna here. Inclusion of כל would give a line of 56 letters, longer than the preceding two, each of which extends further left at the margin (by a couple of letters) than this line. Omission of כל would give a nice fit of 54. But Q at this point must be considered uncertain.

43.6   רב טבחים [M] om. Q₡.

43.6   בן שפן [M] om. Q₡.

43.7   ארץ [MQ] om. ₡. The designations מצרים and ארץ מצרים are both frequent; so that agreement of Q and M here, on a plus, may be coincidental and is not a significant indicator of familial allegiance.

43.7   עד [M] There seems to be no room in the tiny lacuna of Q for עד. Moreover, the tops of the letters for באו seem to be partly visible, immediately before the place name. Cf., in the same verse, ויבאו ארץ מצרים. At both points ₡ reads εἰς. Since ₡ usually renders עד with ἑως (cf. 25.3, 31.38,39, 48.34), ₡ εἰς may render ויבאו + place name. If so, ₡ and Q would agree again against M, at the end of the verse.

43.9   קח בידך [MQ] λαβε σεαυτῳ ₡. At Jer. 38.10, ₡ renders this phrase λαβε εις τας χειρας σου. At 43.9, therefore, it seems that ₡ represents a Hebrew text assimilated to the much more common idiom קח לך.

43.9   In this verse, each text goes its own way: ואבמלט במלבן אשר] om. ₡, probably by haplography, בֶמלטֹבַפתח. Q cannot agree with ₡ here, as even with M text in the lacuna, the reconstructed line would be too short at 39 letters. Clearly Q had a fuller, and perhaps less cryptic, reading than M. On the other hand, בית פרעה [M₡] om. 4Q, likewise probably by haplography, בֶפתחׄבַֹחדׄפנחס. It is tempting to reconstruct Q as

follows: ‏במלט במלבן במשער בית פרעה] אשר בפתח בחהפנחס לעיני אנשים יהודים‎.
This 50-letter line (on the left margin, the shortest of the extant
lines by 3 or 4 letters) would fit nicely. But the ‏ב‎ after ‏פתח‎ spoils
what would otherwise idiomatically resemble Gen. 38.14 (‏בפתח עינים‎), and
gives awkward sense, indicating the likelihood of haplography, and so
leaving the student curious but in the dark.

43.9 ‏אנשים יהודים‎ ₥Q] ανδρων Ιουδα ₵. ₵, or ₵-*Vorlage*, has probably assimilated to more common ‏אנשי יהודה‎.


Note: The first variant in 43.9 (‏קח בידך\לך‎), and the last one in
this same verse (‏אנשים\אנשי‎•••), would tend to suggest that the *Vorlage*
was not a direct ancestor of 4QJer[b], but that, even though it could have
been an older manuscript, it represents a slightly different branch of
the Egyptian family. Thus, while on the one hand its basic character is
resoundingly like that of 4QJer[b], yet these two exemplars were not so
directly, or perhaps I should say, so closely, aligned as ₥ and 4QJer[a]
(most of whose non-₥ readings probably are internal).

3. *50.4-6*

‏ובעח‎
                    ‏נאם יהוה]‎   m
              ‏ראת יהוה אלהיהם]‎   a
                                  r
           ‏אל יהוה ברית עולם]‎    g
            ‏שובבום מהר ]ל גב]‎    i
                                  n

This fragment has only one reading: ‏נאם יהוה‎ ₥Q] om. ₵. This is the
only instance where 4QJer[b] sides with ₥ against a characteristic ₵ zero
variant. Against this we must weigh the much more striking allegiance
with ₵ against ₥, in the two larger fragments.

NOTES

NOTES TO CHAPTER I

1. For bibliography see Frank Moore Cross, *The Ancient Library of Qumrân*, rev. ed. (Garden City, New York: Doubleday and Co., Inc., 1961) hereafter *ALQ*$^2$, esp. chap. 4; "The History of the Biblical Text in the Light of Discoveries in the Judean Desert," *HTR* 57 (1964), 281-299; "The Contribution of the Qumrân Discoveries to the Study of the Biblical Text," *IEJ* 16/2 (1966), 81-95. Also Patrick W. Skehan, "The Biblical Scrolls from Qumran and the Text of the Old Testament," *BA* 28/3 (1965), 87-100. Old problems are treated from the new vantage point by Dominique Barthé-lemy, *Les Devanciers d'Aquila* (Leiden: E. J. Brill, 1963); James D. Shenkel, *Chronology and Recensional Development in the Greek Text of Kings* (Cambridge: Harvard University Press, 1968); Kevin G. O'Connell, *The Theodotionic Revision of the Book of Exodus* (Cambridge: Harvard University Press, 1972); and the Harvard University Ph.D. dissertations of Bruce K. Waltke, "Prolegomena to the Samaritan Pentateuch" (1965), and Ralph W. Klein, "Studies in the Greek Texts of the Chronicler" (1966).

2. H. M. Orlinsky, "The Textual Criticism of the Old Testament," in *The Bible and the Ancient Near East*, ed. G. Ernest Wright (Garden City, New York: Doubleday and Co., Inc., 1961), hereafter *BANE*, p. 121. To imply that previous studies of the problem are all incompetent is simply wrong. The discussion is indeed cluttered with a good deal of deadwood. But it is also studded with a fine display of text-critical acumen. Much remains to be done, yet the final solution, in its broad lines, lies not far from one of the positions held in the last century.

3. About one-eighth of the Masoretic total. This often quoted figure is based on the count of Graf, p. xliii.

4. The term "omission" is used here and throughout in a neutral sense, to indicate the absence of material in one tradition which is present in another, without implying the cause of the divergence or the preferable reading. The term "zero variant," which is coined as a preferable (because less suggestive) synonym of "omission," is used to refer to a textual variant of the sort "X] om. Y," where "Y" may be said to be a zero variant to the text "X." On the other hand, a "content variant" consists of a word or group of words in one text witness which differs from the word or group of words occurring in the corresponding place in another witness.

5.   Johann Gottfried Eichhorn, *Einleitung in das Alte Testament*, vol. 4 (Göttingen, 1824), pp. 170-222.

6.   M. G. L. Spohn, *Ieremias Vates e versione Iudaeorum Alexandrinorum ac reliquorum interpretum graecorum emendatus notisque criticis illustratus*, vol. 1 (Leipzig, 1824), pp. 1-21.

7.   "What the Greek translator omitted, *he either did not have before his eyes, or did not wish to translate a second time*" (italics Spohn's, *ibid.*, p. 4.

8.   The Latin text reads:   "Interpres ille fuit homo privatus, nec publica auctoritate hunc in se suscepit laborem; *quod, quia conceditur, non probo*, sed ex hoc concludo, interpretem ea, quae iam verterat, et iam vertere se meminerat, omittere potuisse" (italics mine), *ibid.*, p. 7.

9.   F. C. Movers, *De utriusque recensionis Vaticinorum Ieremiae, graecae alexandrinae et hebraicae masorethicae, indole et origine commentatio critica* (Hamburg, 1837).

10.   A summary may be found in C. Schulz, *De Jeremiae textus hebraici masorethici et graeci Alexandrini discrepantia* (Treptow, 1861).

11.   K. H. Graf, *Der Prophet Jeremiah* (Leipzig, 1862), pp. xl-lvii.

12.   *Ibid.*, p. xliv.

13.   *Ibid.*, p. xliv.

14.   Graf gives examples of variation in person, number, noun versus pronoun, free translation, of the sort similarly assembled later by Giesebrecht (see chap. V).   It must be stated that the great majority of the examples are entirely unconvincing and that one can only wonder that anyone could have accepted them as evidence for the conclusions which he drew.

15.   Graf, p. lvi.

16.   A. Scholz, *Der masorethische Text und die LXX-Uebersetzung des Buches Jeremias* (Regensburg, 1875).

17.   *Ibid.*, pp. 12-21.

18.   Scholz here cites 30.10-11//46.26-27 and 48.40//49.22, in each instance of which the former is omitted in $\mathfrak{G}$.   However, he overlooks the fact that in $\mathfrak{G}$, with its different order (chap. 46 is before chap. 30, chap. 49 before chap. 48), the two missing occurrences would have been in *second* position, so that his point is mistaken.

19.   G. C. Workman, *The Text of Jeremiah* (Edinburgh, 1889).

20.   See the justly critical reviews of S. R. Driver, "The Double

Text of Jeremiah," *Expositor*, third series, 9 (1889), 321–337, and H. P.
Smith, "Prof. Workman on the Variations between the Hebrew and Greek Text
of Jeremiah," *JBL* 9 (1890), 107–117.

21. A. W. Streane, *The Double Text of Jeremiah* (Cambridge: D. Bell
and Co., 1896). The more recent monograph of Paul Volz, *Studien zum Text
des Jeremia* (Leipzig: J. C. Hinrichs, 1920), is a systematic treatment of
individual textual problems, but does not take up the general question of
the two text types. A Ph.D. dissertation by A. P. Hastoupis, "The Septuagint Text of the Book of Jeremiah" (Northwestern University, 1957),
contains an analysis of the first 25 chapters of Jeremiah. I have examined the dissertation and have found it to be of little use, as it does
not advance the discussion beyond previous works.

22. O. Eissfeldt, *The Old Testament: An Introduction* (New York and
Evanston, 1965).

23. H. Wildberger, "Jeremia," *RGG*, 3rd edition, III, 585.

24. J. Muilenburg, "Jeremiah," *IDB*, II, 834.

25. Wilhelm Rudolph, *Jeremia*, Handbuch zum Alten Testament 12,
second revised edition (Tübingen: J. C. B. Mohr [Paul Siebeck], 1958),
xxi (italics mine).

26. On 4QJer$^a$, see F. M. Cross, *ALQ*$^2$, p. 187 ("The longer recension is also present at Qumrân"). Also, his "The Development of the
Jewish Scripts," *BANE*, p. 137, fig. 1, lines 3, 5, and commentary. Further, D. N. Freedman, "The Massoretic Text and the Qumran Scrolls: A
Study in Orthography," *Textus* 2 (1962), 87–102. A transcription of most
of the fragments of 4QJer$^a$ is given in Appendix D.

27. Official publication of the Jeremiah materials from Cave IV
is in the hands of Professor Cross. In the meantime, he has generously
given me permission to publish a transcription. This is given in Appendix D, along with some textual comments. In addition to these three
Cave IV manuscripts, we have one other piece of evidence, 2QJer, which
generally agrees with 𝕸, though containing the occasional 𝕲 reading (see
chap. III, p. 57 and n. 64).

28. For a minimizing view of the character of 𝕲-*Vorlage*, see
Rudolph, pp. xx–xxi, "Die hebräische Vorlage von 𝕲 steht dem heutigen 𝕸
viel näher als man früher dachte; vollends in 𝕲 und 𝕸 zwei verschiedene
'Rezensionen' zu sehen (Movers u.a.) geht nicht an." A similar statement appeared in Eissfeldt's *Einleitung*, 2nd ed., p. 422, but significantly

was replaced in the third edition with a noncommittal reference to the
new evidence from Qumran. The exegetical approach to Septuagint studies
characterizes the works of H. S. Gehman and his students. See also M.
Goshen-Gottstein, "Theory and Practice of Textual Criticism," *Textus* 3
(1963), 130–158, esp. 137, n. 18.

29. Hyatt, p. 791.

30. "A textual critic engaged upon his business is...like a dog
hunting for fleas. If a dog hunted for fleas on mathematical principles,
basing his researches on statistics of area and population, he would
never catch a flea except by accident. They require to be treated as
individuals; and every problem which presents itself to the textual
critic must be regarded as possibly unique." *A. E. Housman: Selected
Prose*, ed. John Carter (Cambridge: University Press, 1961), 132–133.

31. We may refer to the Samaritan Pentateuch or the Lucianic
recension of the Septuagint. Both contain old, original readings, which
can be ferreted out only by minute analysis of each reading on its own
merits. Yet it is clear that each of these two text types can be described in generalized statements which are both accurate and helpful,
and to say less would be not "prudence" but abdication of the text-
critical task. It is just such abdication, I suspect, which lies behind
the middle position of recent commentators on Jeremiah. It appears that
careful and systematic establishment of the text—the obvious starting
point of study of any ancient written materials—is no longer considered
integral to the exegetical task. While the versions are consulted at
points where the Hebrew text is patently corrupt or secondary, this
"textual criticism" is performed all too frequently, and unsatisfactorily,
in an ad hoc manner. In the absence of systematic textual criticism and
a resultant assessment of the textual character of 𝔊 and 𝔐, a compromise
position is adopted in theory. But since the exegesis proceeds on the
basis of the Hebrew text so long as it yields good sense, in practice
there is an implicit judgment in favor of *Hebraica veritas*. (On this
tendency at the present time, see the discussion and references in Cross,
*ALQ*², pp. 176–177.) Ironically, the result—an implicit general preference for 𝔐—is the exact opposite of the method urged by Hyatt, Rudolph,
*et al.*!

32. In the Pentateuch and the Historical Books the Septuagint
generally contains a fuller text than does 𝔐 (see F. M. Cross, *HTR* 57

[1964], 290, and *IEJ* 16 [1966], 81–95). However this fuller text is to
be explained, it clearly provides no evidence for condensation as a *general* procedure among the Alexandrian Jews who produced the Greek Old
Testament. In this connection, three special problems deserve brief
comment: After lengthy study of the textual problems of Job, Harry M.
Orlinsky has concluded that the shorter Greek text rests on a short
(though not necessarily superior) Hebrew text; see his article, "The
Textual Criticism of the Old Testament," *BANE*, p. 151, and references
there. The short text of the canonical parts of 1 Esdras likewise reflects a correspondingly short (and usually superior) Semitic *Vorlage*,
in comparison with the Masoretic text of Chronicles-Ezra-Nehemiah. See
now Ralph W. Klein, "Studies in the Greek Texts of the Chronicler." The
short Greek text of the latter part of Exodus may be due to translation
procedure (see D. W. Gooding, *The Account of the Tabernacle* [Cambridge,
1959]), though in view of the new developments in textual criticism and
the Exodus manuscripts from Qumrân, this problem needs re-examination. But
even if $\mathfrak{G}$ is condensed here, the reasons for condensation would be closely
linked to the exceptional nature of the material--almost verse-for-verse
reproduction of several chapters of architectural description--so that
this would constitute a special case.

33.  4QJer[b], and the synoptic passage in 2 Kings (see pp. 70 and
69).

34.  "One of the axioms of classical textual criticism is *brevior
lectio potior*, that is, the shorter of two readings is probably original.
This principle,...has been accepted as generally valid by both classical
and Biblical scholars." B. M. Metzger, *The Text of the New Testament*
(New York: Oxford University Press, 1964), p. 161.

35.  This tendency may be illustrated from widely diverse literatures. On secondary expansion in the *Iliad* and the *Mahābhārata*, see B.
M. Metzger, "Recent Trends in the Textual Criticism of the Iliad and the
Mahābhārata," *Chapters in the History of New Testament Textual Criticism*
(Leiden, E. J. Brill, 1963), pp. 142–154, and references there. Among
several texts of the Akkadian Epic section *Gilgamesh and the Land of the
Living*, "there is the very unusual and minutely written UM 29-13-209 +
29-16-414,...[which] seems to have a much more expanded text than our
reconstructed version" (S. N. Kramer, "Gilgamesh and the Land of the
Living," *JCS* 1 [1947], 7). W. F. Albright comments on "the tendency of

ancient Oriental scribes and compilers to add rather than to subtract."
He writes, "successive editions of the Egyptian mortuary texts known as
the Book of the Dead illustrate this process of expansion by addition,
especially when a given text can be traced from the Pyramids of the Sixth
Dynasty through the Coffin Texts of the Twelfth to successive recensions
of the Book of the Dead proper (from the Eighteenth Dynasty to the
Hellenistic-Roman age)," *From Stone Age to Christianity*, 2nd ed. (Garden
City, New York: Doubleday and Co., Inc., 1957), p. 80. The best example
in the New Testament is the Syrian text, where "new omissions...are rare....
New interpolations on the other hand are abundant, most of them being due
to harmonistic or other assimilation" (F. J. Hort, quoted in Metzger, *The
Text of the New Testament*, pp. 131-132). Finally, in the Old Testament
the Samaritan text has long been recognized as a developed text. Recent
studies have shown that this developed text was characteristic of the
Palestinian tradition generally in the Pentateuch. The same is true in
Samuel. (For further characterization of the Palestinian text type, see
chap. VIII, pp. 129-131.)

    36. F. M. Cross, *HTR* 57 (1964), 289-290.

## NOTES TO CHAPTER II

1. Perhaps the prime example of this type of textual development
is the Lucianic recension of the Septuagint. For convenient descriptions
of the character of this recension, see the introductions in Ziegler's
critical editions.

2. For a thorough discussion of the origin and formation of double
readings in the Masoretic text, together with abundant examples, see S.
Talmon, "Double Readings in the Massoretic Text," *Textus* 1 (1960), 144-
184; "Synonymous Readings in the Old Testament," *Scripta Hierosolymitana*,
VIII, *Studies in the Bible*, ed. Chaim Rabin (Jerusalem: Magnes Press,
1961), 335-383, and "Aspects of the Textual Transmission of the Bible in
the Light of Qumran Manuscripts," *Textus* 4 (1964), 95-132.

3. Interestingly, while in 10.25 B (γενεας) = 𝔐, Q-534-613, L' C'
Bo Aeth read βασιλειας, probably reflecting a Hebrew tradition which
read ממלכות.

4. "Leading in the way/wilderness" is a common motif in the O.T.
Note the correction of L-62-613 Arm Tht: εν τω καιρω αγοντος 36 εν τη
ερημω!

5. דל, עני, נקי, אביון, etc., occur interchangeably in parenetic
or accusatory contexts.

6. On 23.17 see, however, p. 28, no. 22.

7. Contrast Paul Volz, *Studien zum Text des Jeremia*, BWAT 25
(Leipzig: J. C. Hinrichs, 1920), p. 60: "Es empfiehlt sich nicht, שררות
zu streichen, da dieser Ausdruck dem Bearbeiter, der hier schreibt, von
jeremian. Texten her geläufig war; andererseits wüsste man nicht zu
sagen, wie מעצות hereingekommen sein sollte." But Volz's attempt to
apply the principle *lectio difficilior* will not stand up. For one thing,
a possible source for במעצות is easily found--as others have already
pointed out, Ps. 81.13 provides ample occasion for the secondary intrusion of this word into Jer. 7.24. On the other hand, it is unlikely
that the original text would have such a variant in an otherwise set
phrase for which (in contrast to the synonymous variants referred to
immediately below) there is no synonymous variant in the O.T. The secondary infection of a standard cliché which originally was fixed in its
literary context may be illustrated in two interestingly related series
of expressions: (i) Jer. 30.11 (שם) הפצותיך אשר הגוים בכל) *vs.* 46.28

(and 10 other places) הֶדִּיחֲךָ. The atypical verb in 30.11 occurs, significantly, in a passage which is omitted in ⅁ and is a secondary doublet of
46.28. (ii) Ezek. 4.13 (שם) אֲדִיחֵם (אֲשֶׁר בַּגּוֹיִם) vs. Ezek. 20.41 (and 5
other places similarly) נְפֹצֹתֶם. Again, the atypical usage in Ezekiel 4.13
is absent in ⅁ and is to be taken as cross-infection from Jeremiah.

8. It is odd that the Hexaplaric "correction" is not really a correction to 𝕸 (*pace* Ziegler's apparatus), but a conflation of ⅁ εξανηλωσαν
and its later replacement, συνετελεσαν. The absence of a Hexaplaric correction to the full text of 𝕸 further suggests the latter's late, conflated character.

9. Cf. ανηγαγεν C'; and ανηγαγεν και συνηγαγεν Q-26-46-239-538-
544-613 Aeth, which may be a conflation of the two readings. Note that
in ⅁, vv. 7-8 appear after v. 40; cf. apparatus to *both* places.

10. For זֶרַע יִשְׂרָאֵל, cf. 2 Kgs. 17.20, and 6 other places.

11. Interestingly, the verb of ⅁-*Vorlage* is the verb of (B)-Ketib!
That is, following לְמַעַן, the form would have to be pointed as an infini-
tive. The Ketib suggests a Hebrew text tradition in which (B) contained
the negative לְמַעַן לֹא, allowing a perfect form to follow.

12. In 7.6, לְרַע לָכֶם is translated εις κακον υμιν. ⅁-*Vorlage* read
לְהָרַע לָכֶם here (Cross has informed me that the development of לְרַע from
לְהָרַע—omitting ה which was not pronounced—is frequent at Qumran). But
in Jer. α, the hiphil otherwise is rendered by κακοποιεω (4.22, 10.5) or
πονηρευω (16.12, 20.13; cf. 23.14), or is mistaken for the noun (13.23:
τα κακα).

13. Syriac has (A) and (B), but in reverse order. For another
example of the variants (A) and (B), compare 1 Kgs. 10.15 כָּל מַלְכֵי הָעֶרֶב//
2 Chr. 9.14 כָּל מַלְכֵי עֲרָב.

14. For similar confusion (in the opposite direction) of כ/ר, cf.
2 Sam. 22.12 חַשְׁרַת/ Ps. 18.12 חֶשְׁכַת.

15. Cf. Rudolph, p. 150, and reference there to F. Perles, *Analek-
ten zur Textkritik des AT*, New Series (1922), 39.100.

16. In this passage another *atbash* cipher in 𝕸 occurs in a secondary addition: v. 26 [וּמֶלֶךְ שֵׁשַׁךְ יִשְׁתֶּה אַחֲרֵיהֶם] om. ⅁ On v. 26, and the
*atbash* in Jeremiah generally, see p. 227, n. 3.

17. וְנָפְלָתֶם כִּכְלִי חֶמְדָּה does not make sense. ⅁ κριοι suits the context, and is to be preferred. While κριοι translates אַדִּירִים in verses
34, 35, 36, it is the standard translation of אַיִל in the Septuagint.

Probably 𝔊 read אֵילֵי; and possibly the variants arose by attraction of
כְּאֵילֵי הַמְדָּה to the phrase כְּלִי הֶמְדָּה (5 times elsewhere in O.T.). The form
וּתְפוֹצוֹתִיכֶם is obscure, but probably reflects some form of the verb נפץ
"to shatter" (cf. Syriac, and other instances of נפץ used to describe
breaking of vessels). In our projected variants we follow John Bright,
*Jeremiah*, The Anchor Bible, vol. 21 (Garden City, New York: Doubleday
and Co., Inc., 1965), p. 159.

18. So, e.g., Rudolph in BH[3] and Bright.

19. With 𝔊, Targum, and 46.16, 50.16; 𝔐 is by anticipation of the
following phrase.

20. As argued in chapter IV, the late spelling נְבוּכַדְנֶאצַּר indicates
the secondary occurrence of the name elsewhere in chapters 27-29, and
probably here also.

21. BH[3]: "3 MSS 𝔊 𝔄"; but Ziegler's apparatus gives no indication
of such a reading in the Arabic version. G. R. Driver's comment (*Textus*
4 [1964], 83), "Jehoiakim must be an error for Zedekiah (LXX)," is inexplicable; 𝔊 contains no such reading.

22. See J. Bright, *A History of Israel*, second edition (Philadelphia: The Westminster Press, 1972), pp. 328-329.

23. If 𝔊 is represented by B-S Bo Aeth Arab (as is probable), then
A-mss. Sa Q-V-(omn) C' represent a very early correction in the direction
of 𝔐, for the genitive absolute construction in this context cannot be so
late as 𝔊^καιγε (βασιλευοντος in O represents the Greek tradition which
was Origen's base text, and which he did not take the trouble to alter).
But further, it is unlikely that in any period the participle was used to
render מַמְלֶכֶת. Rather, βασιλευοντος may reflect a Hebrew מֶלֶךְ = *mulk*,
"kingdom, reign." On the existence of a date formula [x] לִמְלֹךְ [y] בִּשְׁנַת
where מֶלֶךְ = *mulk*, see my Harvard University Ph.D. dissertation, "Studies
in the Text of Jeremiah" (1965), pp. 61-68, Excursus on — מַלְכוּת — מַמְלָכָה
מֶלֶךְ.

24. G. R. Driver, who dates chapters 27-28 בְּרֵאשִׁית מַמְלֶכֶת צִדְקִיָּהוּ,
explains the secondary development of (A) as due to abbreviation of an
original בְּשָׁנָה הָרִאשׁוֹנָה > בְּמ בר [*sic*! printer's error for בְּמ הר], the latter then having been mistaken for בְּשָׁנָה הָרְבִיעִית (*Textus* 4 [1964], p. 86).
But Driver's attempt to explain variation in numbers generally as resulting from abbreviations using only the first letter of the number-name must
be rejected. While the use of the letters of the alphabet in their order

to represent numbers is well known in later extra-biblical materials, Driver can adduce no epigraphic data in support of the practice in early biblical texts. It is incredible to suppose, for example, that ש could represent, variously, שלשה שנים, שמנה שבעים, שבע שמים, שמה שלשים (*Textus* 4 [1964], 82; see also his article, "Abbreviations in the Massoretic Text," *Textus* 1 [1960], 125). The implausible length to which he would take this theory is shown in his treatment of 2 Kgs. 2.24 (*Textus* 1 [1960], 126), involving שתים דבים and ארבעים ושני ילדים. The number 42 "can be extracted from דב 'bear' read as ד = (אַרְבַּע read as ארבע' =) ארבעים 'forty' *plus* ב = שנים 'two,' while the odd 'two' was further taken for the number of the she-bears themselves."

Returning to the problem of Jer. 28.1, we cannot get rid of משנה/ת הרביעית by recourse to Driver's supposed abbreviation. But in any case, his arguments for dating chapters 27-28 בראשית ממלכת צדקיהו are unconvincing. For example, one of his main points is that in Zedekiah's fourth year the king went to Babylon (Jer. 51.59), and (Driver supposes) as the trip would have taken the greater part of the year, there would have been no time in the fourth year for the embassy visit of 27.3. But this is sheer speculation, rendered all the more flimsy by the fact that 51.59 M את צדקיהו "with Z." is rendered in 𝔊 παρα Σεδ.(מאת צדקיהו), so that we cannot even be sure that the king himself went to Babylon!

25. Ziegler, adopting the emendation of Schleusner (= v. 11 ανεωγμενον 106); the form ανεγνωσμενον is in all manuscripts and versions.

26. Cf. Y. Yadin, *IEJ* 12 (1962), pp. 235-238; also Bright and Rudolph in their commentaries on this passage.

27. Usually the two portions are more or less identical, according to Yadin.

28. Or haplography may have occurred in M-𝔊 archetype, and was wrongly restored in proto-M, belonging perhaps after ואת הגלוי.

One cannot argue (as, e.g., Duhm) the secondary character of the phrase from the unique meaning which המצוה is here required to bear. It is entirely possible that the term was a *terminus technicus* applying to legal documents. On the other hand, Bright's suggestion, that 𝔊 omits the words "possibly because they were not understood," is unconvincing. Even if the precise meaning in this context were unclear (which, in view of the common public use of such purchase deeds in Egypt and Palestine, early and late, is highly unlikely), the meaning of the individual words

themselves would be patently obvious. Elsewhere the translator attempted
to render, as conscientiously as he knew, words and phrases which (in the
sense in which he took them) made very awkward sense (cf, 46.25, where
אמון מנא is rendered τον Αμων τον υιον αυτης, reading בנא or בנה). In
the latter instance the text was translated after a fashion, though its
sense must have been anything but clear.

29. It is striking that both pairs of words have letters 1, 2, and
5 in common. In each pair, the fourth letters are easily confused. Duhm
(cf. Ehrlich) espouses a similar explanation. Of course it is also possible that the words in 𝔐 are a later explanatory gloss.

30. Synonymous, that is, in the context of this book, in which Nebuchadrezzar is represented as king of all the earth. On the synonymous
variants ממלכה/ממשלה, see further Talmon, "Synonymous Readings in the
Old Testament," *Scripta Hierosolymitana* VIII, 380, on Isa. 39:2: 𝔐 ממשלתו,
12 Isa^a ממלכתו.

31. Cf. 25.26 𝔐 האדמה על פני הארץ אשר כל הממלכות. הארץ is om. 𝔊
Syr, and ה(ממלכות) indicates that originally in proto-𝔐 also the phrase
was על אשר הממלכות כל. הארץ was filled in according to the common
phrase הארץ ממלכות כל (Jer. 15.4 and parallels), creating a minor inconcinnity.

32. On traces of proto-𝔐 revision in Q-V-etc., see Ziegler, *Ieremias*, pp. 63-64.

33. The development of this conflate reading is mechanically similar to that in 25.6-7 (see p. 13, no. 17). This development is obscured
by the apparatus to BH[3], which has 𝔊 omitting the second variant. Further, BH[3] "dl 𝔊𝔖" is misleading; Syr does not support 𝔊, but omits from
המלך בנות את through to במצפה, and hence is defective by haplography,
במצפה 1°⌐2°, thereby indirectly reflecting the conflate tradition of 𝔐.

34. Cf. Ziegler, *Beiträge*, p. 87, against BH[3] "dittogr."

35. G. R. Driver explains this variation as owing to the abbreviation א or אנ, taken in two different ways (*Textus* 4 [1964], 80-81).
But as both phrases are ubiquitous and as the difference is merely the
presence or absence of ה, his postulated abbreviation is unnecessary, not
to say unlikely.

36. Cf. S. Talmon, *Textus* 1 (1960), 163-164.

37. For (A), see Deut. 29.25, 32.17, Jer. 19.4; for (B) see Deut.
11.28, 13.3, Jer. 7.9.

38. That is, an asterisk represents των κακων των in first occurrence, των κακων where Greek των κακων υμιν = רעתכם, and και των κακων των in all other occurrences. Also, πατ. = πατερων, βασ. = βασιλεων, αρχ. = αρχοντων, γυν. = γυναικων.

39. In these verses, Targ Vulg = Ӎ, while ₲ Syr prefix the conjunction also to מלכי/-.

40. In this instance, the orthographic argument by itself would not bear much weight. But combined with the argument concerning ראו רעתכם, and the textual and stylistic arguments against the originality of any reference in the series to wives, the orthography would appear to be significant.

41. Or perhaps מלכיכם, with C'-613 and 88, unless they are harmonizing with verses 17, 21. Both here and at the end of the series, it is difficult to decide whether 88 represents post-Origenic conflation or a pre-Origenic text basically like C'-613 but with the addition of corrections toward Ӎ. It is odd, too, that 88 and Syh Arm are so divergent from one another and each from Ӎ.

42. Both verbs are used elsewhere with this cliché: 11.22, 21.9, 27.13, 38.2, 42.17, 22; and 44.18, 27.

43. Cf. Scholz, *Commentar zum Buche des Propheten Jeremias* (Würzburg: L. Woerl, 1880), p. 512, "Statt 'Schätze' haben LXX: εν οχυρωματι σου, indem durch Verhören מעשה und מעי(ו)ז miteinander verwechselt wurde."

44. A. W. Streane, *The Double Text of Jeremiah* (Cambridge: D. Bell and Co., 1896); P. Volz, *Der Prophet Jeremia* (Leipzig: Deichert, 1922); F. Nötscher, *Das Buch Jeremias* (Bonn: Hanstein).

45. F. Giesebrecht, *Das Buch Jeremia* (Göttingen: Vandenhoeck and Ruprecht, 1907); cf. A. Scholz, *Der masorethische Text*; Duhm considers either מצוד or מעוז possible.

46. "The Value of Ugaritic for Textual Criticism," *Biblica* 40 (1959), 166-167; followed by Bright.

47. Reading enclitic *mem*, with Bright.

48. Rudolph comments (following Delitzsch): "זב בי ist in der Form זְ(ה)בע' richtige Randbemerkung zu בעמקים: 'das müsste בעמקך heissen.'" This is not impossible, especially if original בעמקם (with enclitic *mem*) became obscured to בעמקים.

49. The pejorative connotations of גלוליה are clear from, e.g., Deut 29.16, 2 Kgs. 23.24. עצביה may have been inspired by Isa. 46.1.

For another example of conflation of the divine name and its pejorative substitute, see p. 12, no. 9.

50. An examination of parallel passages in Jer. 39.9–10 and 2 Kgs. 25.11–12, and the related passage in 2 Kgs. 24.14, in 𝔐 and versions, reveals frequent fluctuation between the synonymous variants דלות הארץ/ דלות העם.

51. Cf. Talmon, *Textus* 1 (1960), 165. For other examples of these synonymous variants, see Jud. 13.7, 1 Sam. 1.11, and the comments of F. M. Cross, "A New Qumran Biblical Fragment Related to the Original Hebrew Underlying the Septuagint," *BASOR* 132 (1953), 18 (on 4QSam[a], v. 22).

52. ע and שׁ are easily confused in some periods; cf. F. M. Cross, *BANE*, p. 137, Fig. 1, lines 3, 5. For a possible similar example of עם/שׁם confusion, see chapter V, n. 30.

53. E.g., 4.29, 29.7, 34.22, 40.5 (cf. 2 Kgs. 25.22): 𝔐 עיר/ 𝔊 ארץ. Also, cf. 44.9, where 𝔐 ארץ = 𝔊, but ארץ is a variant to עיר in all other occurrences of this cliché (7.17, 34, 11.6, 13, 33.10, 44.6, 17, 21).

54. The words occur in this or similar combination nowhere else. הביא with Yhwh as subject generally is followed with a specific object, usually (ה)רעה. Targ reads ואתא וקיים [v ואתא ועבד v₂ (sub נ''ב) zibgofc; v probably represents correction to 𝔐, while the other witnesses may represent a conflation of ויקם/ויבא. Thus, the witness of Targ to וירע is weak.

55. As pointed out above, p. 71, this is the only occurrence in Jer. 𝔐 of the name יוחנן *without* the patronym. It is probable that the phrase was added, as an elaborating gloss, after the period of levelling through of the patronym.

56. αναστρεφειν translates שׁוב ca. 75 times in the Septuagint, including 11 times elsewhere in Jer.; the word never translates סבב in Jer.

57. The reading of A-106 L', etc., probably is to be explained as inner-Greek, under the influence of v. 14; the change involved is only ε/α.

58. On the probable secondary character of this phrase, see no. 57.

59. Compare also:

Jer. 41.1 𝔐                    מזרע המלוכה ורבי המלך ועשרה אנשים אתו

2 Kgs. 25.25 𝔐          ועשרה אנשים אתו          מזרע המלוכה

Jer. 41.1 𝔊  απο γενους του βασιλεως και δεκα ανδρες μετ' αυτου

      L' απο γενους της βασιλειας και τα παιδαρια του βασιλεως...

                                      κ.τ.λ.

2 Kgs.  $\mathcal{G}^{καιγε}$  εκ του σπερματος των βασιλεων και δεκα ανδρες μετ'αυτου
25.25   L Aeth                ... της βασιλειας ...

    In view of the conflated character of Jer. 41 𝔐, we may ask whether, in 41.1, זרע המלוכה and רבי המלך are not old variants. Kgs. $\mathcal{G}^{καιγε}$ and Jer. 𝔊 may indicate the hebrew text מזרע המלך (cf. 1 Kgs. 11.14 מזרע המלך/ εκ του σπερματος της βασιλειας!), which would make the alternate phrases even more similar: מ[זרע/רבי]המלך. Alternatively, רבי המלך may be a variant to עשרה אנשים.

    60. (ο)ανηρ του πολεμου occurs in Ex. 15.3 (F$^b$), Num. 31.28 (p$^b$-), Josh. 5.4 (M$^{mg}$v$^{mg}$z$^{mg}$), 5.6 (εβρ' i$^{mg}$), 6.3 (O𝔛), 1 Sam. 18.5 ($\mathcal{G}^{L\ καιγε}$), 2 Kgs. 25.4 ($\mathcal{G}^{καιγε}$). Significantly, in 1 Sam. 18.5 the old Greek text is absent. Since in this verse $\mathcal{G}^L$ is otherwise infected with $\mathcal{G}^{καιγε}$ readings (εν οφθαλμοις twice [on this as a $\mathcal{G}^{καιγε}$ replacement of earlier ενωπιον in Samuel-Kings, see James D. Shenkel, *Chronology and Recensional Development in the Greek Text of Kings* (Cambridge: Harvard University Press, 1968)]; καιγε once), its agreement with $\mathcal{G}^{καιγε}$ here likewise seems to be due to late infection. On the other hand, in 2 Kgs. 25.4, where $\mathcal{G}^{καιγε}$ reads οι ανδρες του πολεμου, earlier $\mathcal{G}^L$ reads οι ανδρες οι πολεμισται. The recensional character of the former term here, and generally, is clear, especially when taken with the evidence from Jeremiah (see immediately below).

    61. των ανθρωπων των πολεμουντων] τ.α.τ. πολεμιστων A–410 C'–613 Bo. The participle in 𝔊-Ziegler may reflect attraction to 32.24, 29, 37.10 (הנלחמים), either in 𝔊 (with A-etc. original?) or in 𝔊-*Vorlage* (with A-etc. harmonizing to 𝔊 in 49.26, etc.).

    62. 2 Kgs. 25.25 omits כל, which probably is secondary in Jeremiah.

    63. The two passages would have stood at roughly the same place in adjoining columns, and a scribe who did not understand the purpose of the gloss would have attached the phrase to גברים. Compare 42.17 כל האנשים (וכל הזרים = και παντες οι αλλογενεις + [כל האנשים) and 43.2 (האזרים] 𝔊 omits הזדים); the respective plusses are alternate absorptions of the same gloss הזדים, which in 𝔊-*Vorlage* was corrupted to, or mistaken

for, הזרים and prefixed with וכל. Other examples of two-way absorption
of glosses can be adduced.

64. If ανδρας εν πολεμω in fact does represent old Greek, the
related development of the two readings is not affected; then ₵ becomes
a witness to text tradition (B). But the existence in ₵-Ziegler of other
recensional corrections (e.g., twice in 27.6, on which see pp. 54-57, and
the existence of a number of inner-Greek doublets composed of old Greek
and recensional Greek readings (see pp. 25-26), gives plausibility to our
analysis.

65. J. Ziegler, *Beiträge zur Ieremias-Septuaginta* (Göttingen: Vandenhoeck and Ruprecht, 1958), p. 87.

66. "Dritter Beitrag: Dubletten in der Ier.-LXX," *Beiträge*, pp.
87-113.

67. In each reading, the page reference to Ziegler's analysis is
given in brackets after the variants data. The part of the doublet
which is presented in Ziegler's critical text is marked with an asterisk.
In this section, since we are dealing with readings from the point of
view of ₵ text tradition, citation of passages follows the *Greek order*,
with Hebrew order in brackets. This is done to facilitate reference to
Ziegler's analysis, and because of the occasional significance of the
location of a passage in Jer. α or β.

68. Ziegler takes ψευδη as original; we would prefer επ' αδικω.

69. The doublet turns on אזרי, which in old Greek is indicated by
the compound verb (so Ziegler).

70. *Beiträge*, p. 94; cf. also p. 14.

71. *Beiträge*, p. 14.

72. Quoted by Ziegler, *Beiträge*, p. 87.

73. It would be "concealed" only to a blind man! Cf. Lev. 19.14
ולפני עור לא תתן מכשל.

74. 3.17, 7.24, 9.13, 16.12, 18.12, cf. 11.8, 13.10.

75. On Jer. 7.24, see p. 11, no. 4. W. Erbt, *Jeremia und seine
Zeit* (Göttingen: Vandenhoeck and Ruprecht, 1902), p. 285, proposes the
same Hebrew text base for 23.17 ₵. But he takes the ₵ doublet as original,
translating a doublet already in the *Vorlage*. This is unlikely; cf.
*Beiträge*, p. 96.

76. נאם יהוה probably is a secondary gloss, as six other times in
vv. 23-32. Or was the form of variant (B) כה דברי נאם יהוה כפטיש יפצץ

סלע? Note that ουτως οι λογοι μου λεγει κυριος is a pre-Hexaplaric variant, since it renders נאם יהוה with λεγει κυριος (against the usual Hexaplaric addition φησι κυριος).

77. παρελυθη Spohn, 𝔊ᶻⁱ] παρεδοθη codd. gr. et verss.

78. και ουκ εσται αυτω ανθρωπος εν μεσω υμων του ιδειν τα αγαθα α
εγω ποιησω υμιν renders ולא יהיה לו איש בתוככם לראות בטוב אשר אני עשה לכם
cn. 𝔐 לא יהיה לו איש ישב בתוך העם הזה ולא יראה בטוב אשר אני עשה לעמי.
𝔐 has moved away from the direct address of the letter. With the addition of ישב (probably from 39.14, 40.5, 40.6), לראות developed to ולא
יראה to make a two-pronged threat.

79. *Beiträge*, p. 97, n. 1.

80. Working with Ziegler's critical text [καθημενη εκτριβεται],
one might take 𝔐 as a doublet, from variants [בח/דיבון]ישבח](cf. Talmon,
*Textus* 4 [1964], 104, for such variants in Isa. 12.6). But then εκτριβεται would have to be derived (but how?) through דיבון. It is simpler
to suppose dittography > ישבח in 𝔊-*Vorlage*.

81. S. R. Driver, *Notes on the Hebrew Text and the Topography of
the Books of Samuel*, 2nd ed. (Oxford, 1960), p. 296, n. 1.

82. On במלט במלבן, cf. S. R. Driver, *Notes on the Hebrew Text*, pp.
294-296. It should be noted that 2QJer (*Discoveries in the Judaean
Desert of Jordan III: Les 'Petites Grottes' de Qumrân, Textes et Planches*
[2 vols.], ed. M. Baillet, J. T. Milik, R. de Vaux [Oxford: Clarendon
Press, 1962]), though broken at this point, seems not to have room for
the problematic phrase, and may well agree with 𝔊 in omitting במלט במלבן
אשר (see *Textes*, p. 63; *Planches*, pl. XIII.3). (Hereafter *DSD III*.)

83. I confess some uneasiness with Ziegler's argument, which is
as follows: θυμιαμα = זבח in Ex. 23.18, 34.25(bis), 1 Sam. 2.29, 3.14,
2 Kgs. 10.24, but never in Jeremiah. O L Tyc read simply και θυμιαματα
(cf. C και θυσιας), and since we cannot imagine deletion of και θυσιας
to correct toward 𝔐, και θυμιαματα is original. But it is not to be
thought that the translator departed from his practice in 6.20, 7.21, 22
(זבח = θυσια). Therefore θυμιαματα is an erroneous form of θυματα (which
is adopted into Ziegler's critical text).

Though the apparatus to Ex. 34.25, 1 Sam. 3.14, and 2 Kgs. 10.24
illustrates the fluctuation between θυματα/θυμιαματα, and θυμα does
render זבח 9 times in the O.T., it too runs into the objection posed by
6.20, 7.21, 22. Other possibilities may therefore be considered: 𝔊

θυμιαματα translated קטרת (as ca. 40 times elsewhere in LXX) or the like; θυσιαν is old Greek, and θυμιαματα either is an inner-Greek expansion or stems from a Greek recension which rendered זבח with θυμα > θυμιαμα.

84. *Beiträge*, p. 88: "Vermeintliche Dubletten."

85. He points also to a number of other secondary items in 𝔊, derived from Deut. 𝔊.

86. E.g., twice in 34(27).6, S Bo Aeth alone have escaped infection by the late correction to נבוכדנאצר and לעבדו/עבדי. See further above, pp. 54-57.

87. Cf., e.g., Ziegler, *Ieremias*, pp. 42-43, 50-51. Also 39(32).11, where 106 alone preserves the old Greek!

88. Cf., e.g., p. 24, no. 57.

89. Likely instances of such conflation would be nos. 5, 17, and 32, of the Double Readings in 𝔐.

## NOTES TO CHAPTER III

1.  See F. M. Cross, *HTR* 57 (1964), 287.

2.  See, e.g., Num. 14.45, 21.11, 13, in the larger Cambridge Septuagint.

3.  The most obvious reason is the difference in scribal activity in the respective traditions. A text which is much studied and much copied will tend to show more additions than one which is less used, other things being equal.

4.  Similarly Volz. Cornill notes aptly that הדֹּס, as a synonym of נחץ, is redundant in 1.10. This would apply also to 31.28.

5.  34.19 וכל עם הארץ] και τον λαον. עם הארץ is out of place here; we expect העם (as in vv. 8, 10), to give the grouping שרי יהודה'''‎ הסריסים והכהנים והעם. עם הארץ is secondary from elsewhere in Jeremiah (e.g., 1.18, 44.21).

6.  "Jeremiah's Complaints: Observations on Jer. 15.10-21," *JBL* 82 (1963), 403, n. 42.

7.  Note that in 2 Kgs., L καιγε Syr read מערף, which--taken together with other close verbal parallels between 2 Kgs. 17 and Jer. 7.25-26--lends further indirect support to Jer. 7.26 ₵.

8.  It is curious that Syr omits 7.28 from ואמרת to מוסר. Haplography ‎ معل/احمل‎ is doubtful ( معل محـل/احمل‎ would be attractive). Is it possible that in verses 27 and 28 two old variants have been conflated in M?

9.  6.13-15//8.10b-12. The latter passage is om. ₵.

10. So also Skinner, *Prophecy and Religion* (Cambridge at the University Press, 1961), p. 101, n. 1.

11. Streane, Volz, Duhm, Wambacq.

12. Rudolph; similarly F. Giesebrecht, *Das Buch Jeremia*, p. XXXIX.

13. Cf. ης ενετειλαμην ποιειν αυτους O-233 L'-36 which, though it does not reflect on the text of ₵ or ₵-*Vorlage*, indicates the naturalness of such an expansion.

14. Though one should not place too much weight upon it, the orthography of שרירות departs from the usual שררות (7 times). On orthographic aspects of secondary readings, see pp. 95-96.

15. Ex. 20.10 Deut. 5.14 לא תעשה] + בר ₵Ex Deut SyrEx Deut Nash Papyrus (הם). The orthography of Jer. 17.24 M suggests an early date for

the plus, or for its source as a plus. The alignment of the textual witnesses strongly suggests that Jer. M̸ is a Palestinian reading, while Jer.
₵ (with Ex./Deut. M̸) is non-Palestinian.

16. *RSV*, "if that nation, concerning which I have spoken," is
forced; cf. Bright, *Jeremiah*, The Anchor Bible, vol. 21 (Garden City,
New York: Doubleday and Co., Inc., 1965), p. 124, n. 8.

17. Curiously, while the ₵ lacuna is filled as usual by O(※) Arm,
L(※) does *not* restore the clause here, but after v. 13. In view of L's
routine correction to the Hexaplaric text, this is highly unusual. Ziegler's note in the apparatus ("ex 11, 7.32") is doubtful, as the sentence
is not present in v. 11 L'. Perhaps L did not take the O restoration
into his base text because it already had it after v. 13. This would
suggest, however, that his base text represented a manuscript tradition
revised to a proto-M̸ text in which the gloss was taken in at the end of
the חפה-reference, rather than at the beginning.

18. Giesebrecht is wrong in arguing that the clause is "unentbehrlich, da א̈ל 'ח sich schlecht an מסב anschliesst." הסב frequently takes
an indirect object in מן, אל, ל, etc., after the direct object (e.g., 1
Sam. 5.10, 2 Sam. 3.12, 2 Kgs. 20.2, 1 Chr. 10.14, 12.24, 13.3). The
attempt of Volz, Ehrlich, and others to have ואספתי אותם refer to את
הכשדים, is also syntactically improbable. The narrative verbal sequence
clearly is הנני מסב'''(ואספתי)'''ונלחמתי, while the אשר clauses are adjectival, modifying את כלי המלחמה. אותם refers to this primary object much
more naturally than it would to the object of the verb in the adjectival
clause. That O L' ϑ' (※-Q 86) read αυτους (instead of αυτα = τα οπλα)
is no argument against this.

19. (a) 14.12, 21.7,(9), 24.10, 27.(8),13, 29.17,18, 32.(24),36,
34.17, 38.(2), 42.(17,22), 44.(13) (bracketed passages contain zero
variants). (b) 5.12, 14.13,15(bis),16, 16.4, 44.12(bis),18,27 (the short
series is reflected also in the following places: 11.22, 14.18, 15.2,
18.21, 42.16). The order of the terms is: (a) חרב רעב דבר 13 times,
חרב דבר רעב once (= ₵), דבר חרב רעב once (₵'ח'ר'ד). (b) חרב רעב 9 times,
רעב חרב once (₵ חרב רעב). The series thus occurs in fixed sequence, contrary to the random order in Ezek. (10 occurrences) and elsewhere in the
O.T. (6 occurrences).

20. Assuming that the long series is original in three instances
where the whole context is secondarily absent in ₵ (27.13, 29.17,18).

21.  Cf., e.g., S. R. Driver, *An Introduction to the Literature of the Old Testament* (New York, 1957), p. 276.

22.  *RSV*; cf. Cornill "verstossen," Ehrlich "abwerfen," Weiser "wegwerfen," Bright "cast(off)" (alternative, "forsake," p. 151, p-p.).

23.  Though the form apparently is not attested at Qumrân, it is reminiscent of the forms ‎הֻמָּה‎/-, ‎אֻמָּה‎, etc.

24.  Rudolph's comment (following Keil), that "die Zeitbestimmung fehlt in ¢, wohl wegen der Legende im Buch Baruch 1.8f., die den falschen Propheten recht zu geben schien," is not convincing.  Had the translator been motivated by such considerations, the deletion of the temporal phrase would have been insufficient by itself.  One could as plausibly argue that the temporal phrase was added after the erection of the second temple, to vindicate Jeremiah against the false prophets.

25.  Vv. 16-22 therefore relate more closely to chap. 28.

26.  The intervening words, ‎לבלתי‎ to ‎בבלה‎, comprise 53 letters, or about one line in a typical manuscript.  One might have a form of "vertical haplography" aided by ‎בייכי‎.

27.  See chap. V.

28.  Streane comments, "it is clear from considerations of grammar that one or more of the objects specified in M.T. have fallen out of the Greek."  But the construction και των επιλοιπων σκευων,...εις βαβυλωνα εισελευσεται is quite grammatical and may be read "and some of the remaining vessels...shall be taken to Babylon."  Cf. W. W. Goodwin, *A Greek Grammar* (London: Macmillan and Col., Ltd., 1963), p. 233, par. 1097.1.

29.  In a damaged or worn manuscript,  ‎וְיִוָּתֵר‎  could have been read ‎מיתר‎.

30.  Giesebrecht maintains that "solche doppelte Ankündigungen nach einer Unterbrechung sind dem hier redenden Schriftsteller nicht fremd, cf. 27.3 u. 4, 29.8 u. 10, 29.16 u. 17, 29.24f, u. 30."  But three of his examples are irrelevant, as each member of the double proclamation is a completed sentence.  The fourth, 29.16,17, while somewhat analogous, is not cogent, for it does not repeat ‎כי‎, and it does not repeat a relative clause following the second cliché.  The awkwardness of 27.19-22, compared with these examples, is patent.

31.  It is interesting how the conflation in one text tradition of ancient variants which begin or end similarly may make it appear as though a text tradition carrying only one of the variants has suffered

haplography (for a clear example, see p. 14, no. 22).

32. On חרי here, as compared with שרי in 24.1, 29.2, cf. 39.6//
52.12, where the former substitutes חרי for original שרי. On the lateness of the term חרים, see S. R. Driver, *Introduction to the Literature
of the Old Testament*, p. 553 n.

33. Cf. J. Ziegler, *Beiträge zur Ieremias-Septuaginta* (Göttingen:
Vandenhoeck and Ruprecht, 1958), p. 97.

34. Eb 22 supports ₡ also in omitting אלהי ישראל, in v. 13.

35. W. Rudolph, *Jeremia* (Tübingen: J. C. B. Mohr [Paul Siebeck],
1958), p. 203. Compare the discussion of Bright: Though he deletes the
words from his translation, in his note (pp. 221-222, n. 12) he acknowledges that M̸ may be original, because of the characteristic redundancy
of the prose discourses. It is really very difficult to believe that
the general prose style would result in this kind of redundancy in such
stock clichés, except in a secondary manner.

36. On the divergence of M̸ and ₡ in 35.17-19, see pp. 104-106.

37. Of child sacrifice, 7.31, 19.5; of destruction in war, 21.10,
34.2,22, 37.8,10, 38.17,18,23, 39.8, 43.13, 51.32, 52.13. 32.29 and
43.12 conform in substance to this idiom. In 34.5, any such adverbial
construction is impossible.

38. In v. 6, וישלחו את ירמיהו בחבלים ובבור אין מים] και εχαλασαν
αυτον εις τον λακκον, και εν τω λακκω ουκ ην υδωρ = וישלחו אתו אל הבור
ובבור אין מים. M̸ את ירמיהו is characteristic expansion (see chap. IV).
₡ אל הבור may have arisen through confusion (by anticipation?) of בחבלים
with the following ובבור. However, perhaps neither is original. Verse
6 in M̸₡ is not smooth, as the officers first throw Jeremiah in and then
lower him in. Possibly וישלחו אתו and וישליכו אתו were old variants,
conflated early, and glossed in didferent ways in M̸ (בחבלים) and ₡-*Vorlage*
(אל הבור).

39. ερριψεν predominantly renders השליך, never the piel of שלח;
the latter would have been translated χαλαω (see v. 6).

40. See p. 118, no. 24.

41. See no. 88 above.

42. Cf. also Deut. 4.27, 28.64, 30.1,3-4, Ezek. 11.16-17, 20.34,
41, 28.25, 34.12, Dan. 9.7. These passages, and other frequent usage of
נדח and פוץ in similar context, place the point beyond doubt.

43. 40.11 בְּכֹל הָאֲרָצוֹת, from בְּכֹל הָאָרֶץ (∅), represents further influence in this direction.

44. E.g., Graf, *Der Prophet Jeremia* (Leipzig: T. O. Weigel, 1862), p. liv, Giesebrecht, p. 219 ("tendenziöser Natur"), Volz, *Studien zum Text des Jeremia* (Leipzig: J. C. Hinrichs, 1920), p. 212 ("dogmatischen Gründen"), Rudolph, p. 161 ("zu anstössig"), Bright, p. 200 ("application of this title to Nebuchadnezzar was apparently offensive in some circles").

45. *Not* = M, *pace* Ziegler. This reading is an interesting, and perhaps significant, bridge between M and ∅[rel].

46. Werner E. Lemke, "Nebuchadrezzar, My Servant," *CBQ* 28 (1966), 48, n. 9.

47. It is immaterial to the present purpose whether the divergent usage is translational (Thackeray, *The Septuagint and Jewish Worship*, pp. 29-37) or recensional (Ziegler raises the possibility in his critical edition of *Ieremias*, p. 128, n. 1, but, after some study of the problem, I am undecided). In any case, the divergence is attested by numerous striking examples (see Thackeray's list, to which may be added other examples). I am informed that Mr. Emmanuel Tov has given renewed attention to the problem of Jer. α and β, in an unpublished monograph.

48. The verb וְעָבְדוּ is not grammatically necessary to the gloss for joining purposes, as לַעֲבֹד already occurs in 28.14a. It therefore strongly suggests that the Hebrew text from which it was expanded read לַעֲבֹדוּ. The reason for its finite form in 28.14 probably is that, after the addition was taken from the margin into the text, the awkwardness of לַעֲבֹד נ׳מ׳ב׳ לַעֲבֹדוּ was felt, and the second form was altered to read more smoothly.

49. In 27.6 and 28.14, Targ and Vulg agree with M, while Syr is so thorough a conflation of the two passages that it offers no help in recovering the text.

50. The bracketed words are omitted in 27.6 ∅.

51. On M הָאֵלֶּה אֵת כֹּל הָאֲרָצוֹת, see p. 66, n. 5.

52. And with half an eye to Gen. 1.24-30?

53. If this occurred after stage ε[1], the loss of the verbal element would not be felt, as it still existed at the end of the sentence.

54. As noted above, δουλευειν is the regular translation of עָבַד in O and precursors, when correcting the old Greek lacuna toward M.

55. Cf. &#162; apparatus: εργαζεσθαι αυτω] ÷0-Q-86; >233; om. αυτω O
L' Arm / + (※0-Qmg; ÷ pro※L) δεδωκα αυτω (>Qmg; + και L' Tht) δουλευειν
αυτω (v. 7) και δουλευσουσιν αυτω...κ.τ.λ.

56. So Lemke, *CBQ* 28 (1966), p. 48.

57. 534 Tht<sup>cit</sup> are impossible, and have to be the result of correction wrongly inserted (or influenced by a defective text like 26).
In this case, these witnesses reflect an earlier agreement with S Bo
Aeth / 26 is possible (cf. 39.1 B-S A-106') but highly unlikely here.
It may have resulted from haplography (βασ.⌢βαβ.) either before or after
faulty correction to Ɱ (and hence, like 534 Tht<sup>cit</sup>, reflects earlier
agreement with S Bo Aeth / 62 probably originates in the majority reading, with haplography βασ.⌢βαβ./C'-239 is strange; we do not know how to
account for it /※0 Q seems to suggest that some part of the name is a
Hexaplaric addition. But the asterisk may actually apply to εν χειρι.

58. I.e., 15.7 S* 26 La<sup>W</sup> Bo Aeth Or.; 17.25 S 106 Bo Tyc.; 37.17
S 534 Bo Aeth.

59. This may be argued from the general pattern of filling out
names and titles in Ɱ, and apart from one's decision concerning 27.6.

60. On the theological aspects of this problem, see Lemke, *CBQ* 28
(1966). Though we differ somewhat in our interpretation of the textual
evidence, I am in complete agreement with the main thrust of his article.

61. Cf. 26.9, 32.43, 33.10, 34.22.

62. *DSD III, Textes*, p. 64, fig. 5 and notes.

63. See *DSD III, Planches*, Pl. XIII, fig. 5. Instead of a smooth,
slightly left-to-right downstroke (compare פ in line 2), we have the
right arm of א (with a definite tick or "tittle" at the top, and just
the beginning of the arm itself; compare א in lines 3, 5), and the bottom
right end of the diagonal axis.

64. This reconstruction receives support from the letter count.
Compare:

|  |  |  |  | Baillet | My reconstruction |
|---|---|---|---|---|---|
| 1. | ב ‎1 | to 1. 2 | ‎ץ | 48 | 48 |
| 1. | ‎2 ‎ץ | to 1. 3 | ‎ל | 51 | 51 |
| 1. | ‎3 ‎ה | to 1. 4 | ‎ם | 47 | 47 |
| 1. | 4 ‎°וה | to 1. 5 | ‎°ול | 39 | 47 or 51 |

The reconstruction is too short without the phrase (there is no question
of a paragraph break), while מאין בזמה יושב, or better still מאין יושב,

fits perfectly. The latter suggestion is perhaps too nice; moreover, if
2QJer were to have omitted לעבד with 𝔊 in v. 3, בזמה would be required
in v. 2. Note that if 2QJer were reconstructed to agree with 𝔊 in omitting צבאות in v. 2 (fig. 5, line 3), we would have lines of 48, 46, 47,
and 47 characters.

65. Perhaps יהודה 1° and 2° are a conflation of two variant adop-
tions into the text of one gloss on השארית.

66. Both verbs are used elsewhere as alternates with this cliché;
cf. 11.22, 21.9, 27.13, 38.2, and 44.18,27.

67. 𝔊 may be supported by 2QJer. *DSD III, Textes*, p. 65, 1.10,
Baillet reconstructs according to 𝔐:

פלשתים והכרתי לצור ולצ[ל]ון יד[צ]ל כל שריד עוזר כיא שודד יהוה את פלשתים

The line, with 55 letters, seems over long in relation to lines 5-9, 11-
13: 47, 49, 46, 49, 35, (55), 46, 48, 46. Without את פלשתים the line
would have 46 letters, a perfect fit. But we cannot be certain.

68. On the hypothesis that 𝔊 customarily omits the second occurrence of doublets, see chapter V.

69. Note also the occurrence of (ה)קריות in vv. 24 and 41.

70. Cf., e.g., BH[3] " 𝔊, sed cf Jes 13.20."

71. This, and the resulting balanced poetry (at least in v. 39)
suggests that Jer. v. 39 is a literary production, and not just a scribal
gloss reminiscent of Isa. 13.

72. S om. τους 1° and 2°. 86 και precedes τους 1°.

73. These three, the only cursives outside O L' to vary from
reading I, all reflect the same immediate ancestor, which is here reconstructed. 106 has suffered haplography, και πασης της γης 1°⌒2°, while
410 has suffered haplography, αυτου 1°⌒2°. 239 omits τους 2°, with S.

74. Aeth omits και 1°, and αυτους 1°; Arab adds "and" after γης 2°.

75. The text is abbreviated, except for the relevant phrase.

76. Ziegler, *Ieremias: Septuaginta* (Göttingen: Vandenhoeck and
Ruprecht, 1957), pp. 63-64, describes a number of readings in Q-V family
which reflect a pre-Hexaplaric revision toward what we would call proto-𝔐.
In these instances, he suggests, "man kann wohl sagen, dass der Text von
Q-V... oder ein ihm nahe verwandter Text die Vorlage für O gewesen ist."
My posited revision (β) fits nicely into this category and accounts for
the data upon which my questions have focused. Moreover, Ziegler's com-
ments suggest why O (and L) did not retain the old Greek reading--it had

already been excised.  The same phenomenon may be represented in readings
like the following:   14.15 ₵ plus] om. Q-V-46-130-613-710 O L' (⁻³⁶)-198
La^W Bo Arm;  52.17 ₵ plus] om. Q-V-26-46-86'-239-393-534-544 O-233 L'-538
Arm.

77.  The odd position of the first phrase in Aeth Arab (see IV
above) may reflect (β) infected by (δ) and wrongly conflated with (α).
Or, more simply, they may reflect a Greek text (γ) in which the old Greek
phrase was omitted by accident and wrongly restored.

78.  In Jer. α (except for 7.8), לבלתי otherwise (10 times) translated του μη + inf.  But το παραπαν (του) μη = לבלתי in 1 Kgs. 11.10,
Ezek. 20.9,14,15,22, 46.20 (cf. Zeph 3.6 = מבלי), the only occurrences
of this phrase listed in Hatch-Redpath.  οτι, υμας may then be inner-
Greek development.  In view of v. 8 (= οθεν ουκ ωφεληθησεσθε), it is
unlikely that the addition is simply inner-Greek; rather, we suspect an
underlying Hebrew text.  Again, the difference between vv. 4 and 8 may
indicate either alternate attempts by the original translator at rendering the idiom, or later correction to a Hebrew manuscript which had developed לבלתי הועיל.  We cannot be sure.  If Hebrew לבלתי הועיל is reflected
here, it is of course possible that M is defective by homoioarchon:  לַבְלתי
הועיל לַאמר.

79.  Comprising only vv. 16, 17a, 24-25.  So Bright, pp. 289, 298.

80.  A faint trace of evidence that the plus already was in ₵-
*Vorlage* may be seen in the phrase και εγραψα βιβλιον (= ואכתב ספר from
ואכתב בספר) cf. vv. 10, 44...εις βιβλιον.  It is very odd that there is
no trace of Hexaplaric correction in v. 25.

81.  Cf. 32.11, where 106 *alone* carries the old Greek text.

82.  Including 2 Kgs. 23.2, where, however, in ₵ and in the synoptic passage 2 Chr. 34.30, כל 2° is omitted.  כל 2° in Kgs. M probably is
repeated from כל 1°.

83.  About 225 readings to 40.  More than one addition is discussed,
in numbers 1, 17, 40, 45, 55, 99, 166, 175, 194.

84.  See especially number 9, 14, 22, 40, 47, 66, 68, 73, 74, 75,
78, 79, 81, 83, 84, 89, 116, 119, 120, 141, 145, 146, 149, 158, 170, 179,
180, 185, 190.

85.  It might be argued that the awkward reading should be preferred,
as the smoother reading would reflect scribal activity.  But we must distinguish between two at least relatively distinct scribal activities:

intended correction, smoothing, or other "improvement" of the text; and marginal glossing, intended as cross-reference, clarification, commentary, or the like, but originally not meant for inclusion in the text itself. Both kinds of scholarly touches on the manuscript would later be incorporated indiscriminately into the text by a scribe whose primary concern was not with the literary or grammatical context of the text, but merely with its transmission. The latter was a mechanical task, the sometimes pedestrian performance of which may often be seen in the misinsertion of marginal restorations or glosses. The principle of *lectio difficilior* must therefore be used with discrimination.

86.  Numbers 19, 20, 27, 31, 33, 38, 79, 86, 108, 175, 178, 180, 181, 190.

## NOTES TO CHAPTER IV

1. The instances in which the name occurs in 𝕸 in larger contexts omitted in 𝔊 are of course not included in this figure. On the latter two readings, see p. 71, no. 5.

2. Contrast the style in CC1-4, 5-7, 11-13, 14-15, 16-17, 20-21.

3. See p. 73, n. 9.

4. In these chapters, other names also are filled out in 𝕸; D4, 5, S3, T4, and especially H25, 26, 27, 28, 30, 31, 32, 34, I2, 3, 5, 7, 8, 9. In addition, chapters 27-29 contain much secondary expansion of other types.

5. It must be admitted that נבוכדנאצר in chapters 27-29 can be explained in other ways. S. R. Driver (*Introduction to the Literature of the Old Testament* [New York: Meridian Books, 1957], p. 272, n.) has pointed out that other names in this section are spelled atypically. They are:

| | | |
|---|---|---|
| ירמיה | H24-32 | (ירמיהו elsewhere) |
| צדקיה | B7-9 | (צדקיהו B6 and elsewhere) |
| יכניה | D4-6 | (יˈˈכניהו elsewhere) |
| חנניה | I1-9 | (cp. חנניהו 36.12) |
| שמעיה | T2-4 | (but שמעיהו T1) |

This evidence Driver takes as suggesting that 27-29 once had "a history of their own," and that they "reached the compiler through some special channel." Alternately, he conjectures, one could argue simply that in these chapters a later orthographic practice was leveled through.

Driver's first suggestion seems more than the data require. And the alternative does not really contradict our argument, for such secondary leveling could have come into the text at the same time as the secondary additions of נבוכדנאצר.

6. We may have a similar conflation in 27.8: אתו את נב' מלך בבל. But 𝔊 is absent here, probably by homoioteleuton (אשר לא 1°⁀2°).

7. If 39.1-2 were indeed present in the old Greek text. These verses, which are secondary from 52.4-6, are omitted in La^W and under the asterisk in O L.

8. On foreigner-eunuch association, see also Isa. 56.3.

9. Readings of the above three kinds may be found in abundance in the Lucianic text of Kgs., especially in the prophetic narratives.

Especially to be noted are the plusses מלך יהודה + Name (sometimes in L,
sometimes in 𝔐); the noun/pronoun readings; and, in 2 Kgs. 1-3, the systematic addition in L of proper names as subject of the verb.

10.  40.2: ויקח רב טבחים לירמיהו ויאמר אליו] και ελαβον αυτον ο
αρχιμαγειρος και ειπεν αυτω. (לירמיהו)ל is odd here.  Probably לירמיהו
was intended as a clarifying gloss to אליו (···ויאמר אל·· is the predominant
idiom, but ···ויאמר ל does occur; see, e.g., with nouns, 2 Kgs. 4.29,38,
10.23,25, 13.18, 18.22; and at least a dozen times in 2 Kgs. with pronouns) and was wrongly taken into the text.

11.  Some of the above readings (e.g., a, b, f, q, and the instances
of את ירמיהו] ר/אתי, etc.) have been explained as arising from abbreviation of the words in question, or from the scribe's mistaken assumption
of abbreviation.  For example, G. R. Driver has undertaken a survey of
such readings in the O.T. in his article, "Abbreviations in the Massoretic Text," *Textus* 1 (1960), 112-131.  However, many of his examples
are at least open to other interpretations, and some of them disappear
outright upon closer examination.  Cross informs me that, save for
weights and measures, numbers and dates, there are no examples of abbreviations in ancient Hebrew inscriptions.  In Phoenician, especially in late
times, abbreviations were developed, but were not used in literary contexts.  Moreover, while abbreviations have been proposed for the Qumrân
materials, in each case the abbreviations disappeared when more manuscript data became available.  This deals a severe blow to such attempts
to explain variants which arose in pre-Christian times, especially those
which arose as early as the time of the translation of the Septuagint.
In any case, the theory cannot account for the majority of the above
readings.  To be sure, in readings involving יהוה or ירמיהו, and the
like, similarity of pronoun and initial consonant probably aided the development of the variant; but it is risky to explain these by appeal to
a theory of scribal practice of abbreviation.

12.  For example, in the historical books the epithet occurs 19
times in 𝔐, 21 in 𝔊, with 18 of these common to both.  In the Ps., all
15 occurrences are common to both.  In the Minor Prophets, the figures
are 𝔐 108, 𝔊 109, 100 in common.  Only in 1 Isa. is there a divergence
remotely similar to that in Jer.  The figures in 1 Isa. are 𝔐 56, 𝔊 47,
in common 43.  Of the 13 occurrences unique to 𝔐, 3 are in larger contexts which are absent from 𝔊.  Where the presence or absence of only

צבאות is involved, the figures are 10 occurrences unique to M̸, 4 unique
to ₵. But the data in 1 Isa. are not really analogous to those in Jer.

13. So Baumgärtel, "Zu den Gottesnamen in den Büchern Jeremia und
Ezechiel," *Verbannung und Heimkehr* (festschr. Wilhelm Rudolph), ed. Arnulf
Kuschke (Tübingen, 1961), pp. 15-16. For a critique of this article, see
Appendix C. Even if Baumgärtel's point were valid with respect to צבאות,
it could not apply to אלהי ישראל.

14. Baumgärtel argues that the 10 instances of παντοκρατωρ in Jer.
are later insertions in ₵ on the basis of the Hebrew text, and he accounts
for the regular translations of צבאות in Isa. and the Minor Prophets in
similar fashion (pp. 14, 16-18). But such explaining away of the evidence
is totally unacceptable.

15. On this argument as applied to ₵ omissions of some large doublets in Jer., see pp. 91-92.

16. The division of Jer. ₵ into α (1-29) and β (30-52) also bears
on this issue. According to the ₵ order of materials, the M̸ occurrences
of צבאות fall equally in the two halves, 41 in α and 41 in β; likewise,
the 10 occurrences in ₵ are evenly divided between α and β. Now, if α
and β are the work of two collaborators who divided the translation task
between them (so Thackeray), then the omission of צבאות would have to
have been a deliberate methodological decision--a decision which neither
carried out strictly! If, on the other hand, α and β represent an original unified translation partly revised (cf. Ziegler, *Ieremias: Septuaginta*
[Göttingen: Vandenhoeck and Ruprecht, 1957], p. 128, n. 1), then we have
to suppose that the revisor was careful to revise the occurrences of
ταδε λεγει κυριος to ουτως ειπε κυριος (or vice versa), but did not think
it worth the trouble to supply the missing epithet. This point applies
likewise to אלהי ישראל, which occurs 6 times in α, and 8 times in β.

17. Included in this figure is the occurrence in 46.25 of אמר יהוה
צבאות אלהי ישראל, which we take to be a corruption of כה אמר יהוה···, on
the following grounds: M̸ is awkward in initial position preceding הנני
plus participle, in view of the frequent occurrence of כה אמר יהוה הנני
plus participle in Jer. (ca. 30 times); the cliché is absent from ₵, and
is a secondary expansion before הנני פֹקד, following frequent usage and
especially 23.2, 29.32, 50.18. A similar expansion before הנני פקד occurs
in 11.22 (note that הנני plus participle occurs also frequently *without*
the cliché (ca. 25 times). Since the epithet אלהי ישראל otherwise occurs

only in the cliché כה אמר יהוה, its presence in the M gloss to 46.25 gives added support for our conjecture that the gloss originally was כה אמר יהוה צבאות אלהי ישראל.

18. Two occurrences in Chronicles are in synoptic passages and are literarily dependent on 2 Kgs. The only real exceptions are Ex. 5.1 and 32.27. The first at least seems to be late in its full form, since in this context (the struggle with Pharaoh) the formula otherwise occurs in the short form (5 times), or in the form כה אמר יהוה אלהי העברים (3 times).

19. The form does occur in 2 Kgs. 19.20 $\mathcal{G}^{καιγε}$: ταδε λεγει κυριος ο θεος των δυναμεων θεος Ισραηλ (om. ο θεος $\mathcal{G}^{L}$). Even if καιγε and L reflect corresponding Hebrew texts, the readings undoubtedly are secondary, as the parallel reading in Isa. 37.21 M$\mathcal{G}$ supports 2 Kgs. M in כה אמר יהוה אלהי ישראל. But it is likely that $\mathcal{G}^{L}$ has been infected from $\mathcal{G}^{καιγε}$, since it usually follows the old Greek rendering of παντοκρατωρ, while των δυναμεων is distinctively καιγε. See Barthélemy, *Les Devanciers d'Aquila* (Leiden: E. J. Brill, 1963), pp. 82–83.

20. On this occurrence, see p. 76, n. 17.

21. In Hos. 12.6, ויהוה אלהי הצבאות יהוה זכרו is a related phrase, though its context is atypical and the phrase may be secondary.

22. יהוה...שמו occurs primarily in creation/redemption contexts: Ex. 15.3, Isa. 47.4, 48.2, 51.15, 54.5, Am. 4.13, 5.8, 9.6, Jer. 10.16 (//51.19), 31.35, (32.18), 33.2, 50.34. Note especially the formal similarity between many of these passages. Exceptions, where the phrase is in a prophetic formula, are Am. 5.27, Jer. 46.18, Jer. 48.15, Jer. 51.57. Jer. 46.18 and 48.15 are textually suspect; in view of the primary usage, Am. 5.27 and Jer. 51.57 may be secondary also.

23. Whatever $\mathcal{G}$ represents, it does not reflect צבאות. Probably here and in 50.25 (θεω [ημων]), $\mathcal{G}$ is inner-Greek expansion.

24. J. Ziegler, "Die Vorlage der Isaias-Septuaginta (LXX) und die erste Isaias-Rolle von Qumran (1QIs$^a$)," *JBL* 78 (1959), 58.

25. F. Baumgärtel, "Zu den Gottesnamen in den Büchern Jeremia und Ezechiel," *Verbannung und Heimkehr* (Festschr. Wm. Rudolph), ed. Arnulf Kuschke (Tübingen: J. C. B. Mohr, 1961), esp. pp. 15, 18–20.

26. *Verbannung und Heimkehr*, pp. 10–11.

27. Josh. 7.7, Jud. 6.22, Jer. 1.6, 4.10, 14.13, 32.17, Ezek. 4.14, 9.8, 11.13, 21.5. In the four occurrences in Jeremiah, the term

אהיה is curiously translated by ο ων. Thackeray (*The Old Testament and Jewish Worship* [London: The British Academy, 1921], pp. 33-34) suggests that the translator read אהיה, and thought of Ex. 3.14, where 𝔊 translates εγω ειμι ο ων...ο ων απεσταλκεν με.

28. A. Scholz, *Der masorethische Text und die LXX-Uebersetzung des Buches Jeremias* (Regensburg: G. J. Manz, 1875), p. 101.

29. According to the study of R. Rendtorff, "Zum Gebrauch der Formel nᵉ'um jahwe im Jeremiabuch," *ZAW* 66 (1954), 27-37.

30. The one anomalous occurrence in 51.47. The context (51.44b-49a) is missing in 𝔊 by haplography (probably in its *Vorlage*). Interestingly, the Hexaplaric restoration of the passage (in O-Qmg 62-198 Arm o'-86 ϑ'-Syh) contains the cliché φησι κυριος. This may only indicate that a proto-𝔐 text was secondarily harmonized with the other 14 occurrences. But, as others have noted, 51.44b-49a and 51.49b-53 are strikingly similar, and may constitute old, garbled variants of one original text. If this were the case, 51.47 might contain a secondarily defective form of the eschatological formula, with 51.52 preserving the correct full form.

31. The contexts of 33.14 and 51.47 (33.14-26 and 51.44b-49a) are missing in 𝔊.

32. *ZAW* 66 (1954), p. 27, n. 5.

33. Similarly, in secondary occurrences of צבאות: cf., e.g., 19.3, 11,15; 25.8,28,29,32; 27.4,18,19,21; 29.4,8,21,25; 49.5,7,26,35. Also, in secondary human names; see pp. 69-70.

The following statement by Baumgärtel is incomprehensible: "Es fällt auf, dass in c. 1-7 die griechischen Entsprechungen fast völlig vorhanden sind, dass auch hernach bis c. 27 die Ausfälle nur passim zu konstatieren sind, und dass ab c. 28 bis in das c. 31 hinein plötzlich das LXX-Zeugnis so gut wie ganz aussetzt, aber im weiteren Verlauf kann dann wohl nur wieder von einem 'passim' in bezug auf das Minus der LXX gesprochen werden." ("Die Formel nᵉ'um jahwe," *ZAW* 73 [1961], 278-279, n. 6) Our own tabulation, following Baumgärtel's divisions, is as follows:

| 𝔐 order of chapters | | 𝔐 | 𝔊 | |
|---|---|---|---|---|
| | 1-7 | 32 | 29 | |
| | 8-27 | 59 | 30 | |
| | 28-31 | 29 | 15 | (including twice in chap. |
| | 32-end | 55 | 28 | 29, haplography) |

¢ order of chapters     1–7       32       29

8–27      69       35

28–31     26       14

32–end    48       24

While in chapters 1–7 יהוה נאם is indeed in ¢ "fast völlig vorhanden,"
the three following divisions, according to either order, show strikingly
*similar* proportions of Greek minuses!  Baumgärtel's remarks may be based
on superficial use of the Greek evidence, as he cites only the uncial
codices BASQ, and makes no attempt to restore critically the earliest
Greek text.

## NOTES TO CHAPTER V

1. W. Rudolph, *Jeremia* (Tübingen: J. C. B. Mohr [Paul Siebeck], 1958), p. xxi. Also, cf. R. H. Pfeiffer, *Introduction to the Old Testament* (New York: Harper and Brothers, 1941), p. 487; A. Weiser, *The Old Testament: Its Formation and Development* (New York: Association Press, 1961), p. 218; A. Weiser, *Das Buch des Propheten Jeremia*, fourth edition (Göttingen: Vandenhoeck and Ruprecht, 1960), p. xliii; O. Eissfeldt, *Einleitung in das Alten Testament*, third edition (Tübingen: J. C. B. Mohr [Paul Siebeck], 1964), p. 470; J. Muilenburg, "Jeremiah," *Interpreter's Dictionary of the Bible* (Nashville: Abingdon Press, 1962), vol. II, p. 834; H. Wildberger, "Jeremiabuch," *Die Religion in Geschichte und Gegenwart*, third edition (Tübingen: J. C. B. Mohr [Paul Siebeck], 1959), vol. III, p. 585; F. Giesebrecht, *Das Buch Jeremia* (Göttingen: Vandenhoeck and Ruprecht, 1907), pp. xxxvii–xxxix; P. Volz, *Der Prophet Jeremia* (Leipzig: A. Deichert, 1922), p. L; J. Bright, *Jeremiah*, The Anchor Bible, vol. 21 (Garden City, New York: Doubleday and Co., Inc., 1965), pp. cxxiii–cxxiv.

2. Giesebrecht, pp. xxv–xl.

3. *Ibid.*, p. xxxv.

4. κεκαρθαι τας κεφαλας, "to have their heads shorn," Herodotus 2.36. Cited in Liddell-Scott, *A Greek English Lexicon* (Oxford at the Clarendon Press, 1961), p. 935, under κειρω. Numbers 6 (verses 9, 12, 18, 19) demonstrates the extent to which, in this context, נזר and ראש are interchangeable, even in Hebrew.

5. See M. Dahood, *Psalms I*: The Anchor Bible, vol. 16 (Garden City, New York: Doubleday and Co., Inc., 1966), p. 64. Dahood suggests that LXX understood the Hebrew verbal form to be an infixed -t- conjugation of סור.

6. Ezek. 11.15, 20.40, 36.10, Hos. 13.2, Nah. 2.1, Hab. 1.9,15; also (כְּלָה) Ezek. 35.15, Am. 8.8, 9.5.

7. See the discussion above, pp. 27–28, no. 20.

8. Bright, p. cxxiii. Cf. also K. H. Graf, *Der Prophet Jeremia* (Leipzig: T. O. Weigel, 1862), pp. xlviii–ix, Giesebrecht, pp. xxxviii–xxxix, Volz, *Comm.*, p. 1(50) and others *ad loc.*

9. Volz treats only (1), (3), (6), and (7) in this manner. Graf adds five more readings to the list, but his argument in these instances is so strained that it would profit little to consider them here.

10. In each instance the second half of the doublet is missing in 𝔊, except for (4), where the verses are in 𝔊 but at the end of the chapter. In (6) and (7) the omitted readings, while first in the order of 𝔐, are second according to that of 𝔊.

11. Graf, p. xlix. Concerning the difference of translation, it is sufficient to note that differences in translation equivalents are bound up with the general question of the difference between Jer. α and β in 𝔊; other differences are minute and may well indicate differences in the *Vorlage* between the occurrences, such as occur between many doublets in 𝔐.

12. Volz, *Comm.*, p. L: "auf bewusster Überlegung." This is underscored if, as Thackeray has proposed, Jer. α and β are the work of two translators working in concert, for (6), and perhaps (7), straddle the division, and deletion would therefore have to have been an agreed upon policy.

13. Similarly A. Scholz, *Der masorethische Text und die LXX-Uebersetzung des Buches Jeremias* (Regensburg: G. J. Manz, 1875), p. 26.

14. So Giesebrecht, pp. 128-129. But why would this corrector not also restore the other passages similarly deleted by the translator?

15. Whether redactoral or pre-redactoral is immaterial.

16. About half the time, the formula is הנה ימים באים in Jer., the other half of the time it is לכן הנה ימים באים. לכן (which is om. L. Aeth in the latter's text at the old Greek position) may be secondary from the longer form.

17. Transposition of material owing to scribal error and subsequent restoration is a common textual development. Illustrations are found in 31.35-37 (𝔊 37.35-36); in 10.4 where 𝔐 ובמקבות  ובמסמרות is transposed in 𝔊 and 4QJer[b]; and in 8.10b-12 (see below). With respect to 23.7-8, it may be noted that the space between the position in 𝔐 and 𝔊 is roughly that occupied by two columns of a typical biblical scroll from Qumrân. If the top of column A began at or near 23.5, and the gloss were written vertically in the margin between columns A and B (compare the example of such a restoration in the Qumrân manuscript 4QJer[a], fragment 1, transcribed below, Appendix D), it could easily have been taken into the text near the top in one subsequent copy, and near the bottom in another. The further fact  that 23.9-40 is one content unit (לנביאים) and may have been set off by paragraph breaks (or spaces) before and after contributes

to the plausibility of this suggestion.

18. The attempts of Cornill (*Das Buch Jeremia* [Leipzig: C. H. Tauchnitz, 1905], pp. 457-458) and Rudolph (p. 253), for example, to find a reason for their insertion after the Oracle against Egypt are not convincing.

19. The likelihood is increased by the fact that Isa. 14.1-3, following chap. 13 (מַשָּׂא בָּבֶל) and preceding chap. 14.4-23 (מָשָׁל עַל בָּבֶל), constitutes a substantially similar message of weal for Jacob/Israel and woe for their captors. The parallel is too striking to be coincidental, and, in view of the general literary relationship between Isa. 13 and Jer. 50-51, we may conjecture that it was Isa. 14.1-3 which suggested the place where the oracle to Jacob (whether Jeremianic or not) should be inserted.

20. Hitzig argues similarly (*Der Prophet Jeremiah* [Leipzig: S. Hirzel, 1866], p. 348), though linking the gloss more narrowly to 50.2; Cornill's objections (p. 457) are effective against his argument, but do not apply to our proposal, which does not depend upon the evidence Hitzig adduces. It may be noted that it would not be strange to have extended marginal glosses taken into the text at a point other than the one they were meant to gloss. It would be natural to take such a large piece of material in at a paragraph break, or space, to avoid intrusion upon what normally would be a continuous context.

21. Bright, p. 286. His earlier suggestion (p. 278, n. 5) that in vv. 5-7 "words of the people (or the prophet) are quoted, and then answered (in vv. 10f) by the divine oracle," is doubtful, for in this case we have in the words of the people an awkward affirmative anticipation of the divine answer. There is really no difficulty in taking 5-7 as divine speech. The plural of divine address is not unexampled in the O.T. (e.g., Gen. 1.26, 11.7), and v. 7b is most fitting as the climax to this section, before the new beginning in v. 12 (taking the prose verses 8-9 also as an insertion).

22. So, e.g., Rudolph, p. 70.

23. Cf., e.g., the orthography in 30.10//46.27, 10.13//51.16.

24. Note especially the following details: Outside Jer., כְּלוּ occurs 15 times, כָּלָה 10 times; in Jer., כְּלוּ occurs only in 6.13 *bis*, while כָּלָה (8.10 *bis*) occurs also in 2.21, 8.6, 15.10, 20.7, 48.31, 48.38. The hiphil הִכְלִים is inappropriate to the context. What we have in 6.15

is niphal inf. cstr., with full orthography (cf. $\mathcal{G}$, Eb 10 הכלים, and 8.12 M; also 3.3). The phrase (ב)עת פקדתי/- occurs 3 times in Jer. M (6.15, 49.8, 50.31); twice $\mathcal{G}$ reads the noun פקדה/-. On the other hand, the phrase (ב)עת/שנת פקדתם occurs 8 times in Jer. M (8.12, 10.15//51.18, 11.23, 23.12, 31.44, 46.21, 50.27 [see also Isa. 10.3, Hos. 9.7, Mic. 7.4]). The latter form probably is original, while the former arose when the phrase was read as a defectively written פקדתים. Again, therefore, 6.13-15 represents an orthographically more advanced text than 2.10b-12.

25. Aided, conceivably, by one (or both) of the following factors: the passage would take up exactly 3 lines in a column of 50-52 letters; a manuscript with paragraph breaks after the prophetic clichés would be particularly vulnerable to haplography.

26. In the absence of versification, the only way to find one's place in an ancient manuscript would be by context. The relative proximity of the two contexts in a manuscript several yards long and containing dozens of columns would aid in the mistaken identification of context.

27. 6.13-15 presupposes a defectively-written *Vorlage*: συνετελεσαντο for בוצע; την ατιμιαν αυτων for הכלים; εν τη πτωσει αυτων for בנפלים; επισκοπης (αυτων) פקדתים. For a fine illustration of the orthographic contrast between two parts of a conflate reading and orthographic differences generally between text and marginal readings in 1QIsa[a], see S. Talmon, *Textus* 4 (1964), 109f.

28. J. Ziegler, *Beiträge zur Ieremias-Septuaginta* (Göttingen: Vandenhoeck and Ruprecht, 1958), pp. 88-89.

29. The cliché (הרע) ללכת אחרי שררות לבם (ולא) ילכו עוד elsewhere always refers to defecting Israel, and its reference here to כל הגוים makes no sense. For our proposal, see below, n. 30.

30. The gloss may have arisen as follows: 3.17, which begins בעת ההיא יקראו, was glossed with the phrase לעם הזה לירושלם from 4.11, which opens with the almost identical phrase בעת ההיא יאמר. The gloss then was wrongly taken into the text (into 17aβ instead of 17aα), and at some point לעם הזה became the graphically similar לשם יהוה (perhaps mistakenly so read under the influence of contexts like Isa. 18.7, 60.9, Ps. 122.4. Compare Jer. 28.7 and 36.1, where M הזה, $\mathcal{G}$ יהוה; and for שם/עם see p. 21, no. 48 and n. 52). If Cornill and Rudolph are correct in suggesting that 4.10 should read לנו in place of לעם הזה לירושלם, the latter phrase could represent a variant absorption of the proposed gloss on 3.17 (3.17 and

4.10 would stand roughly in the same place in adjacent columns). Alternately, the phrase may originally have been intended as a clarifying
gloss on לנו in 4.10, from 4.11, while some subsequent copyist mistook
it for a gloss on 3.17, because of the above-mentioned similarity in
opening phraseology. In either case, M 3.17 and 4.10 would be the result
of conflation of the variously absorbed gloss.

If, as we hold, לשם יהוה לירושלם is secondary to 3.17, and in origin unrelated to any of the surrounding material, the verse still contains
the problem of the phrase כל הגוים. In our view, the most likely explanation of the verse is that ונקוו אליה כל הגוים is an early gloss. The
rest of the verse makes good sense in the larger context of vv. 14.18,
and the gloss would have arisen by association of the present reference
to eschatological return to Jerusalem, with other such contexts in which
the nations acknowledge the centrality of Jerusalem (e.g., Isa. 2.1-3,
18.7, 60.9).

31. Ehrlich conjectures that אשפתו is corrupt from שפתו; Volz
reads אשר פיהו. The motif of the open lip or mouth of the chthonic deity
is common in Ugaritic contexts (see, e.g., UM 52:61-62 and UM 67:II:2).

32. See also Volz, *Comm.*, p. L: "Begreiflich ist's, wenn 𝔊 in
unjeremianischen oder überarbeiteten Abschnitten kürzt 7.27f; 23.34ff;
27.19 bis 21; 35.17-19." This is to attribute to the translator a
literary-critical interest and competence which we cannot conceive of.

33. His argument from the variation between the versions to the
conclusion that they all abbreviate arbitrarily must be rejected. 𝔊^A
surely contains an inner-Greek variant. Whether or not Syr deliberately
omitted the last three words of the verse, this has no bearing on the
merits of the 𝔊 reading. The statement that "die latein. Väter bewegen
sich in ihren Zitaten hier freier, auch ein Anzeichen, dass sie sich der
mangelnden Authentie ihres vorliegenden Textes bewusst waren" (p. 155)
leads us nowhere.

34. See pp. 73-75, no. 16.

35. Part of the M plus may be secondary: v. 38aα appears to be a
gloss on v. 38, arising out of vv. 34-36; the post positive position of
the introductory formula לכן כה אמר יהוה is suspect. Also, one could
argue that the divine title אלהים חיים identifies the M plus in v. 36 as
from the same glossator who was responsible for the insertion of 10.10
(so also Hitzig). However, it is not impossible that the 𝔊 minus in vv.

36-37 is the result of accidental loss of a line in $\mathcal{C}$-*Vorlage* (the omitted words comprise 58 letters).

36. Cf., e.g., J. Skinner, *Prophecy and Religion* (Cambridge: at the University Press, 1961), pp. 240-241, and Rudolph, pp. 146, 148.

37. Jer. 7.13, 25, 11.7, 26.5, 29.19, 32.33, 35.14, 15, 44.4, 2 Chr. 36.15.

38. It becomes difficult, after a point, to know how to comment upon such improbable theories, which have little or no support from a pattern of readings, but are constructed *ad hoc*. What is offensive about the task of the *posse*, that anyone whould want to excise reference to Jewish participation in it?

39. See p. 14, no. 22, and reference there to Talmon.

40. Cf., e.g., N. K. Gottwald, *All the Kingdoms of the Earth* (New York, 1964), pp. 259-260.

41. So already Graf, who cites Deut. 4.25, 6.2, Ex. 34.7, among biblical passages where this meaning is clear. Compare the phrase ʿ*ly* ʾ*w* ʿ*l bry* ʾ*w* ʿ*l br bry* ʾ*w* ʿ*l* ʿ*qry* in Sefîrē III, lines 1, 25, 26 (J. A. Fitzmyer, "The Aramaic Suzerainty Treaty from Sefîrē in the Museum of Beirut," *CBQ* 20 [1958], 448-449).

42. From the presence of late material in the common text of $M$ and $\mathcal{C}$ we would propose that the divergence occurred not earlier than about 450 Isee further, below, chapter VIII).

43. It is not easy to see Rudolph's point, that 27.7 could be taken as a contradiction *(Widerspruch)* of 29.10. As a matter of fact, 70 years would be a rather good average reckoning of three royal generations.

44. On the other hand, the omission of verse 7 heightens the dramatic force with which v. 8 follows v. 6, especially as we have reconstructed the latter (see pp. 54-57):

נתתי את הארץ ביד מלך בבל לעבדו        6

הגוי והממלכה אשר לא עבדו אתו···אפקד        8

45. *Studies in Daniel* (New York: Jewish Publication Society, 5708-1948), pp. 24-26.

46. J.-T. Milik, "Prière de Nabonide' et Autres Écrits d'un Cycle de Daniel," *Revue Biblique* 63 (1956), 407-415.

47. D. N. Freedman, "The Prayer of Nabonidus," *BASOR* 145 (1957), 32.

48.  See further Ginsberg, *Studies in Daniel*, p. 19 and n. 57, p. 25 and n. 5.

49.  If this explanation is correct, it would suggest that the Palestinian version of the Daniel tradition once told of *three* Kings and that the later transference of the story in Dan. 4 from Nabonidus to Nebuchadrezzar would have taken place after about 450-350 (when, in our judgment, the 𝔐 and 𝔊 archetypes diverged). But this suggestion is offered very tentatively.

50.  Verses 5(*bis*), 6, 10(*bis*), 11, 12(*bis*), 15(*bis*), 17; compare v. 1.

51.  In the absence of specific examples of name reiteration in Deuteronomic--or other biblical--contexts, we suspect that Volz is influenced by familiarity with modern usage ("the word of said witness").

52.  See also chap. IV, esp. p. 71, on the names in 52.24.

53.  Cf. on the one hand 27.22, 29.10; on the other hand 25.12, Num. 16.29, Jer. 34.4-5, 52.11.

54.  καθιζω never translates היה elsewhere, but almost always ישׁב (once גור).

55.  On the equivalence εργαζειν = עבד in Jer. β, see pp. 54-55.

56.  Surely a translator taking liberties would not leave העגל as it is in 𝔐, but would fit it more smoothly into the main narrative.

57.  Giesebrecht's treatment of vv. 18-19, while highly conjectural, is worth consideration. He begins by noting the awkward syntax of העגל. This term usually is taken as a second accusative to ונתתי, meaning "I will make the men...(like) the calf," or the text is emended to כעגל. This meaning agrees with covenant contexts such as Sefîrē I:40 [ואיך יגזר עגלא זנה כן יגזר מתעאל ויגזרן רבוה זי]; see J. A. Fitzmyer, "The Aramaic Inscriptions of Sefîrē I and II," *JAOS* 81 (1961), 181. For other parallels, see the bibliography in Rudolph, p. 205, and in E. Gerstenberger, "Covenant and Commandment," *JBL* 84 (1965), 40, n. 12. But ונתתי האנשים···העגל is strange, and Aquila's rendering ενωπιον του μοσχου ον διειλον points up the syntactic strain involved in the usual interpretation.

In Giesebrecht's view, "die Abgerissenheit des העגל bestätigt, dass die vorausgehenden Relativsätze vom Rand in den Text kamen. Aufklärung bietet v. 19 Schluss העברים בין בתרי העגל, der in LXX nicht gelesen, im Hebr. zu העברים את ברתי העגל v. 18 die Randkorrektur darstellte, nachdem

der obige Satz durch die Relativsätze auseinandergesprengt war. Auch
die auf הָעֵגֶל folgenden Zusätze sind wohl nach dessen Isolierung nach dem
Original gemacht, um das Wort zu halten" (p. 191). Giesebrecht accordingly reconstructs vv. 18-20 to read:

ונתתי את האנשים העברים בין בתרי העגל
שרי יהודה ושרי ירושלם הסרסים והכהנים וכל העם
ונתתי אותם ביד איביהם

with ונתתי in v. 20 resuming ונתתי in v. 18 after the long additions.
His conjecture is radical. But, if correct, it would account not only
for the present awkwardness of הָעֵגֶל and the similarity of העברים את בתרי
to העברים בין בתרי, but it would explain the unique spelling of בתרי
(elsewhere in MT *always* ברית) as arising from corruption of בתרי under
the influence of ברית in vv. 8, 10, 13, 15. If certainty is impossible,
it is clear at least that explanation of Ø variants as tendentious altera-
tions is dubious.

58. Volz, p. 251, Rudolph, p. 203.

59. Cf. v. 13, and the discussion in chap. I.

60. Note the plural כל מצוחיו, in contrast to מצות in v. 14 M, vv.
16, 18.

61. Cf. v. 14 M שמעו את מצות אביהם.

62. Rudolph, p. 208.

63. Alternately, לכן may be secondary expansion from 4. 17. The
introductory prophetic formula in v. 19 could well be a variant witness
to this expansion, in the form of a correction to v. 18 wrongly absorbed
into the text.

64. A. W. Streane, *The Double Text of Jeremiah* (Cambridge: D. Bell
and Co., 1896), p. 238: "The aff. in תקראם is no objection,...as its
antecedent has been *virtually* mentioned in the previous clause" (italics
Streane's).

65. In this repetitive prose style, it is unlikely that the writer
would use such nearly identical phrases, in such close proximity, but in
such a different syntactical construction. In the context, the most
natural reference of את דברי יהוה is to כתבת.

66. Rudolph, p. 212; cf. his note in BH[3]: "G[Bא] ובית יהודה, prb
sic 1."

67. P. 292: "es is klar, dass das Fasten nicht erst ausgerufen
wurde, als die Landleute schon da waren, sondern dass die Ausrufung erst

ihr Zusammenströmen veranlasste."

68. The standard clichés in Jer. for the two groups are איש יהודה
וישבי ירושלם and עְרי יהודה וישבי ירושלם. With the exception of 36.31,
whose order must be secondary, the sequence is always יהודה···ירושלם.

69. Compare the glossed text of 34.8 M (₡ om.bracketed): אחרי כרת
המלך צדקיהו ברית את (כל) העם (אשר בירושלם) לקרא דרור.

70. In an article on "The Synoptic Problem in the Chronicler's
History," *HTR* 58 (1965), 349-363, Werner E. Lemke has some salutary remarks on the precarious nature of attempts to guess the motives of translators or redactors. He writes (p. 262), "...judgments about...personal
reactions...should be used only with great restraint. One should have
recourse to them only when no other, more objective, explanations are
possible, *and when such a proposed motive is clearly discernible in a
number of instances*" (italics mine). In defense of my own explanation
of the ₡ omission in 37.1, it may be pointed out that the triumph of
scribal memory over the text at hand is a common scribal error. My proposal differs from the motive proposals under criticism in that it posits
an oft-observed error in the mechanics of scribal transmission rather
than an *ad hoc*, consciously executed alteration.

71. See pp. 57-58, nos. 161-171. Also, כל (6 times, see pp. 65-
67), צבאות (twice, see chap. IV), אלהי ישראל···אלהי (chap. IV), ואת רעתם
(p. 18, no. 37), ובדבר (pp. 43-44, no. 45), and אדני and נאם יהוה (chap.
IV).

72. E.g., היום הזה (v. 2) and כיום הזה (v. 23), and מן ארץ מצרים
(v. 28).

73. Brown-Driver-Briggs (*A Hebrew and English Lexicon of the Old
Testament* [Oxford: at the Clarendon Press, 1957]) suggest "splash (fall
with a splash) into his vomit"; see Bright, p. 321, n. 26.

74. Cf. Jer. 52.17//2 Kgs. 25.13, which mention just the pillars,
the bases, and the sea; also Jer. 27.19, a gloss from chap. 52. 52.20//
25.16 seem to be a further comment on the weight of just these three
articles, with vv. 21-22//v. 17 a yet further comment on the pillars.

75. Rudolph, p. 46; cf. Volz, p. 56.

76. Rudolph, p. 247; cf. Volz, p. 294.

77. *JBL* 82 (1963), 403 and n. 42. For comments on his view, see
p. 36, no. 9.

78. The formula occurs in 7.1 (om. ₵), 11.1, 18.1, 21.1, 25.1, 30.1, 32.1, 34.1, 34.8, 35.1, 40.1, 44.1 (and, oddly, 46.1, in Syh and L). According to Mowinckel's analysis, all C passages have the formula, but 30.1 and 40.1 do not belong to C. In Rudolph's view, C passages as a rule have the formula, but 30.1, 32.1, 34.1-7, 40.1, 44.1-14 are not C, and 16.1-13 (18), 17.19-27, 22.1-5 (all without the formula) also belong to C. See Mowinckel, *Zur Komposition des Buches Jeremia* (Kristiana, 1914), p. 31, and Rudolph, p. xvi.

79. So, e.g., in 51.64, where עד הנה דברי ירמיהו is absent in ₵, and clearly is a secondary note to demarcate the preceding material from the following synoptic appendix. Compare the similar catch line in 48.47, עד הנה משפט מואב. These two would seem to be related, especially when we note that one occurs at the end of the Oracles against Foreign Nations according to 𝕸 order, the other at the end of the Oracles according to ₵ order. See further in the Excursus to this chapter.

80. An excellent example of the secondary breakdown of literary structure may be seen in 𝕸 of Kings. In *Chronology and Recensional Development in the Greek Text of Kings* (Cambridge: Harvard University Press, 1968), James D. Shenkel has shown that in the original organization of the book of Kings, narrative materials were interspersed with regnal formulas according to a consistent pattern, this pattern is intact in the Greek text tradition, and in 𝕸 the pattern has been disrupted by a number of transpositions of material. Here, however, the controls for identifying the original character of the more systematic structure, and for explaining the cause of the corruption in 𝕸, are clear and indisputable. On the contrary, the attempt to detect a redactoral system in the introductory clichés of the book of Jeremiah suffers from a lack of controls, and the results, if pressed too finely, become arbitrary.

81. Cf. the secondary לאמר (om. ₵ Syr) in 3.1.

82. See the Excursus at the end of this chapter.

83. See p. 14, no. 24.

84. See p. 15.

85. For some strange reason, the Elam superscription stands at the *end* of the Elam oracle in ₵. It may be that ₵ originally read τα αιλαμ εν αρχη βασιλευοντος σεδ. ....περι αιλαμ (compare the superscription to the Oracle against Egypt); that haplography occurred, αιλαμ 1°⌢2°; and that subsequent restoration was made at the end of the Oracle. That 26.1

in substance is old Greek and not recensional correction to M̶ is suggested by the genitive absolute form of the date formula, with βασιλευοντος. This form is consistently early in Greek, with later recensional substitution by other forms. See my Harvard dissertation, "Studies in the Text of Jeremiah" (1965), pp. 61, 67-68.

86. 50.8 and 51.54 בבל//ארץ כשדים; similarly, 50.25, 35; 51.1, 4, 24, 35.

87. See Appendix A, "H. *yrmyhw hnby'* ."

88. We may draw attention again to Lemke's criticism of this type of conjecture, referred to in note 70 above.

89. See below, chapter VI.

90. But rather than suggest that the form of Jer. was modeled on that of the other two, perhaps we should say that with respect to the position of their Oracles against Foreign Nations these three books reflect the same editorial process.

91. Egypt, Philistia, Moab, etc., as against Elam, Egypt, Babylon, etc., in ₵.

92. Rudolph maintains that ₵ understood Elam to be Persia and wanted to place the three great Kingdoms, Persia, Egypt, and Babylon, at the head; in the ₵ order of the small states, on the other hand, there is no ordering principle.

But if there is no recognizable reason for altering the order with respect to the small states, why would ₵ not have been content to follow M̶? Again, Rudolph shoots wide of the mark in trying to guess motives for which there is no clear evidence in the material. By contrast, a secondary reordering of the Oracles toward the order in chapter 25 is quite probable, according to well-attested general text-critical principles.

93. H. St. John Thackeray, *The Septuagint and Jewish Worship*, p. 36.

## NOTES TO CHAPTER VII

1. Published by F. M. Cross, *The Ancient Library of Qumrân*, rev. ed. (Garden City, New York: Doubleday and Co., Inc., 1961), p. 187, n. 38.

2. E.g., 6.13 לילה 14.17 ,,הרעב/והחרב 14.16 ,,ומנביא/ועד כהן /ויומם; in each instance, 𝔊 is transposed.

3. The *atbash* cipher may be an indication of the lateness of the clause. Such ciphers occur also in 51.1, 51.41, and probably 25.25 (where זמרי is to be taken as a corruption of עילם = זמכי). The textual history of these ciphers is varied:

51.41 ששך om. 𝔊, whose text is poetically superior (3 + 2 3 + 2) and original (cf. 50.23). The cipher ששך arose as a gloss on בבל, in v. 41b, but instead of replacing the latter (compare 51.1 below), it was taken into the text after נלכדה, thereby disrupting the metric balance.

51.1 על בבל ואל ישבי לב קמי] επι βαβυλωνα και επι τους κατοικουντας χαλδαιους. It is doubtful that 𝔊 would have understood the cipher (compare O Arm L' α'-86 καρδιαν επεγειροντων, and λεβ/ν καβη σ'-Q 86, λεκκαβη σ'-Anon apud Ghisler. II 897); we may suppose that 𝔊-*Vorlage* read כשדים, and that the phrase originally was על בבל ועל ישבי כשדים, similar to 51.24, 35 (compare also 50.8,35 and 51.54). In this instance the gloss לב קמי replaced כשדים.

25.25 ואת מלכי זמרי ואת מלכי עילם] om. ואת מלכי זמרי 𝔊. Here, 𝔐 has conflated the original reading with a variant text in which זמכי* had replaced עילם.

The *atbash* cipher therefore may be taken throughout as a secondary textual development.

4. The regnal figures of this pericope (7 and 18) agree with those of the Babylonian Chronicle for the capture of Jerusalem in 597 and the fall of Judah in 587; regnal figures and synchronisms in Kings and elsewhere in Jeremiah are uniformly one year higher. For discussion of the data, see W. F. Albright, "The Nebuchadnezzar and Neriglissar Chronicles," *BASOR* 143 (1956), 32, D. N. Freedman, "The Babylonian Chronicle," *BA* 19 (1956), 56-57, and S. Talmon, "Divergences in Calendar-Reckoning in Ephraim and Judah," *VT* 8 (1958), 64-65; also Rudolph, pp. 299-300.

5. Cf. Freedman, *BA* 19 (1956), 57, n. 29, and Albright, *BASOR* 143 (1956), 32, n. 18.

6.  K. H. Graf, *Der Prophet Jeremia* (Leipzig: T. O. Weigel, 1862), p. xlviii; J. Lindblom, *Prophecy in Ancient Israel* (Philadelphia: Muhlenberg Press, 1962), p. 287, n. 111; P. Volz, *Studien zum Text des Jeremia* (Leipzig: J. C. Hinrichs, 1920), p. L.

7.  H. B. Swete, *An Introduction to the Old Testament in Greek* (Cambridge: at the University Press, 1902), p. 259.

8.  For discussion of the contents of the pericope, see the commentaries, esp. W. Rudolph, *Jeremia* (Tübingen: J. C. B. Mohr [Paul Siebeck], 1958), pp. 199-201.

## NOTES TO CHAPTER VIII

1. In the absence of evidence for systematic revision (in the manner of the Greek recensions of proto-Lucian, καιγε, and Aquila), it would not be accurate to refer to 𝔐 as a *recensional* text. The revisions were rather *ad hoc* and cumulative and mark the growth of this local text type, rather than its systematic recension.

2. That is, ca. 150-30 B.C. For the description of 4QJer[b] as a Hasmonaean manuscript, see F. M. Cross, "The Contribution of the Qumrân Discoveries to the Study of the Biblical Text," *IEJ* 16/2 (1966), 81-95.

3. The orthography of Jer. 𝔐 may be described as slightly conservative; but that the text finally chosen is late enough to have come into contact with a newly introduced Egyptian text is suggested by secondary readings with non-Masoretic *plene* orthography (e.g., 6.15 הכלים for הכלם in 𝔊 and the parallel passage in 8.12; 33.8 לכול om. 𝔊; cf. 26.6 הזאת, om. 𝔊).

4. The theory was first sketched in the first edition of *The Ancient Library of Qumrân* (1958), chap. IV, sec. 3, "Early Recensions of the Old Testament," pp. 140-145 (cf. *ALQ*², pp. 188-194), and is presented more fully, with textual examples, in "The History of the Biblical Text in the Light of Discoveries in the Judean Desert," *HTR* 57 (1964), 281-299, and in the article cited in n. 2 above. The summary is from the article last mentioned; this whole discussion is heavily indebted to these works and to discussions in Professor Cross's textual seminar.

5. There is no reason to doubt that 𝔊-*Vorlage* was an Egyptian text. For textual evidence of this, see 43.13 (בית שמש אשר בארץ מצרים/ ηλιουπολεως τους εν ων) and 46.15 (מדוע נסחף/ δια τι εφυγεν ο απις). It is difficult to suppose that these renderings could have been produced anywhere else than in Egypt.

6. Quoted in Waltke, "Prolegomena to the Samaritan Pentateuch," p. 302. The summary of the character of the text is on pp. 300-307.

7. *Ibid.*, p. 303.

8. Compare the expansions common to 𝔊 and the Samaritan Pentateuch, listed for Exodus 1-10, "Prolegomena," pp. 226-227.

9. 4QJer[a]. For references, see p. 7, n. 26.

10. Contrast the later appearance of this text at Masada and Murabba'at.

11.  See his article cited in n. 2 above.

12.  On the date of these two manuscripts, see F. M. Cross in *BANE*, p. 137, fig. 1, lines 3 and 4, and related discussion.

13.  See "Die Eigenart des Q-Textes," in Ziegler, *Ieremias*, pp. 63–66.

14.  See Barthélemy, *Les Devanciers d'Aquila* (Leiden: E. J. Brill, 1963), passim.

15.  On the character of Isa. and Ezek., see F. M. Cross, *HTR* 57 (1964), 286, and the article cited in n. 2 above.  Also, on the secondary expansions in Ezek., see G. Fohrer, "Die Glossen im Buche Ezechiel," *ZAW* 63 (New Series 22; 1951), 33–53.

16.  Cf. D. N. Freedman, "The Law and the Prophets," *VT Supplements* 9 (1963), 260, and J. Bright, *Jeremiah*, The Anchor Bible, vol. 21 (Garden City, New York: Doubleday and Co., Inc., 1965), pp. lxxi, 285, 359–360. On the date of the C source, which H. G. May (*JBL* 61 [1942]) would place in the first half of the fifth century at the earliest, see J. Bright, "The Date of the Prose Sermons of Jeremiah," *JBL* 70 (1951), 15–35.

17.  Cf. D. N. Freedman, *VT Supplements* 9 (1963), 252.

18.  *Ibid.*, pp. 259–260.

19.  Isa. 40.18–20, 41.6–7, 44.9–20, 46.5–7.

20.  Ps. 115.4–8, 135.15ff.

21.  So, e.g., Rudolph and Bright.  Or, if its original position was between verses 3 and 4, the dislocation of the verse would have resulted from haplography, כסף‏‎···‏וכסף (cf. 23.7–8, discussed below).

22.  Baumgartner, *ZAW* 45 (New Series 4; 1927), 101, cf. p. 123, dates the verse to the fifth century, on the basis of ארקא/ארעא.

23.  The common text at each place is כל האנשים.  The respective plusses are alternate absorptions of the same gloss הזדים, which in 𝔊-*Vorlage* was corrupted to, or mistaken for, הזרים and prefixed with וכל.

24.  Whether or not our explanation of 3.17 is correct (see p. 97, no. 2), the phrase seems secondary; see Rudolph.

25.  Gerstenberger's explanation (*JBL* 82 [1963], 394–396) is not convincing.

26.  Cf. pp. 92–93, no. 4, on 23.7–8.

27.  Cf. pp. 95–96, no. 1, on 8.10–12.

28.  Possibly הידד לא הידד is a corruption of הידד לא ידרך, which would have been an old variant of לא ידרך הידד.

29. That the formula, now absent from ₵, once stood in the Egyptian text type, is required to provide the condition for omission of 17.1-5a in ₵ by haplography.

30. For further exemples, see A. Kuenen, *Historisch-kritische Einleitung in die Bücher de Alten Testaments: II* (Leipzig: 1892), p. 243, n. 11.

31. See Bright, pp. lxxv-lxxvi.

32. 23.19-20//30.23-24. On the secondary occurrence in chap. 30, see Hyatt, Rudolph, Bright.

33. Compare the comment of W. F. Albright, "New Light on Early Recensions of the Hebrew Bible," *BASOR* 140 (1955), 33: "Jeremiah...presumably circulated in Egypt as early as the sixth century--thus perhaps accounting for the drastic divergences in content and order between LXX and MT." His presumption concerning the early circulation of a text of Jer. in Egypt is quite plausible. But, as the above analysis has shown, the divergence of 𝔐 and ₵ archetypes cannot be pushed back to the sixth century. His suggestion is correct to the extent that an archaic Egyptian manuscript may have been influential in attracting an early form of the Palestinian text of Jeremiah to Egypt. See further below.

34. Or, perhaps more likely, believed by the community to derive from the prophet himself.

INDEX OF PASSAGES

INDEX OF PASSAGES

The index includes all passages in Jeremiah which have received
analysis, with one exception:   Chapter IV, which contains an analysis of
the proper names, has not been fully indexed.   Zero variants which have
not been analyzed are listed without comment in Chapter VII.